For Surinder Kaur Bhatti

who told stories and taught me to be brave

Gurpreet Kaur Bhatti

PLAYS ONE

BEHSHARAM
BEHZTI
BEHUD
FOURTEEN
KHANDAN

INTRODUCTION BY JATINDER VERMA

OBERON BOOKS
LONDON

WWW.OBERONBOOKS.COM

First published in 2014 by Oberon Books Ltd
521 Caledonian Road, London N7 9RH
Tel: +44 (0) 20 7607 3637 / Fax: +44 (0) 20 7607 3629
e-mail: info@oberonbooks.com
www.oberonbooks.com

A catalogue record for this book is available from the British Library.

PB ISBN: 978-1-78319-130-7
E ISBN: 978-1-78319-629-6

Contents

Introduction   7

Behsharam   13

Behzti   87

Behud   177

Fourteen   253

Khandan   303

Introduction

MAPPING FAMILIES

This collection of Gurpreet Kaur Bhatti's plays is very welcome, confirming her as one of Britain's most significant contemporary playwrights. From her first play, *Behsharam [Shameless]* in 2001 to her latest, *Khandan [Family]*, she has consistently mapped the contours of post-migration families; contours which are as fascinating and illuminating as the first geological map of the ground beneath our feet produced by the great eighteenth-century geologist, Walter Smith.

Reading her plays – and even more, seeing them – is akin to an extended meditation on Philip Larkin's bleak poem, *This Be the Verse*, whose first four lines Bhatti quotes in *Behud*:

> They fuck you up, your mum and dad.
> They may not mean to, but they do.
> They fill you with the faults they had
> And add some extra, just for you.

While family dynamics have been the subject of many plays over the years, Bhatti uniquely dissects the post-migration family, traumatised by transportation from the Punjab to Britain to negotiate the Scylla and Charybdis of alienation and racism.

The effect of migration is inherently characterised by a series of fictions: the fiction of 'back home', of 'rags to riches', of 'preserving culture', of 'authenticity'. Bhatti's art lies in exposing these fictions through an array of splendidly irreverent characters caught in an assortment of familial situations.

Bhatti's debut play *Behsharam* introduces us to her wonderfully zany imagination – from Sati, the younger daughter who lugs around her cardboard cut-out of footballer Ian Wright to the deliciously foul-mouthed matriarch, Beji and her druggie eldest granddaughter Jaspal, who eventually reforms herself as singer 'Kiran Carpenter'. In *Behzti*, she goes further with the middle-aged Polly and Teetee, who have a penchant for stealing smart ladies' shoes from the congregation in their local temple (Gurdwara), and the cocaine-addicted Giani (head priest).

This array of characters provocatively offers us a glimpse of far richer contemporary Asian lives than we are used to seeing in popular media. They help Bhatti expose the fictions by which her characters prop up their lives, provoking us out of a lazy homogenising sense of 'the Asian experience'. One of the most persuasive of pressures migrants feel is that exerted within the family and the extended community to not expose its dirty laundry in public – or, as the journalist Satinder in *Behud* puts it 'draw attention to things that are best left unsaid'. Bhatti's significance in contemporary theatre lies in doing precisely the opposite.

This desire came most sharply to prominence in her second play, *Behzti* in 2005. I first heard about it via an SMS from a friend: 'check this play out – right insult to the community'. Talking to some of the actors whom I knew in the show it was obvious many were very concerned about whether the show, produced by Birmingham Rep, would go on or not as the 'insult' escalated to threats of violence against the writer and the performers. It struck me at the time that there was a very strange, and sad, congruence between the sexual violence Bhatti was exploring in her play and the reaction it was eliciting in some sections of the Asian community.

Following the fatwa against Salman Rushdie's *Satanic Verses*, faith has replaced race, class, ethnicity and culture as the fault-line of social relations; a process accelerated by New Labour post-9/11. Crucially, in the run-up to the controversy surrounding the play, the government proposed new legislation to make incitement to religious hatred a crime. Sensitivity to the charge of 'Faith-crime' was rapidly becoming the litmus-test for multiculturalism.

One of the first taunts doing the rounds on Birmingham streets centred on the poster for the play. The poster depicted a woman peeping over a pair of large knickers which she was holding. Such knickers – boxers, in effect – are one of the five key symbols for male Sikhs. The taunts were aimed at young male Sikhs, who, it was claimed, were too effeminate to do anything about the shameful manner in which their faith was being paraded on the streets. Given the emergent sensitivities surrounding 'faith', it is not too difficult to see how some young Sikh men, when offered 'evidence' by community leaders who had read the play, took to the streets, fuelled by drink (the area surrounding Birmingham Rep is famous for the opportunities it offers for indulging in binge drinking).

This local grievance very rapidly took on the patina of a global 'faith-crime'. And in so doing, ignored the important central issue of sexual violence in religious institutions in Bhatti's play. While today this is no longer a new or even very surprising fact, as we repeatedly hear of such exploitation in the Church, for a racial and religious minority in Britain, exposure of such practices seemed akin at the time to piling yet more pressure on an already beleaguered community. But pandering to religious sensitivities ignored one of the enduring insights of Bhatti's play – the violence victims inflict on each other. As the light-fingered Teetee explains to the carer Elvis, 'Our men are cruel to our women but we get used to it and we follow the rules, letting each slap and tickle and bruise and head-butt go by. And at the end of this rubbish life, we write the rules. We find the beauty in our cruelty. My daughters-in-law suffer just as I suffered. I make sure of it.'

Such cruelty paradoxically stems in part from what is widely perceived as one of the virtues of contemporary Asian life, the strength of family. As the aggressive but physically impotent Balbir says to her daughter Min in *Behzti*, 'Your flesh came out of me, it is mine, my property'.

At the heart of Gurpreet Kaur Bhatti's work is this tension between the desire of parents to determine the destiny of their children and the latter's not unreasonable wish to forge their own lives. Out of this tension arise characters that are, at once, both victims and oppressors; as casually racist towards fellow others – Muslims, black people – as they are burdened by the all-pervasive racism perpetrated on them by the dominant white society. Resisting easy stereotypes, Gurpreet brings to the fore characters from behind the veil of contemporary multiculturalism. Like Liz in *Khandan*, who is more 'Punjabi' than the Punjabi man she's married to, cheerfully making endless cups of chah on the orders of her mother-in-law and obligingly kneading the dough for chappatis, in the hope of having a child with her husband.

In *Fourteen*, Bhatti continues her map of family through the life of Tina, charting her journey from a vivacious Keats-obsessed school-girl to a single mum over the span of thirty years. The redemption for Tina lies not in escaping her working-class roots – despite not having the heart to say 'we go shopping up Southall Broadway, so I say we always visit a special spot in the West Country' – but accepting them: 'Mutton dressed as Mutton'.

Fourteen echoes *Behsharam*, *Behzti* and *Khandan* in having vibrant women characters driving the action of the plays. Bhatti subverts the patriarchy which is conventionally perceived to be the engine of family life to expose another fiction, that of the dominant Asian male looking after his brood. But patriarchal forces achieve focus and are tackled head-on on in her magnificent response to *Behzti*, the play *Behud [Beyond Belief]* in 2010. Police officer Gurpal ('Gary') Singh Mangat, charged with protecting the writer Tarlochan Grewal, speaks for many when he explains to his boss DCI Harris 'I reckon her head's contaminated… Like when animal rights stick dead mice in tins of beans'.

Tarlochan's exchange with bad-boy Khushwant Singh Bains, who's charged to kidnap her, allows Bhatti to probe the confused heart of the protest against *Behzti*, exposing perhaps the most enduring of all migrant fictions, the 'home-land':

TARL: Your head's got all mixed up.

KHUSH: How could it not be living in this shithole?

TARL: But you've got a nice shop.

KHUSH: I mean England.

TARL: You want to nick some notes out of the till and buy one of them round the world tickets. Stick a rucksack on your back and see a bit of life.

KHUSH: I'm going home back to the Punjab. Gonna be a farmer, drive a tractor and work the land, our real proper land.

TARL: Like it out there do you?

KHUSH: I've never been.

TARL: You won't last five minutes.

KHUSH: I'll be with my brothers and sisters.

TARL: They're all getting visas to come here.

In Gurpreet Kaur Bhatti's latest play, *Khandan*, both 'home' and patriarchy appear as flip-sides of the same mythical coin. The ambitious Pal, having dragged his family into the dumps – in-itself an interesting inversion of the immigrant 'rags-to-riches' myth – reclaims his ancestral land in the Punjab on behalf of his son. Except that Pal, the supposed head of the family, is a failure both as a businessman and as a husband. And the son he has is swaddled in another fiction – his mother is not Pal's long-suffering wife but a cousin from India whom he was happy to exploit. The patrimony of ancestral land in the Punjab, which he proudly wants to safeguard for his son, is tainted at its inception. A taint that both Pal and his fiery mother Jeeto wilfully collude in. It is as if they both finally affirm a central truth of migrant lives: that they are built on fictions which, in multiplying over successive generations, take on the reality of myth.

This sense of taint – shameful, dishonourable and outrageously beyond belief – stalks Gurpreet Kaur Bhatti's plays, like the shadow of another life over every migrant's heart, distorting relations between parents and children in an escalating dance to the rhythms of Larkin's bleak prognosis on families. Her collection of plays offers uniquely vivid insights into contemporary British lives with a theatrical aplomb that is suffused with wit and courage to 'draw attention to things that are best left unsaid'.

Jatinder Verma
© May 2014

BEHSHARAM
(SHAMELESS)

Behsharam (Shameless) was first performed on 11 October 2001 at the Soho Theatre and Writers' Centre, in a production by Birmingham Repertory Theatre Company and Soho Theatre Company, with the following cast:

JASPAL, Nathalie Armin
FATHER, Harmage Singh Kalirai
BEJI, Shelley King
SATI, Rina Mahoney
PATRICK, Johann Myers

Director, Deborah Bruce
Designer, Liz Cooke
Lighting designer, Jason Taylor
Choreographer, Shobna Gulati
Dialect, Penny Dyer
Stage Manager, Lorraine Tozer
Deputy Stage Manager, Anna Graf
Assistant Stage Manager, Julia Wickham

SCENE ONE

1998. The sound of applause. A room upstairs in a seedy pub/club in a hopeless Birmingham suburb. Cabaret night. Red velvet curtains are behind a small raised platform on top of which there is an empty microphone.

COMPERE: *(Voiceover.)* Thank you ladies and gentlemen. Remember variety is the spice of life and we've got some red hot vindaloo coming up for you now. Our next act is one of my very own favourites. And she's gorgeous, no really Ladies and Gents, she's… um… she's gorgeous. You'll recognise her from Stars in Their Eyes, where she was pipped at the post by um… by Frankie Goes to Hollywood. *(Bigger voice.)* Coming to you straight from the Handsworth Road, please put your hands together for Kiran Carpenter and her band Asian Invasion!

More applause as JASPAL, a damaged-looking Asian woman in her late twenties, comes out wearing a long sequinned fuschia pink dress. Silhouette/shadow of a band. Intro to 'Yesterday Once More' and she starts to sing with the attitude (though not quite the voice) of a diva.

JASPAL: *(Sings.)* When I was young I'd listen to the radio waiting for my favourite song, when they'd play I'd sing along, it made me smile. Those were such happy times and not so long ago how I wondered where they'd gone. But now they're back again just like a long-lost friend. All the songs I loved so well. Every sha la la la la, every woh oh oh still shines. Every shing a ling a ling that they're starting to sing…

Suddenly the sound system fails, microphones screech and the singing and music become inaudible. JASPAL does her best to carry on but to no avail. The audience become unsettled and sounds of booing and hissing start.

COMPERE: *(Voiceover.)* Well ladies and gents we seem to have a few technical hitches. *(Smaller voice.)* Sorry about that love… er… why don't you er…

JASPAL looks pissed off and walks off the stage.

COMPERE: *(Voiceover)* That's showbusiness folks, up and down quicker than a tart's knickers. We'll have our Kiran back for you in a jiffy. In the meantime, why not make your way to the bar where it's half price for any double with any low calorie mixer. Don't go downstairs!

SCENE TWO

1998. JASPAL's dressing room. A small poky room with a huge old-fashioned dressing table which has three mirrors on it. She is taking her make-up off. Knock at the door.

JASPAL: Piss off.

COMPERE: *(Offstage.)* Someone here to see you love.

JASPAL: Tell them to piss off.

COMPERE: *(Offstage.)* I'll send her up then.

Knock at the door.

JASPAL: Fuck's sake.

She gets up quickly, swings around and goes to open the door.

(Opening door.) All I want is some peace and quiet.

She is silenced by the sight of SATI at the door. SATI is a young pretty Asian girl, dressed in trendy clothes. She is about twenty. They look at each other for a moment.

SATI: Can I come in?

JASPAL moves back as if she is frozen by the sight of her sister. SATI hesitantly enters the room.

SATI: You were good. Out there I mean. Shame about the sound…

JASPAL stares.

SATI: I like your dress.

JASPAL continues to stare. SATI takes out a packet of cigarettes and lights one up.

SATI: Do you want one?

JASPAL: I've stopped.

SATI: What?… Since when?

JASPAL: Since after… never mind. I've stopped.

SATI: Oh.

JASPAL: I didn't know you'd started.

SATI: Oh yeah. It's been a while… soon after… well I started just as you stopped. How about that?

JASPAL: You shouldn't have.

SATI: What?

JASPAL: Started. I thought you'd know better. Never mind about cancer – they dry out your skin and wrinkle up your eyes and deplete your vitamin C. You'll have no immune system left.

SATI: So??

JASPAL grabs the cigarette out of SATI's hand and puts it out hurriedly.

JASPAL: So I'd appreciate it if you stopped stinking out my dressing room. Anyway it's no smoking backstage. Fire hazard.

SATI: Sorry.

JASPAL: I'm a regular here and I don't need any hassle right. Take your dirty habit elsewhere.

JASPAL goes back to her dressing table and carries on taking her make-up off.

SATI: Jaspal.

JASPAL: What.

SATI: I don't believe it. You've changed. I never thought you'd stop. Not you.

JASPAL: Thought you'd be pleased. You were always on at me.

SATI: I was a kid.

JASPAL: And now you're not a kid.

SATI: No.

JASPAL: That's a shame.

SATI: For who?

JASPAL: For you.

SATI: For fuck's sake Jaspal.

JASPAL: Don't you swear in front of me.

SATI: What?

JASPAL: Bad habits. You've picked up some bad habits.

SATI: Maybe it runs in the family.

JASPAL takes out a can of Red Bull, opens it and takes a long swig.

JASPAL: You on your own?

SATI: Yeah.

JASPAL: Didn't fancy bringing a friend?

SATI: Not really.

JASPAL: Not even Mr Cardboard.

SATI: Don't be stupid.

JASPAL: I'm not the one who fell in love with him am I?

SATI: I wasn't in love.

JASPAL: I see him on the telly. What's his name again?

SATI: Stop it.

JASPAL: I'm only asking. Fuck's sake.

SATI: He's gone. Don't you remember?

JASPAL: Oh yeah. His heart got ripped to shreds. Sorry.

SATI: I was a kid.

JASPAL: So you said.

SATI: I stopped all that a long time ago. Anyway, *(she looks her up and down)* you're a fine one to talk.

JASPAL: What?

SATI: Look at you. You've turned yourself into her.

JASPAL: I haven't.

SATI: Mummy 1's favourite.

JASPAL: This is my job right.

SATI: Being a dead pop star?

JASPAL: It's my living.

SATI: Mummy 1 would like it.

JASPAL: Shut up about Mummy 1.

SATI: I saw you on *Stars in Their Eyes*. You were good.

JASPAL: Was I?

SATI: I felt *(pause as she struggles to think)* proud.

JASPAL: Of what?

SATI: You should have won. You looked great, they did a good job on you didn't they? I mean the hair and the make-up and everything… it was all so… believable.

JASPAL: You came to tell me that.

SATI: No.

JASPAL: What do you want?

SATI: Nothing.

JASPAL: Why did you come here?

SATI: To see you. To see how you are.

JASPAL: After four years.

SATI: Yes.

JASPAL: Four fucking years.

SATI: I know it's a long time, a lot's changed…

JASPAL: And don't think you're putting me on any guilt trip. Because I won't have it. I've got no bad habits now. None. I've read the books, I've done the steps, I've even Feng Shui-ed my flat. I'm me, right, ME.

SATI: Is that why you pretend to be Karen Carpenter?

JASPAL: I told you it's my job, it's entertainment. People like it.

SATI: You look like her.

JASPAL: That's what Matthew Kelly said.

SATI: Not like Karen, like Mummy 1.

JASPAL: Will you stop it?

SATI: Remember that photograph, where she's got that beehive and a handbag the size of a suitcase. What did you call it – the Pakis having the picnic in the park. I wanted to look like her. But it was always you.

JASPAL: Shut up.

SATI: I'm just saying…

JASPAL: I don't give a shit. Doesn't affect me any more. Not Mummy 1, not Mummy 2, not Dad, not Patrick, not Beji, not you. And if you think you can walk in here and… well you can fuck off…

SATI: I didn't come here to…

JASPAL: I said sorry.

SATI: You didn't.

JASPAL: You walked out and you left me. You left me. You turn up here, at one of my *performances* and expect me to hug you and kiss you and be all happy and excited. Well I'm not. I did everything for you, everything. You never even bothered about me. No-one ever bothered about me except when they wanted to call someone slag or slut or whore or prostitute. I'm dead to you Sati. Look at me, the living dead. Just get out, get the fuck out, I can't stand looking at you any more.

SATI: Don't… please… don't…

JASPAL: What did you expect?

SATI: I wanted to see you. I've forgiven you…

JASPAL: Fuck off.

SATI: Don't you think I'm the one who should be angry…

JASPAL: You haven't got a right to be angry, like you haven't got a right to forgive. I protected you from all of it, wrapped you in cotton wool. Covered your eyes and your ears and your nose…

SATI: You made it worse.

JASPAL: It was for your own good.

SATI: And you decided that did you, you…

JASPAL: You left me.

SATI: Yeah.

JASPAL: I waited for you.

SATI: I'm here now.

JASPAL: Get lost.

SATI: But… we're family…

JASPAL: I thought you said you'd grown up.

SATI: I'm trying to make things better. You're my sister, my only sister, I feel for you, I really feel…

JASPAL lunges at SATI. She takes her face in her hand and holds it hard against the wall.

JASPAL: You feel for me do you? Feel sorry for me do you?

She releases her and SATI half falls to the floor.

JASPAL: You little cunt.

SATI gathers herself together and exits. JASPAL shouts out after her.

JASPAL: That's a shame. Cos I don't feel anything right. I don't feel fucking anything.

JASPAL is left on her own. She calms down and looks around the room. She catches sight of herself in the mirror, then looks towards the door and goes out after her sister.

SCENE THREE

1994. Day One, The shop. Early evening. The radio is on, 'Whatta Man' by Salt 'n' Pepa and En Vogue plays. Half-empty boxes of tinned produce adorn the dingy space. There are Boots carrier bags everywhere. Sati, sixteen, wears an old shalwar kameez and trendy Nike trainers. She stands behind the shop counter. She vaguely looks over to the shop entrance and when she feels the coast is more or less clear she begins to construct a kind of love seat next to the counter. She creates the seat out of boxes of tinned beans and spaghetti hoops, a small step ladder and a shop stool. She sprays some body spray on herself. She then takes a deep breath and goes to fetch the pièce de résistance – a life-size cardboard cut-out of Ian Wright in Arsenal strip. The cut-out is bendy and can be manipulated into different positions. SATI sits IW on the side of the seat closest to the counter, and sits down next to him.

She begins.

SATI: Ian, I've thought about what you said and I can't. I mean I don't want to. Please understand. It's not that I don't find you attractive. I do. Really I do. But this isn't about that. I respect you Ian, respect you as a footballer. And everything else about you. I mean you and Debbie, what you have is so great, you've got it all – little Stacey, the house in Surrey, the snooker room, I won't let you throw that away Ian. Of course I love you, I mean I have a love for you. But it's more than a physical thing. We share things together. When you got suspended and missed the Cup Winners Cup final against Parma – I cried myself to sleep because I felt your pain. Do you understand? Well I'm not like Dani Behr. This is forever, not a passing thing. I want us to be like Brian Clough and Peter Taylor. Ian, please stop. This has got to be about football, nothing else. Those ninety minutes of epic drama, with heroes, villains, ecstasy and despair. The crowd sings, the players dance… it's a bit like a Bollywood film when you think about it… Have you seen one of those Ian? I'm not changing the subject… I'm just… Ian… Why d'you want to know about them? Alright then. I've got a half-brother, Raju he's six. And there's my older sister Jaspal, she's the black sheep… Oh Ian I didn't mean anything by that… Sorry. They say she's the pretty one… I'm not sure who I look like… I think I look like Mummy 1, that's my real mum. She's on holiday at the moment, she…

Bell rings to indicate shop door is opening. As she hears the bell, SATI pushes IW to the floor and scrambles across the love seat regaining her position behind the counter. PATRICK enters. He is a young, Jamaican male, carrying a big gym bag.

PATRICK: Alright Sati.

SATI: *(Gathers herself together.)* Oh… hello Patrick.

PATRICK: You on your own?

SATI: Yeah… Uncle Comrade's gone to that new Cash & Carry in Smethwick.

PATRICK: Oh yeah?

SATI: You get a free box of Bangladeshi pineapple chunks when you spend over fifty pounds. He couldn't resist that.

PATRICK: I'll have some gum, oh and some of those jammy dodgers for Jaspal.

SATI: She likes them, says they're good for her munchies. *(SATI gets biscuits, serves him, exchange of money etc.)*

PATRICK: Yeah… er… So you getting on alright here?

SATI: It's OK. Fits in with college. Uncle Comrade's not here much, thank god. He found 2p on the floor the other day. And then he starts having a go at me. *(Mimics.)* 'Pennies make pounds, pounds make tens of pounds, tens of pounds make hundreds of pounds, hundreds of pounds make thousands of pounds and that, beti, is the Retail business.'

PATRICK: How much is he paying?

SATI: Pound an hour. So much for his subscription to Marxism Today. I don't mind, he's alright really. *(Gestures to stock cupboard.)* Beji keeps me company and anyway we need the cash. Hey how's your training? You doing the Ali shuffle yet? *(She does some shadow boxing playfully.)*

PATRICK: Getting there. You know training hard, trying to focus. I'm glad to be out of that office, tell you that for nothing.

SATI: It's good to do what you want.

PATRICK: Yeah man.

SATI: Is everything alright with Jaspal?

PATRICK: You know what she's like. Up and down.

SATI: Tell her we miss her. At least I do.

PATRICK: Right.

SATI: So she's alright?

PATRICK: Yeah, yeah. She's getting used to me being in the flat during the day… *(Suddenly remembering.)* … It's Tuesday isn't it, she'll be OK, he always leaves the saag on a Tuesday.

SATI: Hey tell Jaspal that Mummy 2 keeps trying to fix me up.

PATRICK: Yeah?

SATI: She's a right bloody kuthi *[bitch]*. I've told her I'm not interested, but she won't listen. She got me to meet this BMW dealer the other week. And when they left us on our own he started crying, he told me he was in love with his brother-in-law. He pleaded with me to refuse him.

PATRICK: What happened?

SATI: I pretended I was deaf and dumb. Any disability you see, puts the family right off. Anyway Mummy 2 better watch out, Mummy 1 will be back soon.

PATRICK: Been gone a while hasn't she.

SATI: Seven years.

PATRICK: Right… er… Oh, before I forget, I saw this *(Hands her a flyer.)* thought you might like to meet Mr Wright for real.

SATI: *(Reads and gasps.)* Ian Wright's coming to Birmingham.

PATRICK: Yeah, opening some clothes shop in the Pallasades.

SATI: *(Slowly.)* He's coming to Birmingham.

PATRICK: You should go, see him in real life.

SATI: Thanks Patrick. This is incredible, it's…

BEJI: *(Shouting.)* Sati… Sati…

SATI: Oh God. Beji's locked herself in the stock cupboard. Give these to Jaspal from me *(hands PATRICK a box of Milk Tray)* and tell her I'll come and see her after college.

PATRICK: Take it easy Sati.

PATRICK exits. SATI goes to back of shop, lets BEJI out. They come downstage. BEJI is an old Punjabi woman, she has a permanently miserable expression on her face, but her eyes twinkle. She has a hairy face and no teeth and wears an old Punjabi suit, her head is covered with a shawl. BEJI wobbles slightly, she is tipsy. She speaks with an accent.

BEJI: Where's my tic-tacs?

SATI: *(Sniffs as she hands her the box of tic-tacs.)* How's your friend?

BEJI: What?

SATI: Your friend… Jack Daniels!

BEJI: Behsharam, you know it's for my chest *(kindly)*. Come on darling let's go, I'm tired, that cow Mummy 2's going to bite our heads off.

SATI: It's alright, she said she was taking Raju to Shimla's.

BEJI: Raju is a greedy pig.

SATI: Beji! Besides we have to wait for Uncle Comrade. He is supposed to pay us you know.

BEJI: Take it from the till.

SATI: *(As she locks up.)* We can't, it's stealing.

BEJI: Not stealing, borrowing.

SATI: No Beji. *(Pause.)* Beji.

BEJI: Yes, beta.

SATI: Do I look like Mummy 1?

BEJI: Yes beta.

SATI: Mummy 1's prettier than Mummy 2 isn't she?

BEJI: Yes beta. Anyone's prettier than that old bag.

BEJI mutters away to herself and starts to lock up. As she does this SATI picks IW up from behind the counter and holds him close to her face.

SATI: Sometimes I look at my family and I want to heal the differences. Like you did after you smacked David Howells. Make the peace and get on with the game.

She puts him down gently, then turns on a portable TV in the corner of the shop. The voice of Dani Behr comes on, it is 'The Word'. SATI and BEJI start to watch.

SCENE FOUR

1994. Day One, Jaspal and Patrick's flat. The Carpenters' 'Top of the World' plays, and transforms into the music on Jaspal's sound system. Very messy bedsit – two chairs and a beanbag in the middle of the room, there is a bathroom area and a kitchen area. The place is dank and the colours are garish and mismatched. It is like no-one has cleared up for three weeks. There is a messy, packed coffee table, covered with tobacco, rizla papers, bits of food, papers, old makeup and empty takeaway containers. JASPAL is partially dressed, having just had sex with STAN, a punter, friend and dealer.

A door slams. JASPAL is out of it, she slowly puts her clothes back on and at the same time she smokes the end of an old spliff. Her movements are slow and deliberate. She half sings along to the words of the song. JASPAL starts to build another spliff. She lays out rizla paper and fills it with tobacco. She then opens a small packet, it is the wad of weed Stan has left her. On sight of it, she jumps up and goes after him.

JASPAL: Fuck's sake. Come back you bastard.

He's gone, she picks up a Tupperware container wrapped in a Boots carrier bag which has been left on the doorstep and returns inside. She puts the container down on the table and walks around agitated.

JASPAL: Fuck's sake. I told him I want an eighth, I told him. Fuck's sake there's hardly anything here. Stan you fucking bastard. Cheapskate. I told him I'm not a fucking slag, this is business. Bastard. I told him, I do it for an eighth.

She picks up a used condom from the floor, she inspects it.

JASPAL: At least he didn't last long. I'll have words with him Karen. Next time.

She throws the condom in a bin. She takes out saag from the tupperware container and tastes it with a spoon.

JASPAL: Oh shit I can't eat this. It tastes of home. I'll have it after, it'll taste like something else then.

She turns her attention to building the spliff.

Oh shit Karen, ganja alert, ganja alert. There's hardly any left. I'll have to smoke it before… Fuck it, he's on the wagon anyway. I'll just make it last.

She joins in the singing of the song which comes to an end.

You might be a skinny bitch Karen, but you know how to carry a tune. Mummy 1 would have liked this. She liked entertainment didn't she? She loved you Karen. She'd have been proud of me, if I was a bit more like you.

JASPAL is getting more and more out of it.

Not the, you know, not the dying of anorexia bit. She'd have been pissed off at that. Mind you, I'm an entertainer as well aren't I? Sort of.

You and me Karen, we've got a lot in common. *(She looks down at the floor, it's filthy.)*

He'll have to hoover this carpet when he gets back.

(She picks up a face mirror, inspecting the areas of dark hair growth.) Time for beautification Karen. You must have done a bit of that. I bet Richard liked you well groomed.

She starts applying white bleach cream to her upper lip, so this cream now covers her moustache area. She lies in a star shape in the middle of the stage and continues to smoke her spliff.

She hears a door slam, she puts out the spliff, sprays some air freshener, picks up the mirror and viciously starts plucking her eyebrows. PATRICK comes in, puts bag down, goes over to the coffee table and dips some roti into the saag. He chews slowly and watches her.

PATRICK: Can't you do that in the bathroom?

JASPAL: Do you want a woman with a thick black line going across her forehead?

PATRICK: I saw Sati. *(Hands her the chocolates.)* Said she'll come and see you.

JASPAL: What did you tell her?

PATRICK: *(Takes some more food.)* Nothing.

JASPAL: Yeah well, I don't want her getting all upset.

PATRICK: About what?

JASPAL: Anything. She gets upset sometimes. She misses Mummy 1.

PATRICK: Sati said she's coming back.

JASPAL: What's it got to do with you?

PATRICK: I'm just telling you what she told me. Jesus Christ Jaspal. *(Pause.)* Do you know how long your mum's been away?

JASPAL: A while.

PATRICK: Seven years.

JASPAL: And?

PATRICK: Don't you think that's a long time for a holiday.

JASPAL: It's not a holiday. It's a religious pilgrimage. It takes that long to do it.

PATRICK: I see.

JASPAL: Fuck's sake Patrick. It's to do with the culture isn't it?

PATRICK: Right.

JASPAL: Aren't you going to ask if I had a nice day?

PATRICK: I'm the one who's been out all day.

JASPAL: *(Starts taking bleach off with a spatula.)* Of course. How many people did you beat the shit out of today?

PATRICK: *(Moves away.)* Piss off.

JASPAL: *(Moves towards him.)* No tell me. Boxing is a science after all. Between *Richard and Judy* and *Countdown*, I don't get much intellectual stimulation. Maybe you can provide it. I mean you are the one with the degree aren't you.

PATRICK: This place is a tip.

JASPAL: Though having a degree no longer guarantees one a lifetime of security.

PATRICK: *(Sniffs.)* You need a better quality of air freshener.

JASPAL: Especially if your boyfriend leaves his job and starts dreaming of nights out with Prince Naseem.

PATRICK: This place is a tip.

JASPAL: Sorry mum. *(She relights spliff.)*

PATRICK: You could make an effort.

JASPAL: I'll do it later.

PATRICK: I just saw Stan.

JASPAL: Oh yeah.

PATRICK: Has he been round?

JASPAL: No. Why?

PATRICK: Only asking. So what have you been up to?

JASPAL: Loads of things. I sat here… I watched telly…

PATRICK: *(Starts to tidy up.)* There's nothing stopping you going out you know.

JASPAL: There is.

PATRICK: You could go for a nice walk.

JASPAL: Stop that will you. I said I'd do it later.

PATRICK: Bit of exercise, might clear your head.

JASPAL: I don't need my head cleared.

PATRICK: *(Takes spliff from her.)* Give us a toke.

JASPAL: It's the last bit.

PATRICK: I only want a drag.

JASPAL: I'm trying to make it last.

PATRICK: Who paid for it?

JASPAL: *(Takes spliff back off him.)* And you're meant to be in training.

PATRICK: Who paid for it?

JASPAL: I did with my money actually.

PATRICK: I think you'll find I paid for it.

JASPAL: What fucking difference does it make?

PATRICK: I'm just saying.

JASPAL: Stop going on at me willya. It's not my fault you left
your job and we have to live on the fucking poverty line.
What do you want me to say? Two giros are better than
one.

PATRICK: Well they are.

JASPAL: Shut up. Stop going on at me.

PATRICK: I'm sorry. *(He goes over to her, puts his arm around her.)*

JASPAL: My head hurts.

PATRICK: I'm sorry.

JASPAL: Why don't you go out for a bit?

PATRICK: For a bit of what.

JASPAL: You could go and see Stan.

PATRICK: I've just got in.

JASPAL: Go on please. Just a five pound draw.

PATRICK: Jaspal.

JASPAL: Please Patrick please. I only need a bit.

PATRICK: You go.

JASPAL: I can't. I've got a period pain.

PATRICK: Thought it was a headache.

JASPAL: It is as well. *(Pause.)* Please, it'll help me sleep.

PATRICK looks at her, puts his arms around her. They cuddle.

PATRICK: Alright, but I want us to stop. Both of us.

JASPAL: So do I.

PATRICK: Let's make this the last time alright. I need to clean
myself up.

JASPAL: So do I.

PATRICK: The last time. Alright?

JASPAL: Thanks.

They carry on cuddling.

JASPAL: So when are you going.

PATRICK: *(Lets go of her.)* For god's sake. I'll go in a bit.

JASPAL: I'm sorry. *(She puts her arms round him.)* I didn't mean it.

PATRICK: In a bit.

JASPAL: Promise.

PATRICK: I promise. *(They hold each other again.)*

SCENE FIVE

1994. Day Two, The Shop. Afternoon. The FATHER sits on a stool, engrossed in his notebook, he holds a pen. SATI sits on the floor watching TV, fiddling with the remote control. IW cut-out sits on a chair next to SATI. She watches a Football Focus-type programme, which can just about be heard. They both seem to be in their own worlds. The Father talks good English, but has a strong Punjabi accent. He wears old trousers, trainers, mismatched shirt and tie and a red tank top.

SATI: Dad it says on Ceefax that Ian Wright dreams of ending his career at Highbury.

FATHER: *(Not listening.)* Oh yes.

SATI: That's good isn't it.

FATHER: Very good.

SATI: It means that the Gunners' strike force will continue to be led by a man who fuses both explosivity and calm in front of the goal; who uses both legs – left and right.

FATHER: Oh yes, I know.

SATI: He's a lethal weapon Dad.

FATHER: *(With a start.)* Where?

SATI: That rare breed of quick thinkers in the box, always a second faster than any defender.

FATHER: *(Starts to compose a poem.)* Tu... *[You...]*

SATI: Except most probably Tony Adams.

SATI looks intently at the screen. She shakes her fist at it scornfully.

SATI: Forget it Lineker, you're a has-been. Sayonara Gary. Don't you reckon Dad?

FATHER continues to be ignorant of her presence.

FATHER: Tu heh... *[You are...]*

SATI: *(Looks over to cut-out and sings to it.)* Ian Wright, Wright, Wright. Ian Wright, Wright, Wright.

FATHER: Tu heh meri... *[You are my...]*

SATI: I'm coming to see you Ian. In the flesh. Only two days left.

FATHER: Meri... *[My...]*.

SATI: I'll have to get myself ready. Do all the preparation.

FATHER: Tu meri... *[You're my...]*

SATI: *(Looking round the shop.)* We'll close early. Uncle Comrade won't mind.

FATHER: Tu meri zindagi meh... *[In my life you...]*

SATI: I can't wait.

FATHER: *(Looking up.)* Ay *[Came]*. Ah yes... *(He puts his notebook down.)* When is Comrade coming?

SATI: After he's finished at the caucus meeting.

FATHER: I need some money.

SATI: Don't we all dad.

FATHER: Can you ask him for me?

SATI: He's *your* cousin.

FATHER: Yes but he likes you better than he likes me. Always looking down on me because he has this... this shop.

SATI: He doesn't look down on you.

FATHER: *(Looking round.)* What kind of communism is this – where you set up your own small business?

SATI: Leave it will you.

FATHER: Bloody Comrade.

SATI: I'm not asking him.

FATHER: Please.

SATI: No.

FATHER: It's for Raju's tap dancing classes. Mummy 2 says he needs private tuition.

SATI: Tap dancing! He already has piano and tennis lessons.

FATHER: I know.

SATI: He's only six.

FATHER: Mummy 2 says he needs it.

SATI: He's your son dad.

FATHER: He's your brother.

SATI: Half brother. I'm not asking Uncle Comrade for anything except my wages.

FATHER: Suit yourself.

SATI: Stop being so immature.

FATHER: Leave me alone please. I have to finish my poem.

SATI: *(Channel hopping with remote control.)* Where is Raju?

FATHER: *(Ignoring her, recites loudly.)* Tu meri zindagi meh ay. *[You came into my life.]*

SATI: *(Checks watch.)* She must have taken him down the factory with her.

FATHER *(Starts pacing around the shop.)* Tu meri zindagi meh ay.

SATI: Poor Raju. Amount of sweets she force feeds him, he'll end up looking like one of those leather footballs she makes.

FATHER: Tu meri zindagi meh ay.

SATI: Can't you get past the first line?

FATHER: I'm stuck.

SATI: What?

FATHER: I've got writer's block.

BEJI enters holding lots of Boots carrier bags.

BEJI: *(Addressing SATI.)* So many special offers. *(She indicates the bags.)* Everything Three for price of Two.

SATI stares at the screen.

BEJI: *(Starts taking make-up out of bags to show SATI.)* I got you special selection. L'Oreal, Rimmel, Maybelline. Red wine spritzer lip liner, ebony and ivory eye pencil and bridal suite blush creme.

SATI: Thank you Beji.

BEJI: *(Takes SATI's cheek affectionately between her fingers.)* Make-up for day, for evening, for afternoons, for college, for home, for the shop. Anything you want my princess.

SATI: Thanks.

BEJI: Remember is not what you feel like but what you look like. That is the important thing.

SATI: Yes Beji.

BEJI looks disdainfully at IW.

BEJI: Girls are so beautiful and men are so ugly.

SATI: Yes Beji.

BEJI: *(Looks at FATHER with evil eyes.)* What did he make today?

SATI: *(To FATHER.)* What did you make today?

FATHER: Saag.

SATI: Saag.

BEJI: Did he take some to that girl?

SATI: Did you take some to Jaspal, Dad?

FATHER: Yes.

SATI: Yes.

BEJI: Behsharam. Bucharee. Shameless. Poor girl. Would be better if she died in a car crash.

SATI: Beji, don't…

BEJI: Always doing dirty things with bad men.

SATI: She's not.

BEJI: She used to be such a nice girl, before… Anyway tell him I have some good news beta, postcard from Mummy 1. It must have fallen out.

FATHER: Will you please tell her to talk to me? I am her son for God's sake.

SATI: *(To BEJI.)* Dad says will you please talk to him. He is your son for God's…

BEJI: *(Growls with evil eyes at the FATHER.)* Fuck off.

SATI: *(To FATHER.)* She says…

FATHER: Oh for God's sake.

SATI: What did Mummy 1 say?

BEJI: She's having a joyful time.

SATI: Still visiting all the temples.

BEJI: Yes all the gurdwaras.

SATI: Did she say when she'll be back?

BEJI: Soon. She said she'll be back soon.

SATI: Dad, Beji said mum'll be back soon.

BEJI: And we will be one big happy family. Except for Mummy 2 and that behsharam kuthi *[shameless bitch]* Jaspal.

SATI: Mummy 1 is going to live with us isn't she Dad?

FATHER: Sati…

SATI: You said Dad. Remember you said that divorce doesn't matter. You said it's our culture.

FATHER: Yes beta.

SATI: And now you've got Raju it's alright isn't it?

FATHER: Everything is alright.

SATI: I'm glad. I can't wait to see my mum.

FATHER: Sati you have a new mum now and a brother.

SATI: Mummy 2's not my mum.

FATHER: She is your second mum.

BEJI has been observing them. As they have been speaking she has furtively dialled a number on the phone behind the counter.

BEJI: *(Into phone.)* Everyone hates you, you ugly old bag.

FATHER and SATI rush over and FATHER takes the phone off her. SATI leads her away from the phone.

FATHER: Stop it. I told you before no more. *(Into phone.)* Hello yes. I'm sorry, she doesn't mean it.

BEJI: *(Shouts.)* Yes I do. *(Sings.)* Ugly old bag. Ugly old bag.

FATHER: Stop it. *(Into phone.)* Please ignore her. What? OK. OK. I see you later.

He puts the phone down and rejoins SATI who is now watching the TV. BEJI watches them with evil eyes.

FATHER: She is taking Raju for Chinese.

SATI: Again?

FATHER: *(Stands up and points at BEJI.)*

You, I've had enough of you. You are banned from using the phone. Do you understand – banned. *(To SATI.)* Tell her.

SATI: You're banned.

FATHER: And how does she know Mummy 2's mobile number?

SATI: How do you know Mummy 2's...

FATHER: No more of your... your obscene phone calls... My wife and my son. How do you think they feel? I know you don't like them.

BEJI: I don't like them.

FATHER: You never liked me. You're plotting something. I know you.

BEJI: *(To SATI.)* I'm going KFC. You want chicken sandwich?

The FATHER retreats to his seat.

SATI: No thanks.

BEJI: *(Goes out, looks over at the FATHER.)* Now he will start with his rubbish poems.

SATI: Beji, leave him…

The FATHER begins to recite. He does so as if he is in a trance.

FATHER: Mushkal nazar aata tha gala kaught kai marna
Aukhar yai muham bhi teri jambaz nai sir ki

(He translates to himself wistfully.)

It is hard to die by cutting your own throat
Even when you want it, the coward within takes over

SATI: *(She looks over to the cut-out.)* … Sorry, he gets a bit emotional sometimes…

FATHER: Zindgi sai tau khair shikwa tha
Mudtaun Maut nai bhi tarsaya

(He translates to himself wistfully.)

Life is not to one's liking
Yet it takes an age for death to quench the thirst

SATI: Dad, you're depressing Ian.

FATHER: *(Breaking out of trance.)* Where is Comrade?

SATI: I don't know.

FATHER: I'm going.

SATI: Where?

FATHER: To the dole office, to see if they can help me.

SATI: You can't keep going there.

FATHER: I need money.

SATI: For tap dancing lessons?

FATHER: Sati.

SATI: Yes.

FATHER: *(Goes over to her and puts his hand on her shoulder.)* You are a good girl. *(He exits.)*

SATI: *(Gets up and starts tidying all the Boots carrier bags, addresses cut-out.)* Everyone's got problems Ian, everyone. I mean Mummy 2's not the easiest person to get on with, *(imitates Mummy 2)* Sati choose a boy before I choose one for you… I mean I don't understand why she's so keen, she's not exactly over the moon being with my dad. *(Pause.)* Poor dad. It must be terrible being hated by your mother. At least my mum doesn't hate me, even if she is off being a pilgrim somewhere. She'll be like you Ian, she'll be our saviour. And we'll all cheer and sing songs when she comes home. Like I did when you won the Golden Boot. Mummy 1'll sort Mummy 2 out for a start. No more manhunting, no more putting you in the cellar. No more *(imitates)* 'educating your daughter is like watering another man's fields.' No more leather factory smells. No more 'Bad girl, sisters are supposed to look after their brothers'. It's not like I'm going to forget.

'Bad Girl' by Donna Summer starts playing.

SCENE SIX

1994. Day three, early evening. Jaspal's flat. JASPAL sits opposite the IW cut-out. She beholds him suspiciously.

JASPAL: You alright there? *(She waits for him to respond.)* Conversation not your strong point then? *(She gives up on IW and calls out to SATI who's offstage making tea.)* Oy, bring them custard creams in will ya.

SATI: *(Offstage.)* How many sugars?

JASPAL: *(She thinks for a moment before responding.)* Five.

SATI comes in with two mugs of tea and biscuits.

SATI: Bad girl this, bad girl that. Change the record that's what I say.

JASPAL: *(Is building spliff.)* Nothing changes.

SATI: I'm going to meet Ian Wright, no matter what.

JASPAL: Oh good.

SATI: I've planned it all.

JASPAL: It's good to have a goal.

SATI: I don't care what Mummy 2 says, I'm going.

JASPAL: We all need a goal.

SATI: Do you think it's because Ian's black?

JASPAL: I expect there is a connection.

SATI: It's not just Mummy 2. It's Dad and Beji as well. They pretend they don't mind Ian but they do. I've heard them say things.

JASPAL: What things?

SATI: About black people.

JASPAL: You shouldn't listen to their shit.

SATI: I don't. *(Pause.)* Sometimes they say things about you.

JASPAL: Really.

SATI: Beji says you go out with a black bastard.

JASPAL laughs as she continues to build spliff.

SATI: Why do Indian people hate black people?

JASPAL: I don't know do I? Some black people hate Indians as well y'know… do we have to talk about this. It's so depressing.

SATI: That's your answer to everything.

JASPAL: *(Cheerfully.)* Well I *am* depressed.

SATI: You want to be depressed more like.

JASPAL: *(Lights spliff.)* I don't.

SATI: Moping about, listening to that sad woman with anorexia.

JASPAL: She has got a fucking name y'know.

SATI: Is it to remind you of Mummy 1?

JASPAL: No.

SATI: She was her favourite though wasn't she?

JASPAL: Will you shut up? I'm trying to get off my head here.

SATI: It's not right. *(Whips spliff away from JASPAL and puts it out.)* You shouldn't be doing this all the time.

JASPAL: *(Retrieves it and relights.)* What do you know?

SATI: I know.

JASPAL: You'll understand when you get older.

SATI: That stuff keeps the people down. Robs you of your ambition and self-esteem.

JASPAL: *(Smiles as she enjoys her smoke.)* Does it fuck.

SATI: *(Reaches into her bag.)* I've got something for you. *(Hands book over to JASPAL.)* I saw it on *Richard and Judy*, it's recommended by that Raj Persaud. You know the Indian one.

JASPAL: *(Reads.)* HEALING AND FEELING – A GUIDE TO COPING WITH ADDICTIVE BEHAVIOURS – An alcoholic's perspective.

SATI: Only it's not just alcoholics see, its any addiction. *(Reads from a piece of paper.)* Yes see, it's all of them – drugs, sex, gambling… even biscuits. It's for people who… who've got problems. *(Takes out a tape which she gives to her.)* There's a tape as well.

JASPAL holds book and tape and starts laughing uncontrollably until she falls over and continues to laugh on the floor.

SATI: *(Hovers over her.)* Give it a read. You never know.

JASPAL continues to laugh. Eventually subsides.

SATI: You've got a lot Jaspal. You've got this place *(looks around – the flat is a tip)*, even though it's a bit messy. You've got Patrick, and I mean, he cares, he really does care. *(Pause.)* Maybe you should make a bit more of an effort, dinner by candlelight or something. I bet he'd love that.

JASPAL: *(Out of it.)* Drugs advice and relationship counselling. Fucking hell you're only 16.

SATI: I'm trying to…

JASPAL: Maybe you should move in. We need some of that round here.

SATI: I didn't mean…

JASPAL: I know, I'm joking. I mean where would we put you… *(Points to cut-out.)* not to mention your famous footballing friend here… *(Pause.)* … do you take him to college?

SATI: Most days, he sort of keeps me company.

JASPAL: Oh yeah, right. Company, yeah. How is college anyway?

SATI: Boring. Full of saddos.

JASPAL: Oy. Don't neglect your education. Education is freedom. That's what dad used to say. Does he still say that? Does he?

SATI: No.

JASPAL: And make some friends will you please? For once it'd be nice if you brought a real-life human round instead of… *(Points to IW.)* … him.

SATI: *(Gets up.)* If you don't want us here we can always…

JASPAL: For fuck's sake, sit down willya… sit down… I'm only having a joke… fuck's sake… why are you so serious… chill out willya, sit down and chill.

SATI sits back down.

JASPAL: That's better. I'm just saying y'know, maybe you should go out y'know with the other students.

SATI: I'm too busy, Uncle Comrade needs me in the shop, and there's Beji to think of.

JASPAL: So she talks about me, does she?

SATI: No… *(Blurts out.)* well sometimes she says it would be better if you died in a car crash.

Pause. JASPAL laughs.

SATI: *(Hurriedly.)* But she doesn't mean it. You know what it's like.

JASPAL: Yeah I know. Dead but with izzat intact.

SATI: I wish they'd let you come home. They might, one day. Maybe you could make up. *(Pause.)* Couldn't you say sorry?

JASPAL: For what?

SATI: For all the bad things you did.

JASPAL: What things?

SATI: You know, going out with boys and smoking and all that.

JASPAL: Having a boyfriend isn't a crime Sati.

SATI: I know.

JASPAL: You shouldn't believe their lies.

SATI: I don't.

JASPAL: Do you want to know the real reason I left home?

SATI: Tell me.

JASPAL: I wanted to be a performer. I wanted to be in entertainment. They didn't approve.

SATI: What happened?

JASPAL: I left. That's it. Simple.

SATI: They never said.

JASPAL: They wouldn't would they.

SATI: What about your performing?

JASPAL: I stopped all that ages ago.

SATI: You should start again, do a course or something. You never know, you might become a star one day.

JASPAL: I might.

SATI: And I could come and see you in a show.

JASPAL: Yeah.

SATI: I could bring Mummy 1. She'll be home soon.

JASPAL: Who said?

SATI: Beji got a postcard from her. *(Recounts.)* She says she's been to all the gurdwaras in India, and once she's done the ones in Pakistan she'll be back.

JASPAL starts building another spliff.

SATI: Please don't do that.

JASPAL: Why not?

SATI: Can't we be normal and talk?

JASPAL: What's normal?

SATI: Well it changes your state of mind doesn't it – that stuff.

JASPAL: Too fucking right – why do you think I smoke the shit.

SATI: I don't think it's very helpful.

JASPAL: Helpful? Helpful? What the fuck do you know? Just shut up willya, you're doing my head in, man. I know I haven't been out much but I think it's still a free fucking country. Shit I can't even enjoy this now, you've done my head in that much.

SATI: That's your answer to everything isn't it, reach for the rizlas.

JASPAL: *(Angry, screams.)* Why don't you shut the fuck up.

Silence. They are both still for a second. JASPAL then continues to roll.

JASPAL: No-one asked you to come round.

SATI: I want you to be alright.

JASPAL: I'm fine.

SATI: You look terrible, you never go out and this place is disgusting. You've got to sort yourself out, mum'll be back soon.

JASPAL: She won't be back.

SATI: Don't say that.

JASPAL: Well… the pilgrimage…

SATI: What about it?

JASPAL: She's probably turned all religious fundamentalist hasn't she?

SATI: She will be back. I know she will. *(Pause.)* What's Mummy 2 going to do when Mummy 1 comes back?

JASPAL: How should I know?

SATI: I mean someone has to be in charge. Most probably it'll be mum 'cos she's the first wife.

JASPAL: I suppose.

SATI: My mum's a pilgrim. Like the pilgrim fathers, only she's a mother. I could organize a homecoming party. Do you think she'll like that?

JASPAL: I don't know.

SATI: Jaspal, do I look like her?

JASPAL: Will you stop asking me all these questions. I don't know right. I can't remember. Leave me alone willya. I just wanted to chill out, have a puff and you're on at me all the time.

SATI: Sorry Jaspal.

JASPAL: I've got to go to the toilet.

JASPAL exits leaving SATI alone on the sofa. SATI gets up slowly and gets her things together. As she gets IW out of his seat, she talks to him.

SATI: It's because I'm a girl. That's one thing I know for certain. I heard them all saying things, I remember hearing the fights. If I'd been a boy, dad would never have divorced Mummy 1, never married Mummy 2. There would be no Raju. Jaspal most probably would never have got a boyfriend and Mummy 1 would never have gone to India. If I'd been a boy they'd have had more children – another girl, another boy, another girl, another boy. We'd be like an Indian Brady Bunch. Beji would love dad, dad would be rich and not read poems about dying and I might be an apprentice at Highbury, not just a fan. Jaspal would clean her room and Beji wouldn't drink whisky in Uncle

Comrade's stock room. It's an adverse situation Ian. Like when Graham Taylor became England manager. Only there's no-one to sack. Anyway whatever happens, I've got you. I'm going to come and see you at The Pallasades. See you in the flesh. It's going to be a really special day.

Clutching IW, SATI solemnly turns and leaves the flat.

Over to the FATHER who sits in the shop with his notebook. He chews his pen as he contemplates.

At the same time, JASPAL comes back in, she sits on the sofa and hums in her out of it fashion to The Carpenters' 'This Masquerade'. She smokes the end of a spliff.

In the shop the FATHER puts his notebook down, he gets up and recites.

FATHER: I wander'd lonely as a cloud
That floats on high o'er vales and...
(He struggles to remember.) ... something...

He shakes his head and starts again.

FATHER: Ah yes. *(He clears his throat.)*
Shall I compare thee to a summer's day?
Thou art more lovely and more... *(He struggles to remember.)* ... pretty than... .

He gives up and picks up his notebook. He flicks through it. He sits down. At last he's found what he wants. He looks up and recites.

FATHER: Tu meri zindagi meh ay.

He nods contentedly.

PATRICK comes in to the flat.

JASPAL: I feel sick.

PATRICK: What's wrong?

JASPAL: I'm sick.

PATRICK: Don't smoke then.

PATRICK comes and sits beside her and takes the spliff out of her hand and takes a long drag.

JASPAL: Can you not do that please? *(She takes it back.)*

PATRICK: What?

JASPAL: You're meant to have given up.

PATRICK: I'm celebrating. *(He takes it back and finishes it.)*

JASPAL: Don't they teach you about will power in your training. *(She takes it back and tries to take a drag, no joy.)* Oh fuck. Oh fuck Patrick it's dead, it's fucking dead.

PATRICK: I thought you were sick.

JASPAL: I am.

PATRICK: I've got good news.

JASPAL: It was only a skinny one as well. Oh fuck. *(She starts looking around for some more, picking up sofa cushions etc.)*

PATRICK: Don't you want to hear it?

JASPAL: There's a blim here somewhere.

PATRICK: Jaspal!

JASPAL: I know there is.

PATRICK gets up and faces her.

PATRICK: I said I've got good news.

JASPAL stops hunting.

JASPAL: Money?

PATRICK: *(Sits down.)* Not exactly, not yet.

JASPAL: *(Carries on hunting.)* What then?

PATRICK: This American guy's been to see me, they reckon he wants to train me.

JASPAL: What?

PATRICK: He's worked with some of the best boxers in the world, and he wants me to go over there.

JASPAL: But you've got a trainer – Eric or Ernie or whatever his name is.

PATRICK: Eric's not in the same league as this guy. It's a great opportunity.

JASPAL: You're too old.

PATRICK: He doesn't seem to think so.

JASPAL: You're not even that fit. Remember that time we ran for that bus and I beat you.

PATRICK: That was years ago.

JASPAL: You were out of breath in seconds and that was when I had my bad leg.

PATRICK: Can't you be happy for me?

JASPAL: You're living in a dreamworld.

PATRICK: Me?

JASPAL: Hang on. Hang on let me get this straight. You're going to America? You're going to leave me. You're going away.

PATRICK: I didn't say I was going. I'm saying I've got the opportunity.

JASPAL: So you're not going?

PATRICK: I'm telling you about my day.

JASPAL: For fuck's sake Patrick, for fuck's sake. Are you trying to do my head in or what? If you're not going why bother telling me. I don't care.

PATRICK: I want you to be proud.

JASPAL: Because you like beating people up?

PATRICK: It's boxing. I want to box.

JASPAL: But you're wasted. I know I'm wasted. But you, you really are wasted. You had a good job. We had money. I ironed your shirts. We used to have wine.

PATRICK: What are you saying?

JASPAL: Maybe you should go back to work.

PATRICK: What?

JASPAL: Things will get better then.

PATRICK: You don't get it do you?

JASPAL: What don't I get?

PATRICK: I'm doing what I want. For the first time in my life. No office politics, no team-building, no deadlines, no grey-coloured white people sitting opposite me.

JASPAL: *(Hunting again.)* Where's that blim?

PATRICK: I'm not having it – not sitting in an office day by day, suited and booted having my work checked by a Nicola or a Caroline. *(Mimics.)* 'Your girlfriend rang again, she sounded upset, is she not well?'

JASPAL: It's got to be here.

PATRICK: You've got no faith have you.

JASPAL: I'm an atheist.

PATRICK: Not like me. I've always had faith. Faith in lots of things. Father Christmas, Jesus, Allah, Guru Nanak, all them boys. I even thought Muhammed Ali would beat Leon Spinks.

JASPAL: Where is it?

PATRICK: Faith in you and me, even when I had to drag you back home when you were off your face fucking strangers on the streets, I always had faith.

JASPAL: *(Hits him.)* Fuck you.

PATRICK: It's true.

JASPAL: Fuck you.

They have a semi-fight. JASPAL tries to hit him again. He gets her by the wrists and sits her down.

PATRICK: Calm down.

JASPAL: Fuck off.

PATRICK: Let's just calm down.

JASPAL: You have to throw that back in my face don't you.

PATRICK: I meant I've always believed.

JASPAL: Every time.

PATRICK: I didn't mean it like that.

JASPAL: Fuck off Patrick. Just fuck off.

PATRICK: I didn't mean it.

JASPAL: Yes you did. Yes you fucking did. I gave up everything for you. I lost my family because of you.

PATRICK: No Jaspal. No. They were gone long before.

JASPAL: I left my family to be with you.

PATRICK: They chucked you out.

JASPAL: They didn't.

PATRICK: Come on you remember…

JASPAL: Stop it.

PATRICK: First your mum went…

JASPAL: Don't you talk about my mum you bastard.

PATRICK: And then you started on that shit.

JASPAL: Shut your mouth.

PATRICK: Fucking those lowlife losers. Your dad and your gran found out…

JASPAL: Shut your fucking mouth.

PATRICK: And then they chucked you out. And I came for you Jaspal. I came for you. Night after night after night.

JASPAL: Who the fuck do you think you are? Jesus Christ, my saviour? Some knight in shining armour, who came to my rescue cos I used to spread my legs for a few quid.

He moves towards the door.

JASPAL: Where are you going?

PATRICK: I need to get out of here.

JASPAL: I want you to call Stan.

PATRICK: Not today.

JASPAL: Please Patrick.

PATRICK: You ask him. I'm sure he'll oblige.

JASPAL: For fuck's sake Patrick. One little fucking thing I ask you.

PATRICK: I'm going out. *(He leaves.)*

JASPAL: Well fuck off then just fuck off. Go to America. Go with Ernie. *(Pause.)* You don't know what it was like for me. Or for my mum. You bastard. *(Pause. Calls after him.)* Remember to ask Stan if you see him.

JASPAL slumps back into the flat. She's anxious and agitated.

JASPAL: Where's that blim?

She continues to hunt frantically.

SCENE SEVEN

1994. Day four, morning. The Shop. The FATHER sits on his stool with his notebook and pen, trying to compose poetry. BEJI stands at the counter, she aggressively marks tins of beans with a price gun. She is deliberately loud, hoping that the noise disturbs the FATHER. He does his best to ignore her. She finishes all the tins and there is silence. He puts pen to paper. But immediately stops as she starts again, making more noise than before. The FATHER's had enough.

FATHER: Why are you doing this?

BEJI: I'm a worker. I have to work.

FATHER: You are doing it on purpose. To disturb me.

BEJI: Comrade told me to put the prices…

FATHER: Why do you torture me like this?

BEJI: Comrade is my manager. I have to do my work.

FATHER: Bloody Comrade.

BEJI carries on doing the prices.

FATHER: You should be on my side.

BEJI carries on doing the prices.

FATHER: I am your son. Your only son.

BEJI carries on doing the prices.

FATHER: Please stop that noise.

She carries on.

FATHER: Please stop it.

She carries on.

FATHER: I said stop.

He gets up, grabs the gun out of her hands and throws it against the wall. It breaks. They are silent for a moment. BEJI starts to laugh.

FATHER: What's so funny?

BEJI: You broke it. You will have to pay Comrade.

FATHER: I won't.

BEJI: I'll tell Comrade. He will make you.

FATHER: No he won't. He likes me. He helps me…

BEJI: He helps you because he likes your new wife. He likes Mummy 2.

FATHER: Shut up.

BEJI: He likes to do things to her.

FATHER: Stop lying.

BEJI: I have seen them.

FATHER: I'm not listening to you.

BEJI: Who can blame her? With you as a husband, who can blame her?

FATHER: Leave me alone.

BEJI: Comrade gives you money and Mummy 2 pays him back with her fat body.

FATHER: Why do you hate me so much?

BEJI: Why are you so useless? Always going to the dole office, always asking Comrade for money. What sort of man loses control of his family like this?

FATHER: I do my best.

BEJI: And Raju, what about him? Mummy 2 is always overfeeding him, making him do piano lessons and tap dancing.

FATHER: He likes it.

BEJI: Your son is turning into your daughter.

FATHER: Shut up.

BEJI: You let her spoil him, she spends too much money. I wish you'd never brought her here.

FATHER: Mummy 2 is my wife. The mother of my son, she…

BEJI: And what about Mummy 1?

FATHER: It was your fault, you were supposed to look after her.

BEJI: Don't you talk to me like that you bastard, she was your wife. She was your responsibility.

FATHER: Leave me alone.

BEJI: She was weak, she needed you.

FATHER: I'm not listening.

BEJI: You should have kept her. Kept both of them. Mummy 1 and Mummy 2.

FATHER: I did my best.

BEJI: You have no backbone. Is this what I gave birth to? A spineless weak tosser?

FATHER: No-one ever gave me a chance. And you, you were always there waiting for it to go wrong.

BEJI: Sati is beginning to ask questions. She wants to know.

FATHER: Don't you tell her anything.

BEJI: I'm not going to tell, you bastard. I'm not as stupid as you.

FATHER: Why are you doing this?

BEJI: Sati goes to see that behsharam Jaspal. What if she tells her? Then what will you do?

FATHER: She is a drug addict, she doesn't remember.

BEJI: How do you know?

FATHER: I know.

BEJI: Jaspal brought so much shame on us and you did nothing.

FATHER: What did you want me to do? Kill her?

BEJI: You couldn't kill a fly. You're too bloody useless.

FATHER: Leave me alone, I'm trying to write my poem.

The FATHER turns his attention to his notebook again. BEJI goes and retrieves the price gun, she starts the pricing again. Qawaali music starts to play.

BEJI: What about Sati? Always sitting with that black cardboard man, talking to him. It's not normal.

FATHER: Shut up, she will hear you.

BEJI: And what if she becomes like Jaspal? What will you do then?

FATHER: Sati is a good girl.

BEJI: You make me sick. You and your poems. What kind of man are you?

Qawaali music plays louder, as the emotion approaches crescendo, it gets bigger and bigger and ends in a deafening scream.

Silence. The FATHER and BEJI look up at the same time, as though something terrible has happened. They then look down again and carry on with what they were doing. SATI comes running in from the stock room. In one hand she holds the head of IW, in the other the rest of his body from the cardboard cutout. Someone has cut IW's head off.

SATI: LOOK WHAT SHE'S DONE.

FATHER: *(Briefly distracted from the book.)* What happened?

SATI: Mummy 2… she's cut his head off.

FATHER and BEJI are unmoved by this, they carry on with what they are doing.

BEJI: Sit down beta.

SATI: No I won't. I'm sick of this. Sick of her always looking through my stuff, saying this and that, saying I'm bad like Jaspal, not letting me go out, telling me to get married…

BEJI: We not get married. We're not getting you married, no. Men are all dogs... I've heard about those women... you know... there are those women who don't need men, you will be like them, you will be a lesbian. With the lipstick.

SATI: No, you don't understand.

BEJI: You can still have children, they put it in the fridge.

SATI: NO. *(To FATHER.)* You've got to tell her dad. Tell her off, make her stay away from my stuff.

FATHER: What can I do?

SATI: You're my dad.

FATHER: It's not my fault.

SATI: Dad, tell her...

FATHER: Please listen to Mummy 2.

BEJI: Sit down beta, *(points to telly) Fast Show* is coming soon.

SATI: Dad I need you to back me for once. I'm your daughter. Please.

FATHER: I can't do anything.

SATI: Please dad.

FATHER: It's not my fault.

SATI: I want my mum.

FATHER: Don't blame me.

SATI: I want my mum. I want her.

BEJI: She's coming back soon beta.

SATI: When? You keep saying that, but she never comes does she? Does she dad?

FATHER: It was not Mummy 2 who cut his head off, it was her. *(Points to BEJI.)*

BEJI: Kutha, haramzada. Bloody liar, bloody liar. You dog, you bastard, bloody liar.

FATHER: It was her, I saw her cut it.

BEJI grabs the phone and dials. FATHER rushes over to her.

FATHER: No more, no more phone calls, I told you.

BEJI: *(Into phone.)* Next time we'll cut your head off. You bloody cow.

FATHER: Stop it. Stop it. *(He grabs the phone off her, tries to speak to Mummy 2, she has hung up.)*

FATHER: *(To BEJI.)* Go to hell. Just go to hell.

BEJI: I am already in it.

FATHER: *(To SATI.)* It was her, I saw her cut it. She got drunk and then she did it. She's always drunk.

SATI: Dad, stop making things up. She's your wife, you've got to deal with her.

FATHER: It's not my fault.

BEJI: *(To SATI.)* No backbone, he has no backbone, He is a tosser.

FATHER: You call me a tosser.

BEJI: Always writing his rubbish poems.

FATHER: I need to express myself, no-one here listens to me.

BEJI: Rubbish poems.

FATHER: *(To BEJI.)* You are jealous, you have always been jealous of me.

SATI: Dad, you're not listening, Mummy 2's…

FATHER: Mummy 2 what? Mummy 2 what? She is not your enemy. All my life I have done everything for you people. So that you would have a mother.

SATI: I've already got a mother.

FATHER: I can't listen any more. No more. All of you against me.

SATI: Dad.

FATHER: I'm tired of this. Tired of waiting for Comrade. I'm going.

SATI: Dad!

FATHER: I have to sign on.

FATHER exits taking his book with him. There is a pause in the action. BEJI produces another Boots bag, and takes a card out of it.

BEJI: Look beta, postcard from your mum, from a new Gurdwara in Pakistan.

SATI: Well she's not here is she? She's not here.

SATI moves away from BEJI with the head and body of cardboard cut-out. Lights dim on BEJI although her silhouette can still be seen.

Light on SATI at the side of the stage. She is still upset, pulls herself together and manages to talk to IW.

SATI: *(To cut-out.)* I'll put you back together. Don't worry. Cutting you up in pieces, it's not right. I'll be seeing you soon anyway, *(checks watch)* in a few hours. *(Pause.)* I love you Ian Wright. *(Kisses the face passionately.)* I swear that's the God's honest truth.

SATI exits.

SCENE EIGHT

1994. Day four, afternoon. JASPAL lies down alone, she is partially dressed, having just had sex with Stan again. The Carpenters' 'Calling Occupants of Interplanetary Craft' begins to play low. She gets up and slowly puts her clothes back on and at the same time she smokes a spliff. She is out of it.

JASPAL: *(Half-singing/half-speaking.)* In your mind you have capacities to know. To telepath messages through the vast unknown.

JASPAL picks up two used condoms from the floor, she wanders across the room and throws them in the bin.

JASPAL: Please close your eyes and concentrate on every thought you think. Upon the recitation we're about to say. Calling occupants of interplanetary craft. Calling occupants of interplanetary craft. Poor little Karen. Poor Mummy 1. Calling occupants of interplanetary, most extraordinary craft.

JASPAL is like she is in a trance. She is out of it, she takes a long drag and walks about shakily.

JASPAL: Please interstellar policeman. Won't you give us a sign. Give us a sign. Don't shout Mummy, I've told you not to shout. And don't lock this door. Alright Mummy. It's alright. I'm coming now. *(She looks up and her look changes to one of horror.)* Oh no.

She puts a hand between her legs.

JASPAL: Oh no Mummy 1. Look at all this mess, they won't like it you know, they won't have it. Oh Mummy 1, silly, bad Mummy 1. You're not meant to cut down there. Oh no. It's beginning to bleed. There's blood. Hot, dark red blood. It's all on me. You've got it all on me. No Mummy, there's no thing inside. It won't come out because it's not there. They won't like it. They don't want to see all this messy bad Mummy 1.

JASPAL sits down.

It's alright. Does it hurt? It must hurt if it's down there. I'll clean it up for you. They don't want to know about all your messy badness. I'll do it. I said I'll do it. I'll take care of you. I promise. I've asked, they said they don't want to know, they said they're ashamed. Bad bloody messy Mummy 1.

The man said they're on their way. *(Half-singing.)* Please interstellar policeman won't you give us a sign that we've reached you. Poor little thing. What a shame. Poor little Mummy Karen. No, you can't stay now, you've got to go. I'm so sorry, but you have to go now.

Bye Mummy. Bye. *(She waves out to the audience.)* Say bye to Mummy, Sati, say bye. Good girl.

(Motherly.) She's had to go away for a bit, she's gone to help the poor people in India. Like a missionary. Come and sit down.

Do you want some fish fingers?

Poor little Sati, Mummy Karen. *(Half-singing.)* We are your friends. Poor bad Mummy 1. Poor Jaspal. Bad bloody messy girl. Dirty whore. Sucking men on the streets. Fucking black men for a bit of black. *(Half-singing.)* Calling occupants of interplanetary craft. We are your friends.

JASPAL gets under a cover and lies down. PATRICK comes in. He puts his bag down and goes to get a drink.

PATRICK: Jaspal, it's the middle of the afternoon.

No response.

PATRICK: Come on you can't stay in bed all day.

JASPAL: No.

PATRICK: You've got to get up sometime.

PATRICK changes his clothes.

PATRICK: What's wrong with you?

JASPAL: I'm not well.

PATRICK: You're never well.

JASPAL: I miss my mum.

PATRICK comes over and sits by her.

PATRICK: Why don't you try getting in contact with her?

JASPAL: I can't.

PATRICK: Ask Sati to ask your dad.

JASPAL: I can't.

PATRICK: She writes to them doesn't she?

JASPAL: Yeah.

PATRICK: Then ask.

JASPAL: No.

PATRICK: For god's sake Jaspal.

JASPAL: What?

PATRICK: You've got to want to help yourself.

No response.

PATRICK: We need to talk.

JASPAL: We are.

PATRICK: I mean like adults. Like other people do. You know, they weigh things up, consider the options and decide on an outcome.

JASPAL: What?

PATRICK: America.

JASPAL: America?

PATRICK: I want us to go.

JASPAL: It's your life.

PATRICK: It's not.

JASPAL: It is. It so is your life.

PATRICK: It's our life.

JASPAL: I can't.

PATRICK: Why?

JASPAL: I just can't.

PATRICK: But…

JASPAL: Don't Patrick, please don't. Leave me if that's what you want, leave me and go and live with Eric and Ernie in America, but don't ask me… because… I can't… I can't think… about anything…

PATRICK: I didn't say I want to leave you.

JASPAL: Stop please… My head's full as it is. Leave me alone.

PATRICK: *(Looking round.)* Has Stan been here?

JASPAL: What?

PATRICK: Has Stan been here?

JASPAL: No.

PATRICK: *(Picks up tobacco tin.)* What's his tin doing here then?

JASPAL: He lent it me. The other week.

PATRICK: Don't lie.

JASPAL: I'm not. Patrick. Fuck's sake.

PATRICK: You've been fuckin' him haven't you?

JASPAL: What? I haven't.

PATRICK: Don't lie, you have haven't you… you bitch, you fucking bitch.

JASPAL: I haven't. I swear I haven't.

PATRICK: Where's that weed come from then?

JASPAL: It's mine, I found it. I've had it ages… Patrick… please…

PATRICK: You don't care do you, you don't care about anyone else.

JASPAL: I do. I do care… please stop it. I haven't done anything.

PATRICK: What kind of man do you think I am?

JASPAL: A nice one. Please stop shouting… Please… I haven't done anything wrong…

PATRICK: What the fuck am I doing here?

JASPAL: I'm not well… You know what I'm like. I can't help it… you know… my head's full as it is…

JASPAL crumbles on a chair. PATRICK comes right up to her. She tries to move away.

PATRICK: What about me? Have you for one minute ever thought about me? Don't you think my head's full? People have been filling it since I first laid eyes on you.

JASPAL: Go away.

PATRICK: First there's my mum.

(Plays his mother, an older Jamaican woman.) She's a pretty girl, you know your grandmother was Indian. You love her, she love you, don't you pay no mind to her family. Ah the grandchildren will be so beautiful. Hear now, she the same colour as you, one shade lighter maybe, we all the same underneath.

He moves right up to her face, she tries to move away, she can't.

JASPAL: Stop it.

PATRICK: Then there's Carlton.

(Plays his friend Carlton.) Yeah man, Asian girls, boy I'm tellling you, I like a bit of Indian now and again. It's just like the Irish girls at school, they ain't allowed to have it, and when they get it boy – they go like the clappers. They're different P, like the girls in Hawaii Five O used to be, well exotic – that skin, those eyes, that hair. Everyone wants an Asian babe on their arm. You seen that magazine, Raas claat!

And Joe.

(Plays his friend JOE, a Rastafarian.) Why you want to pollute your race, man? You is a black man, try fuckin' a black woman.

JASPAL: Stop.

PATRICK: *(His mother.)* Patrick, I seen her walking the streets with the next man. She selling her body. Oh god, my son, my son, get rid of that slut. She no good.

JASPAL: Stop will you, please.

PATRICK: *(Joe.)* These Pakis man, they look down on us, look at the way she's carrying on. Problems we all got problems, where's your self-respect.

(Carlton.) Alright man, so she's sorted herself out, she likes her weed though don't she, she don't do nothing all day, that's rubbish man.

JASPAL: Get away from me.

She tries to move away, he follows her round the room.

PATRICK: *(Mother.)* Leave her, please, son, she's a nice girl, but she's ill, you can do better.

(Joe.) Why you want to pollute your race?

(Carlton.) You like her don't you. You like that whore.

JASPAL starts to cry, she falls to the floor. PATRICK moves away from her.

JASPAL: Stop, just stop.

PATRICK: I'm going out. *(Begins to exit.)*

JASPAL Patrick… Patrick… I'll stop. I'll be good. I will. I'll change, I will, I promise. Where are you going? *(She clambers after him.)*

PATRICK: Get away from me.

PATRICK picks up his bag and walks out of the flat, past a distraught JASPAL.

JASPAL: Please don't leave me like this… Patrick…

She clambers back to the refuge of her seat.

JASPAL: Don't leave me like this. Not all cut up like this. It hurts. *(She puts her hands between her legs.)*

Help me, please God, help me.

JASPAL sits rocking. She looks around her, she is distressed. She catches sight of the book which SATI bought her. She breathes deeply and picks it up.

SCENE NINE

1994. Day four, afternoon. The Dole Office. The FATHER is sitting down with his poetry book. PATRICK enters, takes a ticket, and sits down, he does not notice the FATHER. PATRICK takes out a book about Muhammed Ali, and starts to read. The Father watches him and moves his hand to the inside of his jacket pocket as though he is checking his wallet.

He looks at PATRICK more intently and notices the book PATRICK is reading.

VOICEOVER: One hundred and forty seven.

Both men look at their tickets and then go back to their books. The FATHER keeps looking at PATRICK. PATRICK does not acknowledge the looks.

FATHER: *(Brightly.)* Too long to wait.

PATRICK looks up briefly. He does not know who the FATHER is and the FATHER does not know who PATRICK is. However, for a split second PATRICK experiences a moment of recognition, which he can't quite work out. It is enough to make him slightly wary at the start of the scene. He nods politely at the FATHER and then looks back down at his book. The FATHER is glad for this acknowledgement and sees it as a way in to talking to PATRICK. FATHER moves a seat closer to PATRICK.

FATHER: *(Indicates PATRICK's book.)* The best.

PATRICK half smiles and nods again.

FATHER: The greatest.

PATRICK: No question.

FATHER: The Rumble in the Jungle is my favourite.

PATRICK: Yeah its a popular one I…

FATHER: The fight of the century.

PATRICK: So they say.

FATHER: *(Points to cover photo of MA.)* I am fan…

PATRICK: Right.

FATHER: You too are… interested…

PATRICK: I am… well I box, I'm a boxer.

FATHER: *(Now delighted, moves closer, loosens tie, takes off glasses.)* Oh, that is wonderful, wonderful, you are real boxer.

PATRICK: I mean I'm hoping to turn professional, maybe try my luck in America…

FATHER: America! America! Very good, very nice. Maybe you will meet the… erm… what is his name… the… Angelo Dundee… He is very nice, I like him.

PATRICK: Well, we'll see.

FATHER: America. Yes, America is very nice, but also the society is very consumerist.

PATRICK: Yes it is.

FATHER: You are real boxer. I think you will be lucky.

PATRICK: I hope so.

FATHER: No hoping, do not hope, you must believe, be clever, quick off the mark, one step ahead. *(He smiles at PATRICK like a child and slowly throws some punches in the air.)*

PATRICK: That's right.

FATHER: One step ahead like him *(Indicates photo of MA on book.)* I remember Zaire 1974 – Muhammed was representing the grace, the beauty and the skill, and George was representing the brutality and the destruction. Everybody in the world thought Muhammed would lose, and even that George might kill him, everybody except ME. I knew that he was too clever you see, too clever for George. All us people, all my Pakistani friends, all of us we used to recite poetry together, he was ours, our hero. Funny if you think, so many of my people all round the country getting together to watch two *(Hesitates.)* of your people fight a boxing match.

PATRICK: Well that's sport for you, bringing people together.

FATHER: And also dividing people. My son he supports Arsenal, he meet a girl from Tottenham, he say *(overacts)* I hate her, I hate her. She is rubbish. *(Pause.)* So the sport is also dividing people.

PATRICK: Yes.

FATHER: *(Comparing hands.)* But we, we are nearly same colour.

PATRICK: Yes.

FATHER: Nearly same colour, but totally different culture. *(He laughs.)*

VOICEOVER: One hundred and forty eight.

FATHER: Too much time.

PATRICK: Yeah.

FATHER: I like people. All people. Not backward like some. Some people from villages, our villages in India you know they have no sense. I am not like that. *(Pause.) (Quietly.)* I am a poet.

PATRICK: Really.

FATHER: *(Points to photo of MA.)* Like Muhammed. *(Eagerly.)* You know – Me. We. You must have heard of it.

PATRICK: Yes I think…

FATHER: He is professor of poetry at Oxford University. Honorary. You should know these things. You must know. You are a boxer.

PATRICK: Well if you…

VOICEOVER: One hundred and fifty.

FATHER: I feel so shame. So much shame. To come here, get Unemployment Benefit.

PATRICK: One of those things.

FATHER: Only temporary measure. I am waiting for new book to be published. Poetry. My wife gone abroad on business, so I must come here. Only temporary measure.

PATRICK: I understand. *(Pause.)* For me too, till it all takes off *(Boxes playfully.)* You know.

They laugh.

FATHER: I know, yes. You have not got wife.

PATRICK: Girlfriend.

FATHER: *(Laughs playfully.)* Girlfriend.

PATRICK: *(Laughs with him.)* Yes.

FATHER: She love you?

PATRICK: Well it's difficult…

FATHER: *(Laughs.)* Yes, I know it.

PATRICK: Well…

FATHER: And you love her.

PATRICK: In a way I…

FATHER: So why not marry.

PATRICK: Well…

FATHER: *(Interrupts.)* She no work?

PATRICK: No.

FATHER: Maybe it is better.

PATRICK: She has a few problems, you know how some families are.

FATHER: Oh yes. I know, I know very well. I feel sorry for them.

PATRICK: Who?

FATHER: The people with the bad families. It is not their fault, they are not educated. Now me, I like the education. For girls as well. My one daughter, she is scientist, doing PhD, gone away to study. My son he will be physiotherapist, he like sports you know. And my other son, well he will be businessman.

PATRICK: That's good.

FATHER: Very good.

PATRICK: So you don't need to worry about them.

FATHER: No. No way. I'm really quite a lucky fellow. Good work. Good family, everything good. *(A beat.)* Very quiet here today.

PATRICK: Yes.

FATHER: Peaceful… Sometimes it is so busy at home. There is no peace.

PATRICK: I know what you mean.

FATHER: Yes. I know you know. I know you are very clever.

PATRICK: Thank you.

FATHER: *(Waves hand at him.)* No need to thank… Sometimes I come here just to think and to write my poems. Sometimes even when I do not have to sign on.

PATRICK: Really?

FATHER: Yes… It is quiet usually.

PATRICK: Usually.

FATHER: Except when there is a rumpus.

PATRICK: Yes.

FATHER: You would like to hear a poem?

PATRICK: Yes. Yes why not?

FATHER: *(Clears his throat.)* Tu meri zindagi meh ay.

PATRICK: That's lovely.

FATHER: It is not finished yet.

PATRICK: Oh I'm sorry, please… carry on.

FATHER: I can't. I have writer's block.

PATRICK: What does it mean?

FATHER: What?

PATRICK: What you just said.

FATHER: Tu meri zindagi meh ay… You came into my life…

PATRICK: You came into my life… *(He starts thinking.)* … you came into my life… And I decided to make you my wife! How about that?

FATHER: No. You are boxer, I am poet. It is better this way.

They continue to wait.

SCENE TEN

1994. The stage is divided into two areas – Jaspal's Flat and a section of Uncle Comrade's Shop. JASPAL sits reading the book SATI left for her. 'Healing and Feeling – A Guide to Coping with Addictive Behaviour – An alcoholic's Perspective.'

She gets up with a start and madly searches for a pen and notepad which she finds under a pile of rubbish. She returns to the book. She has the book in one hand, pen in the other and notepad on her lap. She reads carefully and thoroughly as though she is studying a list.

JASPAL: Yes. *(As though she is answering a question.)* *(Ticks notepad.)*

Reads.

Yes. *(Unsure.) (Ticks notepad.)*

Reads.

Yes. *(Definite.) (Ticks notepad.)*

Reads.

Yeees. *(Anxious.) (Ticks notepad.)*

Reads.

Um. Not sure. Yes. *(Embarrassed.) (Ticks notepad.)*

Reads.

Yes. *(Quickly.) (Ticks notepad.)*

Reads.

Yes. *(Quickly.) (Ticks notepad.)*

Reads.

YES. *(Shouts.) (Ticks notepad.)*

Reads.

Yes. *(Fearful.) (Ticks notepad.)*

She puts the tape in a tape recorder. It starts to play.

TAPE: Six or more yeses – Shit, you have serious addictive tendencies. You could be a risk to yourself as well as others. You need professional help NOW. Or you can simply carry on listening.

Doing this exercise has made JASPAL confused and horrified. She looks around her.

SATI enters the section of Uncle Comrade's shop with IW cut-out.

She grabs some sellotape and sticks his head back on. She stands the mended cut-out on one side. She is still in her shalwar kameez, she looks over at IW and in a coy fashion takes her kameez off to reveal a JVC shirt with number '8' and 'LEGEND' written on the back. She puts a tape in an old cassette recorder and holds the cut-out close to her as though they are poised to start dancing.

JASPAL continues to listen to the tape.

TAPE: Look around you. *(JASPAL looks around the flat.)* Do you see unmanageability? *(She nods.)* Do you feel it deep down inside of you?

JASPAL: Er…yeah…

TAPE: You've got to get rid of it. Let it go. But first, you have to let yourself feel. Once you do that you'll be free. Doesn't that sound good?

JASPAL: Er…

TAPE: Think about it, think about how special it could be. That moment of freedom you've been waiting for all your life.

In the shop 'Chura Liya' [Stolen], a famous Hindi love song plays.

SATI begins a love dance which she does with IW. She mimes the words to the song.

SATI: Chura Liya he tum ne jo dil ko… *[You've stolen my heart…]*

SATI and IW dance together. JASPAL now has her eyes closed and is relaxed.

TAPE: That's it breathe deeply. Now first let's look at that virus which has been attacking your soul. *(JASPAL opens her eyes and looks worried.)* Fear. F. E. A. R fear.

Get it out of your system, out of your body, wash it right out of your hair. Fear. Do you want to *(Spells out letters.)* F.E.A.R Fuck Everything And Run?

JASPAL: Yes.

TAPE: You can change that fear into something good, something new. You can *(Spells out.)* F.E.A.R Face Everything And Resolve. *(Pause.)* I can tell you're feeling nervous, am I right? *(She nods.)* You know at the start sometimes you have to pretend, even if you don't feel it. Remember you got to fake it to make it.

SATI has sat IW down on the shop stool. She does a sensual dance to him and again she mimes the words to the song 'Chura Liya'. Towards the end, she picks him up, they dance close again, this time much more sexually.

By the final crescendo it is as though they have made love. She turns away from him shyly. JASPAL's still listening to the tape.

TAPE: You know that important person from your past. *(JASPAL looks up and nods.)* Well it's time to confront that person. *(Pause.)* Why don't we have a practice?

SATI gets up and walks away from IW. She then turns around and approaches him. She puts on a posh and seductive voice.

SATI: Hello my name's Sati and I live in… *(She shakes her head and says to herself.)* Too much like *Blind Date.*

She starts again and approaches.

SATI: I think we have so much to learn from the continentals don't you? The foreign players are so inventive and… No, no… he won't want to talk shop.

She starts again and approaches.

SATI: Do you think you might?… I mean have you ever… with an Indian girl…

JASPAL fixates on a wooden chair in front of the sofa. She looks at it confused.

TAPE: Forget about the outside world.

There is knocking at the shop door.

SATI: We're closed.

Knocking continues. She ignores it and it subsides. She takes a copy of 19 magazine and a large make-up box from behind the counter. She opens the magazine and goes to sit on a stool.

JASPAL stares at the chair she is obviously ill at ease.

TAPE: How about saying Hi.

JASPAL: *(Slowly, addresses chair.)* Hello.

TAPE: Come on.

JASPAL: Hello… Mummy 1.

TAPE: I want you to follow my instructions very closely.

SATI reads from the magazine.

SATI: *(Reads from magazine in the same way as you would follow a recipe.)* First create your base by dotting foundation on your lids and around the eyes. Stroke it in gently. *(She rubs it in hard and looks at herself in her compact mirror.)* *(Frustrated.)* I can't see any difference *(She slaps more on.)*

(Reads again.) Shade your lids with colour, blending with the fingertips. You can choose your basic colour to tone with your eyes or your clothes. If you want to achieve a really dramatic effect you can combine as many as three contrasting shades.

She appears a bit confused, looks up at IW cardboard cut-out which she has facing her.

SATI: *(Brightens.)* I know. *(She delves into the make-up box and takes two crayons.)*

(To IW cut-out while she is applying.) You'll love this. Dramatic and original.

(She makes a pattern of red and white stripes on her eyes.)

(As she finishes.) What do you think? *(No reply.)*

I hope you like it. I hope you like me. I want to be perfect for you.

JASPAL has moved closer to the chair.

JASPAL: I'm sorry Mummy. I didn't mean it. I didn't look after you. I know I should have. *(She moves closer to the chair.)* Is it hurting Mummy? It's alright now, I'm here. It'll stop hurting now down there. I'm so sorry. For everything. Forgive me mummy, will you do that? Will you? I need some kind of sign. Please.

The shop telephone starts to ring. SATI ignores it. It continues.

SATI: *(To phone.)* I told you, we're closed. *(Continues to apply make-up.)*

JASPAL pleads with the chair.

JASPAL: Talk to me.

SATI finishes – her make-up is completed. As well as the red and white eye shadow, it is all overdone and badly applied. The telephone is still ringing.

SATI: *(Annoyed.)* Right that's it.

She marches over to the telephone and picks it up.

SATI: Uncle I told you I'm on half… *(She stops and her expression changes to one of anxiety.)* … Oh… Hello. Yes it is. Speaking… But she can't be. Are you sure it's her. Oh… Oh… I see. Is she alright? Can I talk to her? *(Pause.)* No way. No I can't. *(Pause.)* She's never been in trouble before. You'll have to tell her no. Someone else will have to come. Tell her to call… What? But I have an important prior engagement. Someone else will have to… Tell her I'll come later. You don't understand. What?… What? … I''ll see what I can do.

SATI stays on the phone. JASPAL's getting frustrated with the chair.

JASPAL: What? *(Pause.)* What do you say? *(Silence. She gets frustrated.)* I said what do you say. *(Shouts.)* For fuck's sake. *(She gets up and accidentally knocks over the chair. She stares for a moment and then it is as if whatever spell she has been under is broken.)*

(Horrified.) For fuck's sake. Someone's trying to fuck me up.

(Paces around, breathing deeply.)

SATI puts the phone down and looks over at IW.

TAPE: Surely after all this work you're not going to Fuck Everything and Run?

JASPAL: *(Gets herself together and smashes up the tape recorder.)* Shut the fuck up. She's got to be told… Patrick… He'll know what to do…

JASPAL picks up an old bag, throws on some shoes and exits. At the same time SATI picks up IW and exits.

SCENE ELEVEN

1994. The Dole Office. FATHER and PATRICK are still waiting.

VOICEOVER: One hundred and fifty three.

FATHER: *(Shouts.)* Please get some more staff here. *(To PATRICK.)* I can see them through there, *(points)* smoking and drinking.

PATRICK: Don't worry about it.

FATHER: I'm not worried. Why should I be worried?

SATI enters with BEJI. They both carry lots of Boots bags, crammed with toiletries and make-up. SATI drags along the IW cut-out. SATI's make-up is by now dishevelled, she is still in her shalwar and JVC shirt. BEJI has her head covered and her head down. FATHER notices them.

FATHER: What happened?

SATI starts emptying contents of Boots bags on to his lap.

FATHER: *(Looks at SATI.)* What… What are you doing?

SATI: *(Brightly/matter of fact.)* Hello dad. How are you?

FATHER: I am fine. What do you think you are doing?

SATI: Can you see me dad? Can you hear me? *(Picks up his hand, pulls it roughly to her cheek.)* Can you feel me?

FATHER: Why are you doing this… I…

SATI: *(Shouts, but still bright.)* Can you dad? Can you see, hear and feel me?

FATHER: Yes.

SATI: Good, Dad, that's good. Very good Dad. You noticed… You noticed that I'm here.

FATHER: Why are you doing this? In front of all the unemployed people?

SATI: I don't give a shit about the unemployed.

FATHER: Have you gone mad?

SATI: It's not even your signing on day. Where's Mummy 2?

FATHER: I… I don't know. I think she took Raju for fencing lesson.

SATI: You've been here all the time haven't you?

FATHER: I need money.

SATI: Sitting here with your rubbishy pitiful poetry.

FATHER: It's not that bad.

SATI: *(Shouts.)* Yes it is!

FATHER: What… what happened?

SATI: *(Points to BEJI who is sitting on the floor, looking away.)* She's been shoplifting, Dad. Your mother has been stealing goods. Vitamin pills, hair accessories and over the counter medicines. They caught her dad, they caught her today, the Boots store detectives have had their eyes on her for months. They caught her dad and I had to deal with it because you were sitting here trying to finish your stupid poem.

FATHER: Beji?

SATI: I had somewhere to go Dad, something to do, it was important. And I had to go and deal with it. *(Gestures to BEJI again.)* She pretended she couldn't speak English. She'd been swearing at the interpreter, reduced her to tears. I had to go Dad, I had to go and translate… It was horrible.

I'm 16 dad, I'm only 16…

BEJI: I won't do it again.

FATHER: What happened?

SATI: She's been cautioned. They're not taking it any further.

FATHER: Thank God.

SATI: I had somewhere to go Dad. It was something. It meant something. And I missed it, you made me miss it.

FATHER: It's not my fault if she is a thief.

PATRICK: She's not a thief, she's just an old woman.

FATHER: What did you say?

PATRICK: She's not…

FATHER: How dare you interfere in my family's business.

PATRICK: Jesus Christ.

FATHER: If I want to call my mother a thief, I will.

PATRICK: Fine.

FATHER: We are not like you people. In my community, we stick together and we look after each other.

PATRICK: Yeah, right.

FATHER: We show respect, we do not cause rumpus.

PATRICK: Of course not.

FATHER: Is this how you behave? Like a nosey parker. After everything I told you. I even read you my poem.

SATI: Dad, he doesn't mean any harm.

FATHER: So you take his side do you? Against your own father? Because he is like your Ian. You like his people, better than you like me.

SATI: *(Holds cut-out protectively.)* Leave Ian Wright out of this.

FATHER: Is this what I deserve? In front of all the unemployed people? Am I such a bad father. Tell me. Am I such a bad father.

JASPAL enters.

JASPAL: Patrick.

She notices SATI, FATHER and BEJI. They all look at her in shock.

JASPAL: Oh shit. *(She laughs nervously.)* Oh God. Oh fuck. Shit.

PATRICK: Let's go.

JASPAL: No. It's alright.

FATHER: I wish I could die now.

BEJI starts ranting like a chant and banging her head with her fist.

BEJI: What are the colours of God like? Oh God our kismet is so bad, oh God, our kismet is so bad.

FATHER: *(To PATRICK.)* Do you know my daughter? I should have known. Always the same with you people. Drug dealer. Pimp?

PATRICK: Here we go.

JASPAL: Shut up dad. Shut up with your racist shit.

FATHER: I am not a racist. Do not call me a racist. Is it true? Am I right? Is he your drug dealer?

JASPAL: Shut up. Drugs come from India anyway.

FATHER: Pakistan, not India. Don't bring India into this.

JASPAL: This is him dad, the black bastard I've been going out with. Who I've been living with, who I've been sleeping with, dad, who I've been having sex with…

FATHER: I am not listening.

JASPAL: Look at him Dad, he's black, he's my boyfriend and we…

FATHER: Don't call me dad. I am not your dad.

JASPAL: I feel sorry for you.

SATI: Jaspal, don't…

JASPAL: *(To SATI.)* Whose side are you on?

SATI: *(Sits rocking with cut-out, she is upset.)* Ian doesn't like fighting.

JASPAL: For fuck's sake.

SATI: Ian wants you to be more understanding.

FATHER: How can you understand this situation?

SATI: Ian says you have to make up.

PATRICK: Come on Sati, you need to get out of here.

FATHER: You leave her alone. One of my daughters is not enough for you?

PATRICK: She's upset, you idiot.

JASPAL: Sati, you've got to stop. He's not real. He doesn't have feelings.

SATI: How do you know?

JASPAL: For fuck's sake. *(To FATHER.)* Are you going to stand by and let this go on.

FATHER: What can I do? You both think you are black.

JASPAL: She's going to turn into a nutter dad, you don't want her to end up like me do you? Don't you care? Can't you see the signs? For fuck's sake.

FATHER: Sati is a good girl, you leave her alone.

JASPAL approaches SATI.

JASPAL: Ian can't hear you. Ian's made out of paper.

SATI: Stop it.

JASPAL: He's a cardboard fucking cut-out.

SATI: Shut up. You're jealous of me. I know you are and I know you used to be a prostitute.

JASPAL: *(To FATHER.)* What did you tell her for? He's not real.

(She moves closer to SATI.)

SATI: And you hate us because mum never writes to you.

JASPAL: *(Screams and goes for the cut-out which she tears up.)* He's not real. He's just paper. He's not real.

SATI in turn screams and tries to salvage IW. There is a scuffle between them. JASPAL grabs hold of her and turns SATI round to face her.

JASPAL: *(To SATI.)* She's not in India.

FATHER: NO.

BEJI stops her chanting and gets up to confront JASPAL.

BEJI: Behsharam, kuthi, behsharam.

JASPAL ignores her and pushes her out of the way.

JASPAL: She didn't have a boy Sati. And he wasn't satisfied with two daughters, so he had to get a new wife.

FATHER: Don't listen.

JASPAL: After Mummy 2 came you didn't like Mummy 1 did you dad? So you didn't mind when she went upstairs and locked herself away listening to her songs while she played with her sewing box.

BEJI: Behsharam.

JASPAL: I found her one day. She was trying to cut up her cunt with a pair of scissors.

FATHER: No.

JASPAL: She said there was a boy inside her and she was trying to get him out. I found her. Found her with all the blood.

FATHER: Stop it Jaspal. Please stop.

JASPAL: She's in a home five miles away, she won't come out now. She doesn't want to.

FATHER: Stop it. Don't listen. *(Points at JASPAL.)* It was her, she signed the papers. She sent her away.

JASPAL: It was only meant to be for a while. But after a bit she said she preferred it in there, at least she could play her music and sing her songs. I was going to tell you, Sati. But then, I couldn't, I didn't want to spoil it, not for you as well.

FATHER: It wasn't my fault. I wanted her to stay. But her *(points at JASPAL)*, she signed the form.

JASPAL goes to take SATI's hand. SATI backs away from her, in utter shock and disbelief, she looks around and runs out of the dole office. BEJI follows her.

BEJI: Sati, Sati, Sati. She tell lies. She is mad. Listen to me.

VOICEOVER: One hundred and fifty four.

PATRICK: *(To FATHER.)* It's great the way you all stick together and look after each other.

PATRICK looks at his ticket and goes to sign on. FATHER and JASPAL sit motionless in the dole office seats. BEJI comes back inside. She approaches JASPAL.

BEJI: Now she is gone. Now you should be happy.

JASPAL: I'm on top of the world.

BEJI turns to the FATHER.

BEJI: You've left me with nothing. With no-one.

FATHER: I wanted us all to be together.

BEJI: Now in the days before I die. I must live in your hell.

FATHER: Please don't…

BEJI: In your hell with you. With nothing but your face to look at. Look at me…

FATHER: No, I…

BEJI: Look at me… *(She pulls his face to her face.)* Every time you look at me. I want you to remember.

FATHER: No…

BEJI: Remember what you did… you took everyone away from me…

FATHER: No, please Beji…

BEJI exits. The FATHER and JASPAL sit in silence.

FATHER: Why Jaspal?

JASPAL: You can't tell lies forever.

FATHER: She is a child. My child.

JASPAL: She's a girl, Dad. Not like Raju.

FATHER: I can't stand to look at you. Get out of my sight.

JASPAL: No. You made me like this. You sit and watch me.

FATHER: You made yourself Jaspal, into this… behsharam…

JASPAL: I'm my father's daughter.

FATHER: And now you want Sati to share your shame.

JASPAL: You fucking hypocrite.

FATHER: She is a good girl, she is clean. I wanted to keep her away from this.

JASPAL: She's my sister. We've got the same blood. You do remember our mother don't you?

FATHER: Do you hate me so much?

JASPAL: I don't hate you dad. I feel sorry for you.

FATHER: Your pity is worse than your hate.

JASPAL: I feel sorry for all of us.

FATHER: So much trouble, there has been so much trouble.

JASPAL: I know.

FATHER: So many bad things have happened.

JASPAL: Yes dad.

FATHER: But it was not my fault.

JASPAL: Like I said dad. You can't tell lies forever.

JASPAL gets up to go.

FATHER: Jaspal… shall I still bring you saag?

JASPAL: No dad. No thanks. I can make my own from now on.

(She goes to leave and looks back.) Why did you bring it dad? Every week. You must have thought of me.

FATHER: After all the shame you brought to us. I didn't want any more.

JASPAL: What do you mean?

FATHER: I brought you food so I would never have to see you begging. So I would not have to see any more of your shame.

JASPAL stops for a moment, then continues on her way out.

JASPAL: There's always Raju dad. You've got a son. Now there's something to be proud of.

She exits. FATHER sits alone on stage.

FATHER: I can't… I can't face looking at him.

He looks to where JASPAL has gone. He breaks down.

FATHER: I feel shame. So much shame. I want my girls. Where are my girls? I want my girls.

He looks around and slowly gathers himself together. He opens his book. He takes out his pen.

FATHER: *(Recites as before.)* Tu meri zindagi meh ay…

SCENE TWELVE

1998. The Dressing Room. JASPAL sits, SATI stands. Silence.

JASPAL: I thought it was for your own good.

SATI: I understand.

JASPAL: I waited for you.

SATI: I know.

SATI takes JASPAL's hands in hers.

JASPAL: I wanted you to come.

SATI: I wanted to.

JASPAL: I waited and waited. I'm clean now.

SATI: I can see.

JASPAL: Really clean.

SATI: Have you ever been to see Mummy 1?

JASPAL: I used to go. Every week. Not any more.

SATI: I'm your family now. You've got me.

JASPAL: What about the others?

SATI: Mummy 2 left. She took Raju on a Mediterranean cruise.

JASPAL: So her and Dad... ?

SATI: She sends pictures. Raju's ten now. She enters him for ballroom dancing competitions, he's won loads of medals.

JASPAL: What about dad?

SATI: The same. And Beji. Both still waiting for Uncle Comrade... What happened to Patrick?

JASPAL: He helped me to get Kiran going. But then he went. He couldn't stand me at the end. I don't blame him.

SATI: I'm sorry.

JASPAL: Don't be. I'm not. Anyway I'm glad you came.

SATI: So am I... Jaspal I need a fag.

JASPAL: You're weak that's what you are.

SATI: Please.

JASPAL: Go on then. I was weak once.

SATI lights up.

SATI: You know. I've been thinking a lot about Mummy 1, I mean mum.

JASPAL: Oh yeah.

SATI: I've been to visit her. I mean she won't leave or anything. I've been on at her but she won't. But she's doing ever so well. I was thinking, we should go and visit her together.

JASPAL is still and has her back to SATI and the audience.

SATI: Well?

JASPAL: What do you want?

SATI: I'm sure she'd like to see us.

JASPAL turns to face SATI.

JASPAL: You've missed your chance.

SATI: What?

JASPAL: She's dead.

SATI: No... no she's not.

JASPAL: She died two years ago of a bleeding heart attack.

SATI: She can't have.

JASPAL: I've got her ashes at home in a jam jar. I couldn't decide what to do with her, so I thought I'd keep her. Keep her with me.

SATI: No.

JASPAL: Oh yes. You lying little cunt. *(She laughs.)* What have you really come for?

SATI: I wanted to see her... *(She starts to cry.)* ... I wanted my mum... I want my mum.

JASPAL: I'll lend you the jar if you like.

SATI: Stop it. I wanted to do something right.

JASPAL: So you thought you'd lie?

SATI: You did.

JASPAL: We're even now. Is that what this is about?

SATI: I was frightened. I thought I might end up like her. Like Mummy 1. It was after I met him.

JASPAL: Who?

SATI: Ian Wright. At this party.

JASPAL: What?

SATI: I kept trying to get close to him but I couldn't get past the bodyguard. I only wanted to talk. Just for a minute. Like I used to. All those times, all the things I used to tell him about. I tried to get near him, but they wouldn't let me through. I had too much to drink. And I was sick in the toilets and I cried. I cried and cried. I thought about Mummy 1, about when she hurt herself and I wanted to copy her. I wanted to make myself bleed like her. And so I did. I made a right old mess.

JASPAL: You silly cow.

SATI: Afterwards I got scared. Scared of myself. Decided I should go and see her. I thought it might help me. Thought you might help me.

JASPAL: You missed your chance.

SATI moves towards JASPAL. Their reflections can be seen in all three mirrors of the dressing table.

SATI: You're my sister.

JASPAL: So?

SATI: We're the same. Same blood. Same badness. As bad as each other.

At this point, both their reflections can be seen in all three mirrors, gradually their reflections overlap and it is hard to make one out from the other.

SATI: Do you see now?

JASPAL: Right pair of cunts aren't we? Who would have thought it?

SATI: What?

JASPAL: You. You turned out as bad as me. Worse by the looks of you.

SATI: What does that mean?

JASPAL: Never mind. Don't do your own head in. That's the worst, when you do your own head in.

SATI: I won't come here again.

COMPERE'S VOICE: *(Offstage.)* Kiran, Jerry wants to know if you're going to do *Ticket to Ride.*

JASPAL: *(Shouts.)* Tell him no. And tell him to get the fucking key right. It's C flat.

COMP: *(Offstage.)* What love?

JASPAL: *(Shouts.)* C fucking flat. *(To SATI.)* Honestly some of these people. Talented as shit.

JASPAL gets up to go out. As she passes SATI she takes her in her arms and kisses her hard on the lips.

SATI: What?

JASPAL: You're my fucking sister aren't you? Come on.

SCENE THIRTEEN

1998. Red velvet curtains are behind a small raised platform on top of which there is an empty microphone.

COMPERE: *(Voiceover.)* And now ladies and gents, it's time to lock up your sons. Here she is, back from the dead, our very own Kiran Carpenter.

The sound of applause again (same as beginning). JASPAL comes out, all dolled-up.

JASPAL: Thank you, thank you all so much. Special thanks to my band the wonderful Asian Invasion. I'm going to leave you with one of my favourites and I'd like to dedicate this one to my sister who came to see the show tonight.

Music starts. JASPAL does a stupendous version of 'Only Yesterday'. She leaves the stage to uproarious applause. Curtains close.

THE END

BEHZTI
(DISHONOUR)

Behzti (Dishonour) was first performed on 9 December 2004 at the Birmingham Repertory Theatre with the following cast:

BALBIR, Shelley King
MIN, Yasmin Wilde
ELVIS, Jimmy Akingbola
GIANI JASWANT, Munir Khairdin
MR SANDHU, Madhav Sharma
TEETEE, Harvey Virdi
POLLY, Pooja Kumar

Director, Janet Steel
Designer, Matthew Wright
Lighting Designer, Mark Doubleday
Stage Manager, Ali Biggs
Assistant Stage Manager, Olly Seviour

PROLOGUE
BATHING, DRESSING AND EATING

BALBIR KAUR, a Sikh woman in her late 50s, sits naked perched on a small stool in a bath. Her face is scarred with disappointment but her eyes are alive with ambition. There is a bucket of water and a plastic mug in front of her. She takes a mugful of water and pours it over her body. She looks around anxiously and shouts out. She speaks with a Punjabi accent.

BALBIR: No soap!

Silence. She looks around again.

BALBIR: No bloddy soap, shitter!

BALBIR pours another mugful of water over herself. MIN, a faithful but simple lump of lard, bustles in. She's a sturdy but ungainly ingenue, prone to outbursts of extreme excitability. MIN is dressed unfashionably in mismatched A line skirt, patterned blouse and pink trainers. Her uncombed hair is in bunches, and she looks younger than her 33 years. She hurriedly unwraps a new bar of household soap.

MIN: It was in the flipping fridge.

BALBIR: You want me to die.

MIN: Those chipolatas smell all carbolic now… I'm at sixes and sevens…

BALBIR: Before I have finished living.

MIN: Most probably butterflies.

MIN hands BALBIR the soap and refills the bucket. MIN goes to lather BALBIR's back and body.

BALBIR: Too hard!

MIN: Oh… shush up.

BALBIR: A lady must be soft. Always soft. Are you a lady or a fellow?

MIN: I'm a flipping well lady and you know it.

BALBIR: You look like a bloddy horse.

BALBIR points towards her vagina.

BALBIR: Polish here please.

MIN: You do it.

BALBIR: I intend to gleam upon my arrival. Make it spick and span!

MIN: Get lost.

BALBIR: That's where you came out of.

MIN: Don't be filthy. Not today.

BALBIR: Or was it my arse?

MIN: I'll wash your mouth out you mucky cow.

BALBIR chuckles as she washes herself.

BALBIR: I bet you eat soap.

MIN: I do not do silly things like that.

MIN pours water over her mother.

BALBIR: That's why you're so clean and shiny inside. Like a brand new penny. Nothing dirty's ever happened in there…

MIN: Flipping well get on with it, Elvis'll be here soon.

BALBIR: I told you to cancel that shitter. *(A beat.)* I want shampoo.

MIN: There's not time. And I've still got to get in the mood.

BALBIR starts to get up.

MIN: Sit down!

BALBIR: You think Elizabeth Taylor leaves her abode without putting shampoo.

BALBIR rises slowly.

MIN: Don't!

BALBIR wobbles on her feet, she grabs a bottle of shampoo and proudly brandishes it around.

BALBIR: Look at me, look at me…

MIN's panicking. BALBIR squirts shampoo onto her hair.

MIN: Stop, I don't like it...

BALBIR teeters awkwardly, she's painfully unsteady on her feet. Shaking, she half works up a lather in her hair and giggles excitedly.

BALBIR: Yes... oh yes... I'm the king of the castle... all over again... The top kitty cat...

Suddenly BALBIR slips and falls, banging her arm. She shrieks as MIN swiftly catches her. There's a moment of disturbed silence. Mother and daughter breathe together quickly, fearfully. BALBIR screws up her face.

BALBIR: *(Low.)* Pain.

MIN: You silly sausage.

MIN rinses BALBIR's hair.

BALBIR: I don't want to die.

MIN: Don't depress yourself.

BALBIR starts to cry like a child. MIN beams with encouragement.

MIN: Guess what... I've only gone and booked us a taximan!

BALBIR: I mustn't die. Not yet.

MIN holds her sobbing mother tightly to her significant breast. MIN then carefully wraps the towel around BALBIR and starts drying her body. Next she skilfully lifts her up and places her onto a slender single bed, which is revealed to be next to the bath. Clothes are laid out at the back of the bed and there's an NHS commode next to it.

MIN: Arms up.

BALBIR complies. MIN picks up a plain white cotton slip from the back of the bed and puts it on her. This is a routine they know well.

BALBIR: I thought seeing as... it's today... I might wear a padded brassiere.

MIN: Knickers!

MIN searches around and finds a huge pair of white cotton pants. She dangles them in front of BALBIR who eyes them with disappointment.

BALBIR: Don't I have any frilly ones left?

MIN: You know you don't.

MIN puts the knickers to one side and finds a pot of extra strength E45 cream.

BALBIR: What am I supposed to do on a special occasion?

MIN: None of those left either.

MIN vigorously applies cream to her mother's legs and arms. Then MIN picks up BALBIR and carefully places her on the commode. BALBIR regards her with fury.

BALBIR: I don't want to.

MIN: Put your sensible hat on please.

MIN turns away and wraps a scarf around her head. She takes off her shoes and sits cross-legged on the floor. She clasps her hands together and starts a religious chant (Salokh). Her Punjabi is broken and her accent, imperfect.

MIN: Thum Thakur, thum pay ardas, jiyo pind sabh theri ras…

BALBIR: What you doing that for?

MIN: Practice for later. I want to move my mouth in time with all the other Sikhs.

BALBIR: Those fat shitters.

MIN: You ought to join in. We want to give a good impression.

BALBIR: I'm having beef cobbler for my dinner.

MIN: Get lost. Cod in parsley or vegetarian.

BALBIR: Cobbler.

MIN: You're not going there with cow's meat in your tummy.

Sound of trickling urine into the commode.

MIN: See.

BALBIR: I didn't want to. I made myself.

MIN gets up to wipe her mother and puts the knickers on her.

BALBIR: I am exercising control you see. Omnipotence.

MIN resumes her chanting as she lifts BALBIR back onto the bed.

MIN: What does it mean?

BALBIR: Heh?

MIN: What I'm saying.

BALBIR: Who cares?

MIN: God! And me.

BALBIR: I told you before.

MIN: Again…

BALBIR: I want beef.

MIN: Mother…

BALBIR: Cobbler with gravy and duchess potatoes. I want it!

MIN hurries offstage.

BALBIR: Beef, naughty beef! Yippee.

Sound of a microwave being turned on offstage. MIN comes back in.

MIN: Tell me.

Exasperated BALBIR rolls her eyes and translates/talks double speed.

BALBIR: You are the Lord, to you we pray, Body and soul are your gifts to us, You are the mother and the father, we are your children, In your grace lies abundant peace, your bounds are beyond us, you are higher than the highest. The whole creation is threaded together through you, And abides in your Will, you alone know your mystery, Nanak your servant, is forever your sacrifice.

MIN: Is forever your sacrifice… *(MIN breathes in deeply as though she is smelling sweet flowers.)* … I love it. I love all that… hmmm… it's getting me all going…

BALBIR: Do my make-up now.

MIN ignores her and produces a rickety old tape recorder.

BALBIR: Min!

MIN presses play on the tape recorder. 'Billie Jean' by Michael Jackson blares out. MIN starts to move her body in time with the music. With the freedom and energy of a child, she skips around and soaks up the rhythm. She dances joyfully but without much expertise.

BALBIR: Oh shitter…

MIN: Shush up!

BALBIR: Rubbish… you look so rubbish…

MIN does the moonwalk rather brilliantly.

MIN: I'm not listening!

MIN carries on. The frenzy of her movement brings MIN close to hysteria.

MIN: Watch me Mother… watch!

BALBIR crawls onto the floor and just about reaches the tape recorder. She presses stop.

BALBIR: Help me.

Breathless MIN stands over her.

MIN: That was… absolutely outstanding… I feel… almost perfect. Like a royal blue slush puppy.

BALBIR: Please!

MIN slowly moves towards BALBIR as though she is about to pick her up, but instead tugs harshly at BALBIR's hair. BALBIR yelps with pain.

MIN: You don't interrupt. Not when I'm moving about.

BALBIR: That hurt. You hurt me.

MIN: You hurt people.

BALBIR: If I had a knife I'd stick it up your arse.

MIN: Oh shush up!

BALBIR: You're illegal.

MIN: Capital punishment is illegal but corporal isn't.

BALBIR: You are an evil criminal.

MIN: I'm trying not to be.

MIN helps BALBIR up.

MIN: Didn't even pull that hard.

BALBIR pretends to cry silently. MIN's knocked.

MIN: Come on… don't be unhappy… I'll say I'm sorry…

MIN gaily and genuinely yanks one of her bunches.

MIN: Look I'm doing it to myself.

BALBIR isn't having it. MIN disappears under the bed and delves into a suitcase. She finds a shiny red and gold shalwar kameez, clearly suitable for a young woman. MIN endeavours to tantalise her mother with the suit.

MIN: How about this then?

BALBIR: Doesn't fit any more.

MIN: We'll squeeze you in. You'll be the belle of the ball.

BALBIR touches the material.

MIN: Imagine all those ladies, being jealous of you.

MIN carefully puts the shalwar on BALBIR.

BALBIR: What about my make-up?

MIN finds blue eyeshadow and bright red lipstick in the suitcase. She hands them to BALBIR who with a quivering hand starts applying them badly to her face. MIN tidies up.

BALBIR: You should put some. You need it more than me.

MIN: I'm not bothering with that hokum.

BALBIR: You have to start. Otherwise you will never stop.

MIN: What?

BALBIR: Looking like a bloddy horse. *(A beat.)* Put some. Please.

MIN solemnly applies blue eyeshadow to her eyelids. BALBIR chuckles as she watches her.

BALBIR: And the lips, go on.

MIN applies the lipstick. MIN eyes herself in the compact mirror.

MIN: Doesn't look like me any more.

BALBIR: Thank bloddy God.

MIN: Suppose it's still me inside.

BALBIR: Nothing you can do about the insides.

BALBIR holds MIN's face in her hands. BALBIR smiles.

BALBIR: Now we have hope ducks, now we have hope.

MIN: Hope?

BALBIR: That the world is a big fat oyster, slimy and sticky in the hand. Always leaving some oyster optimism on the fingers.

MIN: Don't be mucky.

BALBIR: Hope that it is all still to come.

MIN: What's to come?

BALBIR: Sunbathing on the Riviera, balloon trips over Manhattan and cocktails till dawn with Richard Burton. That if you work hard and present your arguments with focus and precision, tomorrow will be another day.

MIN starts to pack a bag.

MIN: Shall I pack some extra pads in case your bladder can't cope?

BALBIR: You can keep your pads and pensions and prescriptions.

MIN: They're all for you.

BALBIR: I want long, silly, tipsy days with naughty men who shout and laugh. I want to play with glamorous bits and bobs that sparkle and twinkle.

MIN: Mother! Think about where we're going, think about the holy things that are written in the book.

BALBIR: I can't be bothered.

A microwave pings offstage.

MIN: You want to lend some attention to Guru Nanak.

MIN wheels out the commode.

BALBIR: Who is he? My dad?

MIN brings in a high chair and a ready meal for one.

MIN: It's his day.

MIN helps BALBIR into the high chair and puts the meal in front of her.

MIN: You tuck in to your cobbler.

MIN heads out.

BALBIR: Min…

MIN: What?

BALBIR: Please do effort to look a bit more nice.

MIN: What flipping well for?

BALBIR: Min!

MIN: Alright!

MIN exits. BALBIR eats ravenously and every so often spits into a small bowl. She mutters to herself.

BALBIR: Mmm… Min… poor fatty Min… You should try the meat of the magnificent cow… they say I can't chew it but… look… *(She chews and then spits.)* … those lumpy molecules don't want to pass down my throat but I still get the effect of the red meat entering my blood, you see, I need my red blood flowing to be this living thing. Watch the juice inside me grab life by the scruff of its neck. I'll show those fat shitters what it is to transform into a creature of splendour and win the final battle of the war.

Unseen by BALBIR, a skinny young black man enters. This is ELVIS, BALBIR's home carer. He is in his 20s, gawky and gormless, but with razor sharp edges. Carrying a zimmerframe with wheels, he listens to BALBIR as she eats.

BALBIR: Beef! Mincey, chewy, naughty, beefy beef! Makes you stronger than cod and parsley and vegetarian. And even if it turns my shit stinky doesn't matter.

ELVIS: You are disgusting, do you know that?

BALBIR: You are not supposed to come today.

ELVIS indicates the frame.

ELVIS: I've tightened the screws.

BALBIR: My purse.

ELVIS passes her a purse from under the pillow. He rolls the frame forward.

ELVIS: No more squeaks. See. You'll be floating like a butterfly. Whee… whee…

He pushes the frame in a circle around BALBIR. She takes a coin out of her purse and holds it out.

BALBIR: Take it.

ELVIS: Why?

BALBIR: For your birthday.

ELVIS: It's gone. Ages ago.

BALBIR: Is my present to you.

ELVIS: One pound?

BALBIR: Take it and go.

ELVIS: You know it's against the rules.

BALBIR: Please go.

ELVIS: We're off out soon.

BALBIR: You don't come.

ELVIS: I'm booked for the day. Time and a half.

BALBIR: If you leave… I… I will let you kiss me… darling…

BALBIR offers up her lips. ELVIS recoils.

BALBIR: We won't tell the girl.

ELVIS picks up a hair dryer.

ELVIS: I'd actually rather not. Thanks.

ELVIS starts drying BALBIR's hair. BALBIR screams.

BALBIR: Get out, get out of my house you shitter!

ELVIS carries on, unfazed by BALBIR's outburst. MIN comes back in.

BALBIR: Min, he's hitting me…

MIN: Elvis doesn't hit mother.

ELVIS turns off the hair dryer. MIN's wearing a simple shalwar kameez and looks rather fetching. She's carrying a pair of old tap shoes.

ELVIS: You look… quite radiant. If you don't mind me saying.

MIN picks up BALBIR's red and gold kameez.

MIN: Arms up.

BALBIR sticks her arms up. MIN and ELVIS put the top on BALBIR.
It's a very tight squeeze.

BALBIR: He called me a smelly P.A.K.I.

MIN: Stop fibbing and finish that cobbler.

MIN sits on the floor and puts on the shoes. BALBIR attacks her food
again. ELVIS starts styling BALBIR's hair. He indicates MIN's shoes.

ELVIS: Where did you get them?

MIN: Oxfam. She needed a new balaclava.

MIN starts to tap dance. BALBIR covers her ears. MIN dances without
skill but manages to make a constant tap tap noise.

MIN: *(Breathless.)* Do you like the noise?

ELVIS: Yeah.

MIN: I love it.

ELVIS: You should go to a club.

MIN: Like a disco?

ELVIS: That's it.

MIN: We had them at school. You can't move in a disco, not
like you can at home. Too many bodies and all them traffic
lights going off at the same time. *(A beat.)* Ooh... I'm in the
mood now.

MIN stops. With her hands on her hips she bends over like an athlete.

ELVIS: Hey... perhaps... I could take you.

BALBIR: *(Screams.)* No!

MIN: Don't you start a rumpus mother.

MIN takes off her shoes.

BALBIR: I said you to do effort.

ELVIS: She looks lovely.

BALBIR: You are sex maniac virgin, to you even bloddy horse
is lovely.

ELVIS takes away BALBIR's plate and cutlery.

BALBIR: Send that shitter away.

MIN: I need him. I can't manage the frame and the chair on my own.

BALBIR: I will carry it all.

MIN: You can't wipe your own bottom.

BALBIR: Someone else might aid us.

MIN: *(Shouts.)* There is no-one flipping else! Now shush up!

BALBIR retreats into herself and closes her eyes. ELVIS comes back in and wipes down BALBIR's high chair, he places a glass of water in front of her and ELVIS and MIN watch BALBIR fall asleep. They speak in hushed tones so as not to wake BALBIR.

ELVIS: Is there singing, in your church?

MIN: You won't understand the words.

ELVIS: Then I'll hum. I need the practice.

MIN: Just get us in and out. You don't have to stay.

ELVIS: I want to. Tell me what to do?

MIN: Can't remember. Haven't been since I was little.

ELVIS: Thought you'd go every Sunday. See all your mates.

MIN: It's too much bother with the frame and the chair…you know.

ELVIS: Don't her mates help?

MIN: I don't like to make silly demands…

ELVIS: You should ask me.

MIN: Going out's not part of her package. I've had to make a special request.

ELVIS: I'd come anyway.

MIN: If you hold the frame, I'll push the chair.

ELVIS: I reckon you need more than fifteen minutes a day. I'll put in a word.

MIN: No, don't.

ELVIS: You shouldn't have to miss out on your culture.

MIN: She's never been interested before. This leaflet about Guruji's special day popped through the letterbox and she went all keen.

ELVIS: Tell me what it's like. In there.

MIN thinks hard.

MIN: You have to take your shoes off and cover your head.

ELVIS: Show me.

MIN giggles. She takes off her shoes and covers her head.

MIN: Then you go in and make sure you've got 2p in your hand or even a twenty.

She takes out a coin and holds it tightly in her hand.

MIN: You walk on the white sheets, there's women on one side and men on the other, but don't worry about them. *(She walks.)* Carry on straight towards the man with the beard, he'll be waving his wand, and the book's there in front of you.

ELVIS: Right.

MIN: You put your hands together *(she puts her hands together)* and in that moment you have to think really quickly.

ELVIS: About what?

MIN: About God and what you want to say to him. Only don't speak it out loud, keep it deeply, deeply inside. *(She does the following action.)* You kneel down, look at the book, make sure your forehead touches the ground and then you whisper it, ever so quietly. Now get up, but don't turn your back on him, and go and sit down.

ELVIS: What do you want to say to him?

MIN: That... I love God and Guru Nanak and all the gurus as well, and I want to be a good disciple.

ELVIS: *(Hopeful.)* What else you gonna say?

MIN: Er... that... he... might perhaps... show me the way through... So that things can stay. For me and her.

ELVIS: But things change.

MIN: Change isn't always for the better Elvis.

ELVIS takes this in. MIN turns away uneasily.

MIN: Perhaps you wouldn't mind sorting out the chair?

ELVIS nods and turns to go.

MIN: Elvis!

He stops. MIN giggles nervously.

MIN: I feel funny… all sort of… a bit… nervous… I'm not used to so many bodies.

ELVIS: You'll be alright.

He turns to go again.

MIN: What if I get it wrong?

ELVIS nods to the ceiling.

ELVIS: He'll be watching over.

ELVIS exits. MIN gently shakes BALBIR to awaken her. MIN takes out a coat, a headscarf and a bag from under the bed. She puts them on the bed and then lifts her mother out of the chair. BALBIR stiffens her body.

MIN: What's the matter?

MIN just about manages to place her mother on the bed.

BALBIR: I don't want to go.

MIN: But I've done all the preparations. I've worked myself up.

BALBIR: You go. On your own.

MIN: I can't… you know I can't. I've booked a taximan mother. I've even started to look forward… You're flipping well going.

BALBIR: Why does he have to come?

MIN: It's his job.

BALBIR: People will see us with him and think…

MIN: What?

BALBIR: That he is my son in law.

MIN: It's a new century, people understand about Social Services.

BALBIR: You don't care about me.

MIN: Don't you dare…

BALBIR: Only about yourself, you only bother about yourself.

MIN's getting to the end of her tether. She shouts.

MIN: Please, shush up.

BALBIR: I wish you'd never come out of me. I wish you'd never taken a breath and that I'd burnt you and buried you before anyone knew what a thicko you would turn out to be.

MIN: Don't call me that!

BALBIR: *(Chanting.)* Thicko… thicko…

MIN: I could have got CSEs…

BALBIR: Thickhead, thickhead…

MIN: And O'levels perhaps. I would have taken them as well if I hadn't had to keep bringing you down the hospital.

BALBIR: Thicko… thicko… thickhead… thickhead… Just like your black Elvis.

Almost in tears, MIN takes some sellotape out of a bag. She pulls some off and plasters it over BALBIR's mouth. BALBIR struggles, but MIN suppresses her.

MIN: You're forcing me. I'm only doing this because you are forcing me.

She puts two more rounds of sellotape over BALBIR's mouth and then ties her mother's wrists together.

MIN: I don't care what you say about me. But there's no need to be rude about other people.

BALBIR is finally silenced. MIN paces around, she speaks as though she is thinking very hard.

MIN: I'm trying mother. I'm trying. But sometimes I can't cope very well, not in here and especially… not… out there. And I know you seem to find Elvis… difficult and his presence deeply odious. But I derive a great deal of encouragement from him. That's how I manage. I should improve, that's true. And I will try. Maybe that's what I ought to say to God, that I'd like to be better. And perhaps he'll make me… turn me into something good, a thing to be proud of. *(A beat.)* But for now, for today, on this auspicious occasion of the birth of Guru Nanak, please let's put our trust and hope in God. *(A beat.)* And in Elvis.

BALBIR half nods.

MIN: I mean it.

BALBIR nods vigorously. MIN takes the sellotape off. BALBIR breathes out with relief.

BALBIR: Make sure you tell them he is not your boyfriend.

MIN: I don't do things like that.

BALBIR: Why don't you?

MIN: I'm not a party person.

BALBIR: Then what person are you?

MIN: We'd better get our skates on.

BALBIR: After a certain age, a lady should not be on her own.

MIN: That's why I stay with you.

BALBIR: Forget me.

MIN: I can't.

BALBIR reaches for the headscarf and puts it on.

BALBIR: Today is my wedding anniversary.

MIN: *(Shocked.)* Oh mother.

BALBIR: In those times, girls used to be married in anticipation of the full moon, on the Guru's birthday.

MIN: How romantic.

BALBIR: Now they get married on Saturdays and Sundays.

MIN: I didn't realise.

BALBIR: Before your father went, we used to imagine your wedding.

MIN: Was it like yours?

BALBIR: No. It was bigger and grander, hugely expensive and wildly flamboyant. Your groom would arrive on a white stallion, your body would drip in 24 carat gold, and you would be demure and expertly made up, the envy of all womanhood.

MIN: Me?

BALBIR: Like a photograph in a magazine. A moment of perfection, captured, to be remembered and yearned for, forever.

MIN: I know I'm a disappointment.

BALBIR: Yes. *(A beat.)* But it doesn't have to be that way. When we get there… I plan to ask Him Upstairs to bless us. Blessings are always granted on the Guruji's special day.

MIN: But you don't believe in God.

BALBIR: That doesn't stop him believing in me. *(A beat.)* You remember Mr Sandhu?

MIN: Did he used to have a curly perm?

BALBIR: I gather he wears a turban now.

MIN: Did my dad go on walks with him? In the park, while I rode my bike?

BALBIR: Possibly.

MIN: I can't ride a bike any more.

BALBIR: He is Chairman of the Gurdwara's Renovation Committee.

MIN: I thought he sold the pools.

BALBIR: Local councillor!

MIN: Done very well for himself.

BALBIR: You know he washed your father's body.

MIN: I don't have any vague recollections of anyone.

BALBIR: And he has always taken a great interest in me. And you.

MIN: He's never been round.

ELVIS enters with the wheelchair, starts clearing up.

BALBIR: A very busy person like that doesn't come round. *(A beat.)* When I detected his mobile telephone number on that leaflet, I rang it. He is going to aid us.

MIN: How?

BALBIR: He has a list. The cream of the cream of all lists.

MIN starts getting distressed.

MIN: I don't understand lists.

BALBIR: He is going to find someone for you.

MIN: Someone?

BALBIR: You will go to his office in the Gurdwara and talk to him.

MIN: I can't talk.

BALBIR: He will see what a nice young lady you are and he will match you up. And if you are a good girl, by this afternoon you might have a rich, handsome, successful fiancé.

MIN: You shouldn't have.

ELVIS can't bear any more.

ELVIS: Min!

BALBIR and MIN look round at him.

ELVIS: Shall I wait downstairs for the taxi?

MIN: Yes please.

ELVIS retreats and exits.

BALBIR: I have to protect you from external forces. I must look after you.

MIN: But I look after you.

BALBIR: You are one of Nature's cruel jokes.

MIN: You've got nobody except me. And I won't leave you.

BALBIR: It will be a big property no doubt and I will have my own quarters. And when you bear your first son…

MIN: No…

BALBIR: I will be there to guide him through life's rocky road. And what a success he will be.

MIN: No mother. I won't.

BALBIR: This is something… perhaps the last thing I can do for you before they set me alight on a pauper's pyre.

MIN: No.

BALBIR: Finally there will be someone to… keep you company, instead of boring old me. Doesn't that sound… appealing?

MIN veers between desperation and defiance.

MIN: I won't. I shall not.

This fuels BALBIR's fury.

BALBIR: You think you can say no to such a thing? You think a bloddy horse like you can say no to Mr Sandhu?

MIN: I'm nothing to do with him.

BALBIR: He is trying to help you, to help us get out of this shitter hole your father left us in.

MIN: Don't you blame my dad, you're the one that ruins things.

BALBIR: He ruined me. And you. Embarrassing us, leaving us stinking of his dishonour…

MIN: It wasn't his fault.

BALBIR: Your father flushed my life down the toilet.

MIN: You kept smacking him round the face!

BALBIR: He deserved it.

MIN's crying now. BALBIR feels for her.

BALBIR: Min! I know what sacrifices you've made.

MIN: I don't care about any of them.

BALBIR: It's because of me you've turned into this lump of lard, I know, and I'm sorry.

MIN: Why can't you be happy as we are?

BALBIR: How? Eating plastic frozen school dinners, waiting for you to wipe my arse, being wheeled about like shopping in a supermarket trolley? You think it is pleasant watching a fat virgin become infertile? I want to live a life that is something. I want to be seen and noticed and invited by people. I want anything… that is not this.

MIN: I'm scared.

BALBIR: Of what.

MIN: Of all of it.

BALBIR: There isn't a brave bone in your body.

BALBIR gets up using her frame and picks up her coat. She wobbles briefly but the familiar feel and support of the frame gives her a certain confidence. She puts on the coat and eyes MIN with disdain.

BALBIR: If I can show my face, you can open your mouth. You're going to talk to Mr Sandhu, and if you're lucky you'll end up with half a chance.

MIN: You won't make me Mother. I do what I like and there's nothing you can do about it.

BALBIR: We'll see.

MIN: I'm going to wish Guru Nanak a happy birthday and that's all. He loves me and he's going to show me the way.

BALBIR: And I want none of your bloddy dancing in front of people. Always giving me the bloddy embarrassment.

MIN: *(Shouts.)* And you try not to poo yourself mother!

BALBIR wobbles but clutches her zimmerframe tightly and stumbles out. MIN is left alone, sobbing. After a few moments, she gets up, wipes away her tears, straightens herself out and follows her mother outside.

SCENE ONE
GURDWARA – ARRIVAL

A vast dimly lit empty space. This whole space may give rise to several areas, but the significant action takes place centre stage. There is the sense that parts of the space can be, or might turn, into anything.

Hypnotic Sikh religious music plays. On a square area, defined by white sheets on the floor, sits one of the Gurdwara's priests, GIANI JASWANT, forty-seven, a pensive, heavy-hearted soul. He has a long black/grey beard and wears a blue turban and a white kurtha pyjama. He holds a stick of horse hair. GIANI JASWANT waves the stick about and gently chants to the music.

At one side, an edgy, frightened-looking balding man throws darts at a dartboard. Above the board hangs an ornate Kirpan (Sikh religious sword). This man is MR SANDHU, fifty-five. Wearing a suit from Asda, he has a fastidious air and on first sight is utterly forgettable. There is a small desk and chair behind him. On the desk is writing paper, a pen and a bag of mint humbugs. MR SANDHU nervously beholds the dart in his hand.

MR SANDHU: Double top… double top for a sweetie…

MR SANDHU throws the dart and quickly goes to retrieve it, as he wanders back he inserts a humbug into his mouth.

Lights reveal a small dank area centre stage. A shoe rack displays assorted footwear. POLLY DHODHAR, forty-eight, a capable woman who's losing her once sensational looks, sashays towards the rack.

She wears a spangly shalwar kameez and carries a large shoulder bag.

POLLY carefully inspects different shoes. Eventually she finds a pair of black patent stilettos. She briefly checks that no-one's looking and puts them on. She walks around in a circle, takes the shoes off, checks again that she's not being watched and hurriedly stuffs them in her bag. A hard-faced but curvaceous woman, TEETEE PARMAR, fifty-two, approaches unseen by POLLY. She too carries a shoulder bag and shouts out angrily. Both women speak with broad Punjabi accents.

TEETEE: Joo naughty thief!

POLLY jumps. When she sees TEETEE, the two women burst into peals of laughter.

POLLY: Meh tha Darghi! *[You scared me!]*

> *TEETEE starts looking through the shoes.*

TEETEE: That bitch from the Post Office got Manolo Blahniks.

POLLY: I saw.

TEETEE: Probably took them in with her. Greedy cow.

> *They continue to rummage. TEETEE's getting frustrated.*

TEETEE: All these cheapie people, coming to the Gurdwara in their stinking chappals *[sandals]* they bought in 1973. Don't they have no respect for God?

> *POLLY finds some smart leather loafers.*

POLLY: Patrick's Coxes! Your size.

> *TEETEE eagerly puts them on. They fit perfectly. She walks about proudly.*

TEETEE: Oh yes… this is more like it, very much more like it indeed. These are the foot holders of a queen, a goddess with a decent pair of trotters at the end of her tree trunks.

POLLY: Sandhu's daugher's.

TEETEE: That runt who vomits her dinner down the carsey?

> *She admires her feet. As they talk, POLLY and TEETEE try on different shoes from the rack.*

TEETEE: Least daddy can buy her some new ones. Is she married yet?

POLLY: I heard she's a muff diver.

TEETEE: Someone'll still have her. *(A beat.)* Bet there'll be some proper decent shoes at that wedding.

POLLY: Your Billoo could do worse.

TEETEE: That stick insect can't handle one of mine.

POLLY: What's there to handle?

TEETEE: Billoo only likes big things. Big boobs, big bottoms, big houses, big cars… everything big…

POLLY: I like the sound of that.

TEETEE: And he has big ideas for his business. Expansion. He is buying a crane and a what you call it… scaffolding… oh and a tractor even… so you see he is not likely to mate with a lezzer.

POLLY: I thought I saw him up the dole.

TEETEE: He meets his uneducated friends there. He tries to direct those unlucky boys onto the right path. And then they go for chips.

POLLY reaches inside her bag.

POLLY: How proud you must be Teeteeji.

POLLY takes out a pamphlet of assorted paint colours and pointedly flicks through it.

TEETEE: I am but… I don't like to flaunt what I've got. What is that you are flicking Pollyji?

POLLY: Did I mention that while I was at the Cash and Carry, performing my weekly task for the Gurdwara, loading extra large bags of granulated sugar and 20kg sacks of chappati flour, into my spacious Four by Four, I received a call on my mobile phone?

TEETEE: No.

POLLY: From Mr Sandhu…

TEETEE: No!

POLLY: Asking me to trawl the local DIY superstore for a pamphlet of assorted paint colours. He is choosing a design scheme for the new extension to the Gurdwara.

TEETEE: Already?

POLLY: And judging by his amicable tone, I would not be surprised if he requested my opinion before making a final decision.

TEETEE: *(A beat.)* Do you want to know a big fat secret?

POLLY: Yes please.

TEETEE: Guess who will be building the new extension to the Gurdwara?

POLLY: That gora cowboy Thompson I expect.

TEETEE: *(Thrown.)* Who told you that?

POLLY: I saw his van parked outside yesterday. He was chewing his bacon roll with great confidence.

TEETEE: His confident chewing is about to be terminated. Guess again.

POLLY: Mr Sandhu is in charge of the new extension.

TEETEE: I know, but who will be building it?

POLLY: Not your Billoo?

TEETEE: And I am going to see Mr Sandhu later…

POLLY: No!

TEETEE: Because Billoo is making me his manager.

POLLY: No!

TEETEE: Yes! That boy is going to be extremely huge around these parts. You mark my words. He has a large brain and long fingers. Always a winning combination.

TEETEE stuffs a few pairs of shoes into POLLY's bag.

POLLY: *(Cheeky.)* You should tell him to come and visit me.

TEETEE: What?

POLLY: I could make him some aloo paratha to keep him fit and strong. *(A beat/sighs.)* No-one's tasted my aloo paratha in quite some time.

TEETEE grabs POLLY by the scruff of the neck and violently pushes her to the floor. TEETEE sits astride POLLY and tightens her grip around POLLY's throat.

POLLY: *(Choking.)* Teeteeji!

TEETEE: You leave him alone. You don't go near my son, understand?

POLLY: I was joking, only joking.

TEETEE releases her.

TEETEE: Find some other boy to molest.

POLLY: *(Coughing.)* I've tried. They've all got blondie girlfriends.

They exchange a conciliatory smile. TEETEE sighs.

TEETEE: Today, I feel old.

POLLY: I don't. I feel damn well gorgeous.

TEETEE examines her hands.

TEETEE: I must have made a hundred rotis this morning.

POLLY: And I chopped a thousand onions.

In the worship area, GIANI JASWANT gets up and bows respectfully towards the holy book.

TEETEE: God will appreciate it, you will see.

GIANI JASWANT exits the worship area.

POLLY: *(Downbeat.)* Always we are just passing time. Over and over and over and over…

TEETEE playfully pokes POLLY in the ribs.

TEETEE: But what a time it is! All us ladies together, giving each other the company.

POLLY: *(Unsure.)* Yes.

TEETEE: So much fun God gives us, under his roof. We should be thankful.

GIANI JASWANT walks past. On seeing him, TEETEE adjusts her chooni (scarf). POLLY quickly greets him with a traditional Sikh salutation.

POLLY: Sat siri akal Gianiji…

TEETEE: Very busy today Gianiji, you must be pleased.

POLLY: Like a church at Christmas.

There's an awkward silence.

TEETEE: Shall we bring you some chah Gianiji?

He shakes his head. They all stare at each other, not knowing what to say. The GIANI opens his mouth to speak, the ladies regard him with anticipation, it seems as though he is about to say something very important.

GIANI: I have been pondering… when a fly sits on an orange, it is up to the warrior to eat the pith. Then perhaps the dolphins will fly in the sky. It is only by such devotion that one can understand the true limitless power of the divine, enlightened one.

POLLY and TEETEE nod in bemused agreement.

POLLY: Perhaps you would like some methi dhi roti *[fenugreek bread]*.

GIANI: No thank you. I prefer to arrange my own thali *[plate]*. Actually I was just on my way to relieve myself.

The GIANI heads off. Watching him go, POLLY turns to TEETEE.

POLLY: Bucharah *[poor thing]*, after so long, the drugs are still affecting his brain.

TEETEE: No-one was forcing him to put white powders up his nose.

POLLY: Still, he has had a hard life. You remember what it was like in that house…

TEETEE: Perhaps you should make him some aloo paratha.

POLLY: Giani Jaswant is far too old for me.

TEETEE: Stupid! He is at least two years younger than you.

POLLY: Exactly.

TEETEE gathers their things together.

POLLY: Time to do more sayva?

(Sayva [service to God] – this means helping out. The selfless and menial nature of this work is deemed to be an essential part of being a good Sikh.) TEETEE nods and releases a long suffering sigh.

TEETEE: God is waiting. *(A beat.)* And that Binder Kaur always leaves her gold on the side when she's stirring the kheer *[rice pudding]*.

The women laugh and go to leave when ELVIS enters (carrying BALBIR's bag and frame) followed by MIN who pushes BALBIR in her wheelchair. POLLY and TEETEE stop in their tracks, frozen by shock. They both stare at BALBIR who stares back.

ELVIS and MIN don't know what to do, so stand awkwardly and look to the ground. BALBIR starts to gently sing a traditional, poignant bridal farewell (bidhai).

BALBIR: Babel bidya carendea menoo rakleh aaj dee rath veh
Kiken rukha beti mehria meh sujan sudahleh app

*[Please father let me stay at home for just one more night
How can I daughter? I've asked them to take you away.]*

TEETEE joins in, softly, almost as if she's on automatic.

B&T: Theri melah dhi bich bich veh, doli meeri nay nungdee
Ick itt cudvahdeh mangat behti car jah aap dhi

*[I can't leave father, my doli won't pass through your door
Then I'll take this wall apart, brick by brick, until you can pass,
go now daughter to your new home.]*

BALBIR points a finger at POLLY and chuckles warmly.

BALBIR: You remember?

POLLY's eyes well with tears. She nods and drops to her knees, throwing her arms lovingly around BALBIR's legs. BALBIR turns to MIN and indicates POLLY.

BALBIR: You think you have seen beauty?

No response. BALBIR shouts.

BALBIR: You think you have seen beauty?

MIN: *(Anxious.)* I don't know.

BALBIR: Well you bloddy haven't. None of you bloddy lot
have. Not like this one on her wedding day. Nineteen she
was. We sang that song and we sent her on her way...
and we sobbed and we wailed. She was the jewel in our
crown, our Audrey Hepburn. The skin, the eyes, the hair,
the figure. Bloddy shitter, if she possessed a swimsuit she
would have won Miss World.

BALBIR eyes TEETEE.

BALBIR: You remember that day Teetee Parmar?

TEETEE: We have missed you Bhanji.

POLLY: You are a mother to us Bhanji.

TEETEE indicates MIN.

TEETEE: This must be…

POLLY: Yes! How big she has become.

TEETEE: She used to be a girl, now she is a woman.

An intrigued POLLY regards ELVIS.

POLLY: And this…

TEETEE: Must be her friend.

BALBIR: No… he is our help… you understand…

ELVIS: I'm Elvis.

POLLY: That's what they all say.

TEETEE and POLLY laugh heartily. BALBIR joins in. The three women embrace and hold hands. MIN and ELVIS take off their shoes. BALBIR proudly indicates the women to MIN.

BALBIR: When your poor useless father brought me to this country, we purchased a filthy, crumbling end of terrace…

TEETEE: Me and my old man lived in the cellar.

POLLY: And I lived in the cellar of the cellar, until I was married…

BALBIR: What days they were!

TEETEE: Bringing the coal in from outside…

BALBIR: Boiling the men's underwear…

POLLY: No carpet and no television…

TEETEE: Being spat at by little goreh *[white]* children…

POLLY: Carrying big shiny handbags…

BALBIR: Big plops of rain falling through the ceiling…

TEETEE: Always some beating and shouting coming from one room or another…

POLLY: No proper food…

BALBIR: Bloddy marvellous days…

POLLY: *(To MIN.)* You used to do dancing for us.

MIN: I still can!

TEETEE: So pretty you were.

MIN: At school, they used to say I looked like a buffalo.

Embarrassed laughter. MIN goes to take off BALBIR's shoes.

POLLY: So lucky to have this kind of daughter Bhanji.

TEETEE: God will bless her. Not every girl would make such a sacrifice.

POLLY: And we miss her daddy so much. He is in our hearts and souls every second of every moment…

TEETEE: Who can believe that such a thing would happen…

BALBIR: *(Interrupts.)* Time to think of the future now.

TEETEE: You still have the toilet trouble Bhanji?

BALBIR: I grow stronger every day. You see I am not over yet. Plenty more pages of my story to be fingered. And you?

TEETEE: Oh I have been lucky. Blessed by good fortune and three sons. Strong as oxes, they are rich, playboy businessmen.

BALBIR: The old man?

TEETEE: Building a kauthi *[big house]* back home. He draws pictures of all the rooms in those blue airmail letters. When he finds a pen.

BALBIR: And your husband Pollyji?

POLLY: Dead as a doorknob… Heart attack… Sudden it was.

BALBIR: No-one told me.

TEETEE: But… I phoned you and left a message.

POLLY: I am alright now.

BALBIR: Really?

TEETEE: Oh I am one hundred and ten per cent positive.

BALBIR: Of course. Maninder forgets things sometimes.

MIN: When?

POLLY: We wept very hard.

BALBIR: I am sorry Pollyji, I would like to have joined in with your weeping.

MIN: Perhaps I did forget.

TEETEE: You are only human.

MIN: *(Excited.)* You'll have to come round one day. I'll make a ginormous pan of sweet milky tea.

POLLY: We will come. One day.

MIN: I'll buy new biscuits to mark the occasion.

She takes a pen and paper out of her pocket and starts writing.

MIN: Ours is the tallest block on the estate. It's four pound fifty with a taximan.

BALBIR: They know the way.

MIN: But they've never been.

BALBIR grabs the paper from MIN and tosses it aside.

TEETEE: *(Uneasy.)* Bhanji, you know we are thinking about you and remembering you every day of our lives.

BALBIR: Sisters… you do not have to explain.

POLLY: *(Sad.)* But always God is keeping us so damn well busy.

TEETEE: I am pushing the tea trolley around the hospital.

POLLY: I am packaging the airport food.

TEETEE: And then God calls us here.

POLLY: To do his never-ending work.

BALBIR: Of course! Maninder, tell the boy to get my things ready…

MIN joins ELVIS, they organise BALBIR's stuff and set up her frame.

BALBIR: So many things have changed… over the years. You must tell me… I have been starved of things you see. What of my husband's dearest friend?

POLLY: A great success.

TEETEE: He has an office here now.

POLLY: Without Mr Sandhu, the Gurdwara would have no stainless steel utensils.

BALBIR: And the house? What has he done with my old house?

TEETEE: Converted into penthouse apartments. He rents them out.

POLLY: To students and DSS claimants. Did you know his little brother is now the head Giani at the Gurdwara?

BALBIR: Jaswant? But he was a most ungodly individual. *(A beat.)* I would… like to see our esteemed Beerji.

POLLY: Do you have an appointment?

BALBIR: No.

POLLY: You need a visa to see Mr Sandhu.

BALBIR: Just point me in the right direction.

TEETEE: Do you have some… special business Bhanji?

BALBIR: *(A beat.)* The girl you see… she is in need of help.

TEETEE: Help?

BALBIR: I understand he has a list.

TEETEE: Are you sure Bhanji… that that is what you want for her?

BALBIR: Oh yes. The old ways never did us any harm.

TEETEE: No.

BALBIR: So shall we go?

MIN and ELVIS approach with BALBIR's frame and things.

MIN: *(To ELVIS.)* Where's your baseball cap?

ELVIS: I left it.

TEETEE: You have to cover your head…

POLLY: … before you enter God's house.

BALBIR: He doesn't understand.

TEETEE rummages in her bag.

TEETEE: Lucky I have something spare.

She takes out a patterned floral ladies' headscarf.

ELVIS: What's that for?

TEETEE and POLLY tie the headscarf round ELVIS' head in the typical way Sikh men tie scarves to cover their heads before entering a religious space. ELVIS tears himself away.

ELVIS: Oy... I ain't a woman.

MIN: They're normally white hankies.

ELVIS: I ain't wearing that.

TEETEE: Please do not insult our culture.

BALBIR: Put it!

MIN: You have to have something.

Seeing MIN's imploring face, ELVIS slowly moves towards the women.

POLLY ties the scarf on him.

POLLY: Now he is Elvis Singh.

POLLY and TEETEE clap their hands to do a gidha (traditional folk dance).

TEETEE: *(Chants.)* One for the money, two for the show.

They dance around ELVIS, clap and make blowing, spitting sounds with their mouths (part of the gidha).

MIN: Don't!

ELVIS angrily tears off the scarf.

ELVIS: Stop it right.

POLLY: Oh Elvis... We were only playing.

TEETEE: Such anger! It is not usual to see such anger in the Gurdwara.

BALBIR: Rest assured ladies, I will be making a comprehensive complaint to the relevant authorities.

POLLY: No Bhanji… it is our sillibilliness… we are sorry
    Elvis… Come with me and I will find you a spare scarf.

ELVIS: I'm staying here.

POLLY: All the men borrow them.

MIN: Go on.

ELVIS: I'm not supposed to leave you.

MIN: We'll see you inside in a minute.

*ELVIS reluctantly heads off with POLLY. MIN goes to lift BALBIR
out of her wheelchair. BALBIR gets up and holds onto her frame, she
wobbles towards TEETEE.*

BALBIR: How about you and me go for a wander?

TEETEE: *(Reluctant.)* Bhanji…

BALBIR: Let's see who we bump into… for old times sake…

MIN: Mother! Stop bothering the nice lady.

BALBIR moves closer to TEETEE out of MIN's earshot.

BALBIR: *(Clipped.)* After all these years, don't you think you
    owe me a bloddy wander?

TEETEE picks up her bag and turns to MIN.

TEETEE: You!

MIN: What?

TEETEE: I am taking your mummy for a walk.

MIN: You can't.

BALBIR: Shut up shitter!

Using her frame, BALBIR follows TEETEE.

MIN: *(Fearful.)* What am I supposed to do?

*MIN looks around nervously. She spots GIANI JASWANT walking to
the kitchen area and follows him.*

SCENE TWO
GURDWARA – COVERING THE HEAD

POLLY and ELVIS stand in front of a large, open petthi (Indian trunk).
POLLY takes out a pink turban.

ELVIS: No.

POLLY: Why?

ELVIS: I'm not a Sikh am I?

POLLY: Try it.

> *She puts it on his head.*

POLLY: *(Admiring.)* Very handsome. You look like a
bridegroom, burning with passion, hungry for his ravishing
bride.

> *ELVIS quickly takes the turban off.*

ELVIS: Can I have one of them scarves?

> *POLLY continues to rummage.*

POLLY: You are their helper?

ELVIS: Home care. From Social Services. I heat her dinner
up and wash the plates. And I bring shopping round if
Min can't carry it and I comb her mum's hair most days.
Usually I've only got fifteen minutes but I try and stay
longer.

POLLY: Do you care for other people?

ELVIS: Mostly old folks. I shave and wash and wipe them till
they look like million dollar grannies and granddads.

POLLY: Very nice. And what does your girlfriend do?

ELVIS: I ain't got a girl.

POLLY: Single?

> *ELVIS nods.*

POLLY: Like me. *(A beat.)* Tell me, these days how does one
meet people?

ELVIS: How do you mean?

POLLY: You know… a gentleman… and a lady…

ELVIS: Er… I dunno… down the pub, or in shops or at bus stops?

POLLY: How lovely to have such… opportunities.

ELVIS: Oh I don't. But that's what people do, I reckon.

POLLY: You know… I am not a racialist.

ELVIS: Good.

POLLY: And my husband… well he was an open-minded man.

ELVIS: Can I please have one of them scarves?

POLLY: You're in a rush.

ELVIS: I've got to get back… I'm supposed to be responsible.

POLLY puts a white headscarf on ELVIS. They can't take their eyes off each other and this moment is loaded with sexual tension. It sizzles, silently.

ELVIS: You must miss him.

POLLY: Deeply. I miss him deeply.

ELVIS: I can see.

POLLY: Thank you. For seeing.

ELVIS: You wanna get out and about.

POLLY: I can't.

ELVIS: Why?

POLLY: It doesn't look… nice. When he ended, so did I.

POLLY moves close to ELVIS.

POLLY: I just need to…

POLLY adjusts his scarf.

POLLY: How does that feel?

ELVIS: Good.

POLLY: It looks… perfect…

They freeze for a moment. ELVIS hurriedly turns away.

ELVIS: I'd better get back. Thanks yeah.

POLLY: Elvis!

ELVIS: Yeah?

POLLY: What is your favourite colour?

ELVIS: Er… blue's… alright…

ELVIS turns to go.

POLLY: Will I see you later?

ELVIS smiles at her cheerfully.

ELVIS: I'm booked for the day.

He goes off. POLLY beams to herself excitedly, she takes out the paint pamphlet and flicks through it. She stops at a page of blues.

POLLY: *(Whispers/Reads.)* Sapphire lagoon.

She gently places a hand on her heart.

SCENE THREE
GURDWARA – PREPARING FOR MR SANDHU

MR SANDHU throws darts at the board as before. He goes to retrieve the darts and stuffs a handful of sweets into his mouth. TEETEE and BALBIR approach. A screen separates SANDHU's office area and he remains unseen.

POLLY enters the worship area. She bows in front of the book and sits down cross-legged. She clasps her hands together and meditates. TEETEE nods towards the screen.

TEETEE: Through there.

BALBIR: A visa you say?

TEETEE doesn't respond. BALBIR regards the screen apprehensively.

BALBIR: I mean we spoke on the phone, but it is always better to confirm in the flesh.

TEETEE: Yes.

BALBIR: And I must prepare him for the girl. You see… she is not your usual type of individual.

TEETEE: No.

BALBIR: He is a man who can make things happen, am I right?

TEETEE: Certainly.

BALBIR: We need ones like him. Doers. If only I had had one like him… Now quickly, do my make-up…

TEETEE takes the make-up out of BALBIR's bag and retouches BALBIR's face.

BALBIR: It is good to see you Teetee.

TEETEE: And you Bhanji.

BALBIR: Thank God we are all still living up to our expectations.

BALBIR hobbles towards the screen. Suddenly TEETEE screams out.

TEETEE: Don't go in there!

BALBIR: Why not?

TEETEE: *(A beat.)* You… you… don't have an appointment.

BALBIR: *(Quiet.)* Do you remember who I am? What I was?

TEETEE: Bhanji…

BALBIR: *(Shouts.)* Bloddy shitter, you used to scrub my floor and press my clothes and weep at my feet when all your thieving trash relatives murdered each other. All of you shitters, taking refuge under my roof. No murmurings or mutterings when the bricks and mortar slipped through my fingers and my name… *(Louder.)* my name was no longer spoken, instead ended up written in red ink on a pocket blue rent book.

TEETEE: I am sorry Bhanji for what you have endured.

BALBIR: You know you can't ever touch me Teetee… You can't ever, won't ever be Me. And you are jealous. You can't stand the idea of him helping me. Can you?

TEETEE: No.

BALBIR: Always the same Teetee, spoiling the happiness of others.

TEETEE: Actually Bhanji… I was joking.

BALBIR: *(A beat.)* So was I.

They smile at each other uneasily.

TEETEE: Wait a few moments, gather your thoughts, then knock loudly. Always best to enter such a room, prepared.

TEETEE turns to go.

TEETEE: He will be happy to see you.

TEETEE heads off. BALBIR beholds the screen anxiously. In the background ELVIS hovers around the shoe rack, he is clearly lost.

SCENE FOUR
GURDWARA – GOD IS LOVE

A stainless steel workstation. A sink and a pile of stainless steel utensils. The GIANI eats a samosa. MIN stands at the sink and looks around. She approaches the GIANI.

MIN: Excuse me... Sat siri akal...

He stares at her, unmoved.

MIN: What am I meant to do?

GIANI: What?

MIN: I don't know what I'm supposed to do. In here.

GIANI: I am an empty void, and know only of empty voids... if you want to ask a question... you must ask...

He points to the sky.

MIN: Is there anyone else about... who could tell me about such things?

GIANI: I try not to see people... or things. But sometimes I cannot prevent it.

Confused MIN picks up some of the kitchen utensils.

MIN: Perhaps I'll do some washing up.

She starts washing up.

MIN: Will you teach me a hymn?

GIANI: I don't teach... I am a learner still...

MIN: I bet you love God. A lot.

GIANI: I want... very badly... to serve him well.

MIN: So do I... Can you please tell me what is it exactly God wants?

The GIANI regards her, puzzled.

GIANI: All I know is this. Once upon a time there was a bedraggled man who woke up regularly in the front room of a small, abject house... in front of the test card as it happens... smelling. His mouth was always fixed around an empty bottle and there were tubes of five pound notes lying on mirrors all around... Ladies often left mugs of sweet milky tea by his side. They laughed and held their noses before slamming the door shut.

This continued. Other men came and went but the bedraggled man had blurred vision and couldn't make much out. One day there was the sound of screaming and some kerfuffle about a body on a railway track. They pulled the bedraggled man out of the front room as they had to make way for a coffin. Someone gave him a fizzy potion and he fell asleep on a 747, which eventually came to a halt outside Indira Gandhi Airport. At the end of the GT road he found himself in a wheatfield and finally woke up.

The village people hosed him down and brought him fresh saag and mackee dhi roti. They taught him to pray and he started wearing white cotton underwear. The man was no longer bedraggled and now God was happy.

MIN: *(Slowly.)* That is brilliant!

GIANI: Excuse me. I want to go to sleep now.

MIN: The begaggled man became... like a butterfly.

GIANI JASWANT lies down and closes his eyes.

MIN: Suppose you haven't been... very good inside... for a very long time... and what if you can't... become a butterfly?

The GIANI doesn't respond.

MIN: Please… tell me…

GIANI: You stay sleeping and smelling in the house.

The GIANI goes to sleep. ELVIS enters with BALBIR's wheelchair.

ELVIS: I've been looking for you everywhere! Where's Balbir?

MIN: Off praying with that kind lady.

ELVIS: I was worried.

MIN: Do you think a person can be different, from what he is Elvis?

ELVIS: Dunno… yeah… I think… Otherwise there'd never be any new days or times would there?

MIN: Perhaps you could sing a hymn while I do these cups.

ELVIS: Min…

MIN: *(Interrupts.)* I think God might like that Elvis.

SCENE FIVE
GURDWARA – THE DEAL

BALBIR tentatively moves towards MR SANDHU's screen. She knocks. He immediately jumps.

SANDHU: Wait!

He sits down behind his desk. He frantically finds an old-fashioned fountain pen and starts writing on a sheet of paper with meticulous precision.

SANDHU: Yes?

BALBIR wobbles in with her frame. She stops in front of his desk and grins.

BALBIR: How is it going?

SANDHU is paralysed with shock.

BALBIR: Don't get up. I've been shown around already. I've been all over and I must say you've done a spectacular job with this place. Whoever chose the carpet in the entry area is a genius.

So very soft, but yet firm which is what the ball of the foot requires. And proper cotton sheets for a change, not those market ones that bobble. Were they from a department store?

SANDHU nods uncomfortably. BALBIR indicates the Kirpan, she nods with approval.

BALBIR: A healthy reminder that we are a warrior race.

SANDHU: *(Nervous.)* I do not have any appointments today.

BALBIR: You are free then?

SANDHU: *(Shy.)* No-one is supposed to come.

BALBIR: Took me a while to find you. But I didn't let a couple of flights stop me! I pushed and pulled and yanked myself up. *(Deep breath.)* Like Hillary and Tensing when they reached the top of the world.

SANDHU: You are not supposed to be here. There are no appointments... today.

BALBIR: I thought after we spoke on the phone, I supposed we had an... understanding.

SANDHU: Please... who are you?

BALBIR: Oh... how silly of me... of course... I am not the... *(She means to say beauty but can't.)* ... person... I once was, Sandhuji... beerji *[brother]*. I am... er... Tej's wife.

SANDHU: Tej?

BALBIR nods.

SANDHU: Tej?

SANDHU thinks hard.

SANDHU: He jumped out of that train.

SANDHU's mood starts to change. He starts to come into his own.

BALBIR: The man was endlessly irresponsible. But now there is the girl to think of.

SANDHU: I remember... Tej was taking pills.

BALBIR: You mentioned a list.

SANDHU: And he liked to drink pints of lager with a teaspoon in The Rose and Crown.

BALBIR: You said it was the cream of the cream.

SANDHU: Afterwards he'd have a whisky chaser.

BALBIR: The list… beerji… I thought you could help…

SANDHU: I do recall now.

BALBIR: Marvellous.

SANDHU: You know I haven't considered Tej for many years. And now suddenly I miss him.

BALBIR: You do?

SANDHU: He was always so very…

BALBIR: … drunk.

SANDHU: Yes he was, but he was far more than that. He was a soft man, gentle and quite shy.

BALBIR: The girl is in her prime. More or less.

SANDHU: Tell me about Tej's girl.

BALBIR: Sadly she has been lumbered with many of her father's attributes. And she's no spring chicken, but she has a certain something.

SANDHU: Does she resemble him?

BALBIR: Er… yes… and she is strangely vital. And… er… domesticated. Very reliable and honest.

SANDHU: She wants someone?

BALBIR: From the list.

SANDHU: Boyfriends?

BALBIR: No such luck.

SANDHU: They all have boyfriends these days.

BALBIR: Not her. Never. Ever.

SANDHU reaches for a book, which sits on his desk. It's the Sikh guide to first names. He puts on a pair of glasses.

SANDHU: She sounds… special.

BALBIR: Oh… she is.

SANDHU: What is her name?

BALBIR: Maninder.

SANDHU flicks through the book and stops at a page.

SANDHU: *(Reads.)* Maninder – Goddess of the soul. An inexact but charming translation. *(A beat.)* Tell me, does she desire love?

BALBIR: Oh yes.

SANDHU takes off his glasses.

SANDHU: Love. Love is a gift from God, the purest and yet most complex aspect of being. It makes you feel warm, exuberant, expansive. *(He sighs.)* Ah… to give love… to receive love… to be blessed with a lover.

BALBIR: *(Unsure.)* Yes.

SANDHU: But a lover is not the one who is happy only in happy times and miserable in adversity. A lover is the one who is yours, who is inside you, who you are inside. Who makes you feel like hot chocolate sauce on milky vanilla ice cream or treacle sponge with extra thick double custard or pink roast lamb with thin garlicky juices and buttery jersey royals. Someone who makes you feel you are worth something… anything… who will let you play and fight and be simple. And who won't hate you. Ever. No matter how disgusting or disgraceful you really are.

Silence. BALBIR's rather taken aback. She thinks for a moment.

BALBIR: And how… er… is the lovely Madhu?

SANDHU: *(A beat.)* Having spent the afternoon in a seaweed body wrap, my wife came home one day and unfortunately… drank a bottle of dettol. Needless to say, she expired.

BALBIR: Depression?

SANDHU: She seemed alright to me.

BALBIR: What a sad story.

SANDHU: Tej… was my friend.

BALBIR: I remember.

SANDHU: Perhaps you should go now.

BALBIR: Go?

SANDHU: A man needs time to reflect.

BALBIR: I have been reflecting for twenty years. Dreaming of red and gold wallpaper in my front room. Burgundy velvet drapes, a white leather settee and an avocado green bathroom suite. *(A beat.)* I hear you are something of a property magnate Sandhuji.

SANDHU: I do my best for my people.

BALBIR: I had plans once. Of entrepreneurship and empire. My husband squandered them.

SANDHU: Please do not speak ill of him.

BALBIR: Before his ashes were flung over Brighton Pier, my home was taken away.

SANDHU: The property was about to be repossessed and the purchase ensured that Tej had a first class funeral. As I recall I managed the funds expertly and us men were able to give him a special send-off at the Rose and Crown. Whisky chasers were served with pints of lager as a fitting tribute. George, the landlord, was most impressed.

BALBIR: I lost my place.

SANDHU: Luckily I fought for the names of his dependents to be inserted at the top of the Council's list.

BALBIR: Yet you have never visited our humble domicile?

SANDHU: I have such… painful recollections. Of his departure.

BALBIR: Our existence has been overwhelmed by the vile selfishness of my husband's pathetic act. If it were possible I too would obliterate myself and the girl from my own memory.

SANDHU: I have subsequently become accustomed to solitude.

BALBIR: Someone must now take charge of the girl. She and I were never compensated… So the list… beerji… you understand… I thought you should see her… so that an appropriate choice can be chosen.

SANDHU: I would like to meet Tej's girl.

BALBIR: When?

SANDHU: Tell her to go and pray first.

BALBIR: *(Clipped.)* You know… fate has been immeasurably unkind to her.

SANDHU: Just like her father.

BALBIR hobbles out. Unseen by BALBIR, TEETEE watches her go. SANDHU resumes his game of darts. TEETEE approaches the screen and knocks.

SCENE SIX
GURDWARA – A HAPPY TIME BEFORE IT

ELVIS and MIN are doing sayva – washing up glasses and pans at the stainless steel workstation. GIANI JASWANT is asleep as before. ELVIS sings with beautiful gospel undertones.

ELVIS: Precious Lord, take my hand, lead me on, let me stand, I am tired, I am weak, I am worn… Through the storm, through the night, lead me on, to the light, take my hand, precious lord, lead me on.

MIN: Oooh… you got to love that.

ELVIS: Teach me one of yours.

MIN considers this and starts to chant.

MIN: Satnam, satnam, satnamji, vaheguru, vaheguru, vaheguruji, japo, satnam, satnam…

She continues, ELVIS joins in. The chant ends.

MIN: It's brilliant here.

ELVIS: What do you like about it?

MIN: All of it. Like when you wash up and clean in here, you're doing it for everyone. Not yourself. But you're still doing it because you want to.

ELVIS: *(Tentative.)* Do you ever go out to other places?

MIN: Oh… yes… hospital, post office, chemist. Sometimes I buy clothes if there's a blue cross sale.

ELVIS: What about when it gets late?

MIN shakes her head awkwardly.

ELVIS: I'm in the pub most evenings. After the last granny's tucked up in bed and I've fed my dad, that's where you'll find me. I don't say much, I'm just there. Quiet, trying not to think about anything, cos I know tomorrow's gonna be just the same as today. Belter, that's the barman, he makes sure my glass is half full and sometimes when it's nearly closing time, when there's not been a broken window and Belter's not got his hands on a pair of schoolgirl tits, he tells me to get on the stage. And then it's my turn to shine.

Nervous ELVIS moves closer to MIN.

ELVIS: If you like… I could bring you down there. One night.

MIN: How about… how about another song?

ELVIS nods. He starts singing Bob Marley's 'One Drop'. Unseen by MIN and ELVIS, GIANI JASWANT gets up.

ELVIS: Feel it in the one drop, and we still find time to rap
We're making the one stop, the generation gap
So feel this drum beat, as it beats within

Out of the blue, GIANI JASWANT joins in with the chorus.

ELVIS/GIANI: Playing a rhythm resisting against the system
Ooh-we I know JAH'd never let us down

ELVIS is immediately silenced.

MIN: Sorry Sir. He's a Christian.

ELVIS: I'm not.

MIN: He's not used to performing selfless service to God.

GIANI: There is no Christian or Hindu or Muslim or Jew or Buddhist or Rastafarian or Sikh. Only the divine being. *(A beat.)* Ek Umkar, Satnam *[One God, named Truth]. (A beat.)* Have you ever been to the Notting Hill Carnival?

ELVIS and MIN shake their heads.

GIANI: You should go. It is free and you get to blow a whistle. I haven't been for many years, not since I started growing my hair. If you don't get stuck behind a float and manage to avoid the knife-wielding girl gangs and the ladies with sequinned bikini bottoms, it is possible to find the spirit of the Guru's unique illumination. From that experience of truth and enlightenment, one can come forth from the darkness and like an insect around a light bulb be exposed to the brightness of purity and wholeness.

MIN and ELVIS look on mystified. GIANI JASWANT takes a paratha lying on the side and munches on it.

GIANI: In the company of saints and holy people
No more is there a feeling of 'us' and 'them'
No-one an enemy, none a stranger
I get along with all

(Guru Arjan, Guru Granth Sahib p. 1299.)

The GIANI exits.

ELVIS: I don't get it.

MIN: People like us aren't supposed to.

ELVIS: What?

MIN: We have to make do with listening to him.

ELVIS: Min… there's something I'd like to say to you…

BALBIR staggers in.

BALBIR: Who loves you baby!

BALBIR stumbles to the floor.

MIN: Where's your lady?

MIN and ELVIS rush to her aid, they pick her up and sit her down.

ELVIS: Better get her to the toilet.

ELVIS puts her in the chair.

BALBIR: No! I feel born again. Like I'm wearing a brand new nappy. I want to receive the Guru's wisdom and to sing the song of the holy word. I've found God Min. I've found him.

MIN: Flip!

BALBIR: I feel the need to worship, to make my peace… Will you take me inside?

MIN: Yes mother… yes…

ELVIS starts pushing the chair. BALBIR turns to face him.

BALBIR: Stop! You don't come Elvis darling… this is to be a private time for me and my girl.

MIN: Oh mother, thank you… thank you…

MIN goes to wheel BALBIR out.

ELVIS: Wait… you can't go off like this.

MIN: We won't be long.

ELVIS watches them go.

SCENE SEVEN
GURDWARA – A GENTLEMAN'S AGREEMENT

MR SANDHU plays darts as before. TEETEE stands close by him.

SANDHU: Pala?

TEETEE: India.

SANDHU: He'll be back soon.

TEETEE: He won't be back. He doesn't want England any more. Or me.

SANDHU: These things pass.

TEETEE: He called me an ugly old bitch.

SANDHU: Words… mean nothing.

In the background MIN and BALBIR enter the worship area. They bow in front of the book and place coins down. They go to sit by POLLY.

TEETEE: I hope it's not long before he dies.

SANDHU: You shouldn't utter such phrases.

TEETEE: I try not to.

SANDHU: You have your boys.

TEETEE: Oh yes… them…

SANDHU: Any sign of grandchildren?

TEETEE: Sunny's wife has left and Channa's isn't far behind. They are sometimes not very good boys. They like too much television and also quite young girls.

SANDHU: You should give them a chance.

TEETEE: I know it is not their fault.

SANDHU: Boys need chances.

TEETEE: And I am hopeful for Billoo…

SANDHU: The unmarried one?

TEETEE: Yes. The others have never suffered you see. Have never been hit or punched or anything. And now I have to suffer their lack of suffering. They are spoilt, and so they spoil everything they get their hands on. But Billoo was lucky, from an early age, when I saw my failures with the others, I would remember to kick him often and also pull his hair at regular intervals. We understand one another's many past afflictions and so you see he is the only person who loves me. Who I can rely on.

SANDHU: What are you talking about?

TEETEE: He is setting up his building firm you know. And his aspirations… give me some hope.

SANDHU: What do you want Bhanji?

TEETEE: For Billoo… to build the extension to the Gurdwara.

SANDHU: That that… is a big task.

TEETEE: I will help him, don't you worry about that. *(A beat.)* You haven't made your decision yet have you Beerji?

SANDHU: Does your son have access to all the necessary technical advisory people?

TEETEE: All of them. He has done labour and his friend is a plumber, another an electrician, one more a carpet fitter.

SANDHU: Can he understand an architect's plans?

TEETEE: Certainly. He communicates brilliantly with persons at all levels of society.

SANDHU: And he will give me a good price?

TEETEE: The cheapest gora cowboy cannot compete with my Billoo.

POLLY exits the worship area.

SANDHU: Why Bhanji do you want this?

TEETEE: He needs something. Of standing. For his future.

SANDHU: There is nothing else you can attempt?

TEETEE: No-one else I can ask. I will do anything Beerji, to help my boy.

SANDHU: I require only one thing.

TEETEE: Yes?

SANDHU: That I can count on you.

TEETEE's face almost crumbles, it's as if this is the worst thing MR SANDHU could have said to her.

SANDHU: I need people I can depend on.

TEETEE: I know.

SCENE EIGHT
GURDWARA – SOFT AND LOVELY FEELINGS

A toilet cubicle and a sink. ELVIS washes his hands. POLLY approaches but spots GIANI JASWANT coming out of the cubicle and quickly retreats.

She moves out of his sight and hovers nearby.

The GIANI sits down cross-legged next to the sink and starts clipping his toenails. ELVIS regards him anxiously.

ELVIS: Are you confidential?

POLLY moves closer and listens in.

GIANI: I don't really like to know things.

ELVIS: Please… I need some advice.

GIANI: I've already told my story today.

ELVIS: *(Urgent.)* What do you do if you like someone, and you wanna tell them, but if they don't like you back, you don't wanna make it all funny between you.

POLLY moves away out of earshot. She starts jumping around and throws her hands into the air joyfully.

ELVIS: Cos you have to keep seeing that person, twice a day and when you leave you're all soft and dreamy about it. About them.

Excited POLLY turns back to eavesdrop.

ELVIS: You keep imagining what it'd be like, you know if you got on a bus and sat next to each other or gave them a present. What do you do?

GIANI: I could… er… ask the one above… and see what he says…

ELVIS: There's not time. She's probably already met some dreamboat with all prospects and stuff. Today. It's got to happen today. Cos tomorrow, everything's gonna be back like it always is.

POLLY moves out of earshot and delves into her bag. She excitedly sprays her body with Impulse. She checks her make-up and starts to do her hair.

ELVIS: Do you know Min?

GIANI: My brother... knows people... I don't...

ELVIS: Her mum had that stroke.

GIANI shakes his head.

ELVIS: The dad topped himself ages ago. It was in the papers.

GIANI: I have always been in his shadow. He is a more capable individual than myself, so perhaps you should turn to my brother.

ELVIS: *(Not listening.)* Min's the one. So good she is... so kind and pretty and decent. I mean I see her give Balbir a slap now and again, but only when she warrants it, which is most days if you ask me. After I've had a morning of cleaning and feeding, I go round and she's there all high and happy. She likes to move about and dance, oh you should see her. And really she deserves a proper dreamboat. I know she does. *(A beat.)* But I love her. And I don't see how he could love her like I do.

GIANI: That is quite wonderful.

ELVIS: What do I do?

GIANI: You want to apply action to this problem?

ELVIS: Yes.

The GIANI springs up, perturbed.

GIANI: I am sorry. But I must go and change my undergarments.

The GIANI hurries out. ELVIS is flummoxed. An overjoyed POLLY appears in front of him.

POLLY: Thank you Elvis.

ELVIS: For what?

POLLY: You sillybilly...

ELVIS is about to say something but POLLY places a finger on his lips.

POLLY: No more words... or questions or doubts. The answer to everything you are wondering... is yes.

ELVIS: Yes?

POLLY: Yes, yes, yes, yes, yes and a thousand yeses more.

ELVIS: I don't…

POLLY silences him again with her finger.

POLLY: When I was young… people used to say I was beautiful.

ELVIS: I heard…

POLLY: But I haven't felt beautiful, not for the longest time. You see so very deeply don't you? Inside people.

ELVIS: What?

POLLY: And you can see it in me now?

ELVIS: Oh… yeah… right… well you're lovely… of course.

POLLY: Really?

ELVIS: You are, honestly. Bet you were a proper stunner when…

POLLY moves towards ELVIS and kisses him on the lips. He responds and they embrace passionately. After a moment he hurriedly withdraws.

ELVIS: *(Mortified.)* I'm sorry…

POLLY: For what you silly?

She kisses him again and he responds. The GIANI comes back in. He stares at them. ELVIS notices him and recoils.

GIANI: I was under the impression this was the men's…

POLLY: Please Gianiji… I assure you…

ELVIS: I've never done this before.

GIANI: My toenail clippers…

POLLY: Things aren't what they seem.

GIANI: I don't want to see things…

ELVIS: Please don't tell anyone…

GIANI: But I keep being shown things… .

POLLY: We were just discussing... er...

POLLY hurriedly produces the paint pamphlet. The GIANI grabs his toenail clippers.

POLLY: What is your favoured choice of colour for the new extension?

The GIANI hurries out. POLLY goes to take ELVIS' hand, but he moves away and runs out.

SCENE NINE
GURDWARA – PERSUASION

MR SANDHU throws one last dart but doesn't bother retrieving it. He heads off in the opposite direction from the screen. Using her frame, BALBIR walks towards the screen. MIN has her arms around BALBIR and guides her gently. MIN looks around confused.

MIN: I think the girls' toilets are the other way.

BALBIR: Coming here has given my bladder renewed strength and vigour.

BALBIR indicates the screen.

BALBIR: He's in there.

MIN pulls away from her mother.

MIN: No mother. I can't...

BALBIR: Please... Min...

MIN: I want us to worship.

BALBIR: But I've already said my piece.

MIN: Then let's do sayva.

BALBIR: I'm disabled.

MIN: You could hold a tea towel and dry some kitchen utensils.

BALBIR: If you're not going in, how do you plan to pass your life?

MIN: Isn't it time to go home now?

BALBIR: No.

MIN: We've been outside long enough… I'm not really sure how to behave any more…

BALBIR: Before your father went, there was an outside…

MIN: Elvis must be starving. He's too well mannered to help himself.

BALBIR: When I am gone… there will be no Elvis.

MIN: Don't say that.

BALBIR: Bloddy shitter! No father, no mother, no friend, no job, no place, no hope. The council will put you in a ticked box… you will have to pay for everything and if you are lucky you will go to work with angry people who laugh at you and steal your money and ping your bra strap.

MIN: *(Unsure.)* I'll be alright.

BALBIR: Your flesh came out of me, it is mine, my property, and I won't let those shitter social workers file you away.

MIN: They won't.

BALBIR: You'll never belong or fit or be anything, not on your own… Not with your father's blood in your veins…

MIN: He was sad.

BALBIR: And useless. He is the reason I have to protect you and plan for you.

BALBIR puts her arms around her daughter, this is the first affection she's shown MIN in a long time. She hugs MIN warmly and then falls over.

MIN: *(Heartfelt.)* Mother…

MIN helps BALBIR up.

BALBIR: My beta, all I want is to take care of you… pay back the devotion you have shown me…

MIN's deeply touched.

MIN: Sometimes I suppose I expect the worst.

BALBIR: Like your dad.

MIN: I don't want to be sad like my dad.

BALBIR: Whatever those fat shitters think... I say you are a winner. And that you deserve a prize.

MIN: I always fancied an Olympic bronze. In gymnastics.

BALBIR: Yes.

MIN: Or showjumping even.

BALBIR: I have been reflecting. And have concluded that this is the only way forward. If you really want to get that medal.

MIN: I might.

BALBIR: And one day... you might find that you can become... something else...

MIN: Like the begaggled man...

BALBIR: A champion even.

MIN: Like a butterfly.

BALBIR: Moreover there is a side of you, a feminine angle that it is time to explore.

MIN: Explore.

BALBIR: Feelings that you have never felt. Sensations you have never sensed.

MIN: Sometimes I think I may have feelings and sensations.

BALBIR: All you have to do is have a natter with Mr Sandhu.

MIN: I'm not sure...

BALBIR: There is no time to wallow in the luxury of self-doubt. Think of all the others who will be affected by your sorry vacillation.

MIN: Others?

BALBIR: A government compelled to pay you billions in social security, charity workers forced to call on you with dustbin bags full of used underwear and non-perishable goods. And my restless soul, tortured by the knowledge of your fleabag solitude.

MIN: I don't want anyone else to suffer. Because of me.

BALBIR: Go forth. Then and only then is there the chance that Things and You might have a different outcome.

MIN: For God's sake.

BALBIR: I imagine that… God will be extremely pleased with you.

MIN: Will I be free then mother?

BALBIR: Free?

MIN: Of all that's criminal and… wrong about me…

BALBIR: Oh yes.

MIN: Does he remember me?

BALBIR: The years appear to have withered away his mental faculties.

MIN: *(Awkward.)* What's he like?

BALBIR: A gentle mouse, a widower whose wife's tragic departure was not unlike your father's.

MIN: I don't have to do anything… I mean I don't have to do anything today?

BALBIR: Just go and talk to him.

MIN: Do you really think I can?

BALBIR: I'm almost certain.

MIN tentatively regards the screen. She slowly stands up.

MIN: Say a prayer for me mother.

SCENE TEN
GURDWARA – TRUE COLOURS

Having covered his head, MR SANDHU walks towards the book. He kneels down, moves his head to the floor and then stands up. He puts his hands together and closes his eyes as though he is deep in prayer. He retreats slowly and sits down. He assumes a meditative pose and rocks gently to mesmerising Punjabi chanting. ELVIS hovers by the stainless steel workstation. POLLY approaches cautiously.

POLLY: Do you want some rice pudding Elvis? It's extra milky Golden Temple style. Eat it and you will turn into a Jat Sikh farmer, big and strong, two metres tall and three metres wide.

ELVIS: No thanks.

POLLY: Why would you want to anyway? When you are perfect as you are.

ELVIS: About before... I didn't mean to offend you or anyone...

POLLY rushes towards him and takes his hands.

POLLY: Let's get out! Now!

ELVIS: I don't know what happened.

POLLY: I have a jeep-style vehicle in the car park, we can find a country road, recline the seats and let the love songs blare out loud and proud.

POLLY moves to kiss him again, and again he responds, but then draws away.

ELVIS: I do like you... But this isn't right...

POLLY: You have given me such hope.

ELVIS: I never meant to.

POLLY: I am breathing and feeling and seeing and tasting like never before.

ELVIS: Tasting what?

POLLY: *(Laughs.)* You poor, strange, wild child!

ELVIS: That bloke's gonna tell on me... and it'll all be over before it's even started.

POLLY: Let him tell.

ELVIS: No!

POLLY: We'll live like outcasts and hold our heads up high and sell our story to the papers if there's enough interest. We'll shop together in anonymous supermarkets and scour holiday brochures for cottages in remote hilly locations.

I'll wear micro-minis and drink babycham! We'll live like Kings!

POLLY kisses him again but ELVIS quickly pushes her away.

ELVIS: *(Shouts.)* Get off me!

POLLY: But before… I felt…

ELVIS: I'm sorry…

POLLY: You said you liked me. That you wanted to get on a bus and give me a present.

ELVIS: It's not you.

POLLY: Then who?

Silence. The truth dawns on POLLY.

POLLY: I made you feel… sexy… I know I did.

ELVIS: I couldn't help it…

POLLY: You would choose a buffalo over me?

ELVIS: I don't know you.

POLLY: But I'm beautiful.

ELVIS: So's she.

POLLY: *(Vehement.)* No she isn't!

ELVIS: This is my fault. I shouldn't have…

POLLY: *(Hisses.)* No you shouldn't love people and then take your love away just because there's a buffalo in the distance.

ELVIS: I didn't intend…

POLLY: To torment my soul?

ELVIS: Please…

POLLY: *(Upset.)* To hurt me? You think you can come in here and play with me as though I am an empty can of fanta?

POLLY goes to attack ELVIS, however he manages to hold her at arm's length. She tries to hit him and they struggle. TEETEE enters.

TEETEE: Bhanji?

ELVIS lets go of POLLY, she stumbles but manages to hold herself up.

ELVIS: I'd better go and find Balbir.

POLLY: Teeteeji… this boy…

ELVIS: I have to fill out a sheet you see.

POLLY: He is not what he seems.

TEETEE moves in front of ELVIS blocking his way.

TEETEE: What has happened?

ELVIS: There's been a misunderstanding.

POLLY: He… he… insulted me…

ELVIS: I'm trying to do my job.

TEETEE: You don't come in here and insult the ladies of the Gurdwara.

ELVIS: I never.

TEETEE: That is for the ladies to do.

POLLY: Gianiji witnessed the incident.

TEETEE: That is extremely serious cause for concern.

POLLY: And *(points)* he and the buffalo girl are up to something.

TEETEE: I might have known… Did he insult you… badly?

POLLY: Yes but… I managed to… protect my honour.

TEETEE: What shall we do?

POLLY: Tell him off Bhanji, you tell him off good and proper!

TEETEE: No rules in here boy. No police, no evidence, no witnesses, nothing.

ELVIS: You threatening me?

TEETEE: Remember one thing boy. There is a man's soul in this woman's body. Our men are cruel to our women but we get used to it and we follow the rules, letting each slap and tickle and bruise and headbutt go by. And at the end of this rubbish life, we write the rules. We find the beauty in our cruelty. My daughter-in-laws suffer just as I suffered.

I make sure of it. Things happen. And no-one can do nothing. Because everything must stay the same.

ELVIS: I don't know what you're on about.

POLLY: Tell him Bhanji!

TEETEE: You be careful boy.

ELVIS pushes past TEETEE and heads out.

BALBIR watches MR SANDHU walk out of the worship area.

Agitated ELVIS walks into the GIANI.

ELVIS: Please don't say anything. To Min.

GIANI: I don't like to speak, but people keep asking me things.

ELVIS: I don't want her to know me like this. I couldn't stand it.

GIANI: Before the bedraggled man entered the front room… He was like you… And God was truly happy. I have concluded… that you must tell the person in question.

ELVIS: Tell her?

GIANI: *(Chants.)* Jo bole so nihal: Sat Sri Akal.

ELVIS shakes his head, perplexed.

GIANI: He who says this is saved: Truth is the immortal Lord.

Sikh religious music plays. The GIANI holds his hands together and walks towards the worship area.

He bows respectfully to the holy book and then goes to sit behind it. TEETEE and POLLY also advance and kneel down before the book. GIANI JASWANT soberly waves the stick of horse-hair. TEETEE and POLLY sit cross-legged with their heads covered on the women's side. ELVIS leads BALBIR in.

ELVIS: *(Anxious.)* Where's Min?

ELVIS helps BALBIR MUTHATECK pray respectfully in front of the book. He does the same and then walks her over to the women's side.

BALBIR: Leave her alone.

ELVIS: You better tell me.

BALBIR: What are you going to do? Wipe my arse to death?

ELVIS: I'll find her.

ELVIS turns to go, BALBIR clutches onto his arm for dear life.

BALBIR: If you go, I won't sign your sheet. *(A beat.)* I'll say you went off and left me. They won't let you come round any more, they'll send someone else.

BALBIR is now seated. TEETEE and POLLY regard ELVIS disdainfully. He stands desperately on the ladies' side.

BALBIR: *(Hissing at ELVIS.)* You are causing the embarrassment!

ELVIS uneasily goes to sit on the men's side. BALBIR turns to the ladies.

BALBIR: He is not my usual staff.

GIANI JASWANT starts a religious chant in Punjabi.

GIANI: *(Translation.)*
God cares for all forever
Sees all beings in the sea and on land
Does not dwell on their past sinful deeds
Benevolent to the poor, an ocean of compassion
Watches sinners but does not stop bestowing gifts on them.

(Guru Gobind Singh, Dasam Granth, Swayyai.)

SCENE ELEVEN
GURDWARA – GULTHEE (MISTAKE/WRONGDOING)

MIN is alone in SANDHU's office area. She paces around, not knowing what to do. She picks up the kirpan. She starts having a swordfight with an imaginary opponent. She moves around vigorously and becomes increasingly relaxed. On the desk she notices a BeeGees CD and regards it, surprised. She hums 'How Deep Is Your Love' and sways while still holding onto the kirpan. As the musical feelings rise inside her, she starts to dance with the kirpan, her movements are big and bold and fill the space. While she is humming and dancing, MR SANDHU enters. He watches MIN. Suddenly she spots him, and stops dead. They contemplate each other. She hands him the kirpan. He puts it back in its place.

SANDHU: You looked like you were enjoying yourself.

MIN: I didn't mean to… enjoy myself.

SANDHU: How are you?

MIN: I don't know.

SANDHU: We met when you were little. In the park. You were riding a purple tomahawk.

MIN: Did you have a greasy face?

SANDHU: No… I'm sure I was well groomed.

MIN: I don't remember much.

MIN shuffles around awkwardly.

SANDHU: Please sit.

MIN: What… me?

SANDHU nods. MIN obediently goes to sit behind the desk. Awkward silence. MIN indicates the CD.

MIN: What you doing with music?

SANDHU: It keeps me… *(Thinks for a second.)* … going.

MIN: I know what you mean.

SANDHU: Through all the bad moments… and believe me there've been enough of those. Sometimes…

MR SANDHU breaks down.

SANDHU: I find it all very hard…

Concerned MIN watches him cry like a baby.

SANDHU: No-one understands my plight.

MIN: Don't depress yourself.

MIN reaches in her pocket and takes out a scrunched up tissue.

MIN: Here you are…

SANDHU: Thank you. For being so caring.

MIN: It's only been used once.

SANDHU: Guilt is a very difficult feeling to bear.

MIN: I know.

SANDHU: Yes I suppose you do. How on earth... is one supposed to cope?

MIN: Put a smile on God's face, and he'll forgive us all.

MR SANDHU composes himself.

MIN: Are you better now?

SANDHU: Much better. Yes. Much better. *(A beat.)* I... er... understand you are looking for someone.

MIN: Sort of.

SANDHU: What kind of individual?

MIN: Any.

SANDHU: And what kind of person are you?

MIN thinks on this.

MIN: Female.

SANDHU: You have a beautiful name.

MIN: I always wanted to be called Sally.

SANDHU: I expect you want to see the list?

MIN: I don't... not really.

SANDHU: Then why are you here?

MIN: My mum told me to come.

SANDHU: I see.

MIN: Can I go now?

SANDHU: If you like.

MIN: I don't want to miss the paug.

MIN gets up to leave.

SANDHU: Tej would have been proud of you.

MIN stops.

MIN: I haven't done anything.

SANDHU: You seem to follow your own mind.

MIN: Do I?

SANDHU: Just like your dad. He... also followed his heart. Do you do that?

MIN: I couldn't say.

SANDHU: Is there anyone... inside your heart?

MIN: Sometimes... I think so.

SANDHU: His name?

MIN: Secret.

SANDHU: What does it begin with?

MIN: E...

SANDHU: Next letter?

MIN: That's enough...

She heads out.

SANDHU: You know, your father was extremely melancholic.

MIN turns to face him.

MIN: Did you help him put my stabilizers on?

SANDHU: Yes I did, he and I... we used to go on long walks.

MIN: While I went round and round.

(In the worship area, the congregation stand and chant the last Aardas – traditional Sikh song at the end of the reading of the Granth Sahib.)

SANDHU: You know when we came to this country, we were all so hopeful. We wanted possibilities, to wear ties and frequent pubs. And to feel carpet underneath our feet. I wanted to be a man, not a son or a brother or a husband.

MIN: *(Confused.)* You... you are...

SANDHU: You buy and sell and eat and excrete and do all the things you said and that you wanted. And all that happens is that you end up. You just end up.

MIN: End up what?

SANDHU: Tej knew.

MIN: I don't understand all this.

SANDHU: I'm a very selfish person.

MIN: *(Encouraging.)* Bet you're not.

SANDHU: After a while we get used to the disappointment. And we pass our failures onto our children. Then everything becomes your problem.

MIN: Shall I go now?

SANDHU: I have failed.

MIN: You haven't. You've got a desk and a chair. And loads of other bits and pieces. *(Pointing to the Kirpan.)* Look.

SANDHU: You must have heard about my wife.

MIN shakes her head.

SANDHU: I can see the blame and the pity in your eyes.

MIN: Who is she?

SANDHU: But you see I am so lonely, so very damn well lonely.

MIN: You want to get a telly.

SANDHU: So good. You are so so good. I can see it. I can see Tej in you.

MIN: My dad was sad.

SANDHU: I need someone you see.

MIN: Is she gone... your wife?

SANDHU: Yes. Thank you for realising.

MIN: Do you want to marry my mum?

SANDHU: You remind me of him... you remind me of my Tej... he... he used to kiss me... on the lips... hard... so hard...

MIN: *(Disturbed.)* What?

SANDHU: You remember don't you?

MIN: No...

SANDHU: But you saw us... together...

MIN's getting distressed.

MIN: Please stop...

SANDHU: You watched didn't you? When you were going round and round. Your eyes met mine. And his.

MIN: No.

SANDHU: He felt sick with himself for what you'd seen.

MIN: I didn't want to see. I didn't mean to.

MIN's sobbing.

SANDHU: Then he got on that train.

MIN: I know... I'm all criminal...

SANDHU: If you hadn't been there, he'd still be here. With me.

MIN: Please don't tell my mum.

SANDHU: I loved him so much... If he was alive, if I could be with him I'd be a much better person. If people would only let me be, I'd be happy. It's not fair. It's not fair...

MIN: Stop talking... please...

She turns to exit. MR SANDHU follows her.

SANDHU: He was a fine man, such a nice person. Good to be around and spend time with...

Before MIN can head out. MR SANDHU grabs her. She struggles.

MIN: Get off me... get off... please get off...

Her screams and shouts merge with the end of the Aardas (song) in the worship area.

SCENE TWELVE
GURDWARA – MY FLESH AND YOUR BLOOD

GIANI JASWANT distributes parshad (religious food). He first goes to ELVIS, who eats it, then to POLLY and TEETEE who surreptitiously stuff it in tissues and put it in their handbags, and finally to BALBIR who solemnly eats it. ELVIS helps BALBIR up. TEETEE and POLLY head out. BALBIR shakes ELVIS off and using her frame, follows the ladies. ELVIS comes forward and approaches the shoe rack. He looks around. ELVIS starts to sing with simple, beautiful clarity.

ELVIS: You are the sunshine of my life, that's why I'll always be around. You are the apple of my eye, forever you'll stay in my heart

A blank-faced MIN appears. She hobbles along slowly and sits down on a small stool a distance away from ELVIS. He stops singing.

ELVIS: Coming here. I'm starting to feel like you feel. You know when you dance. Like I can do deeds and speak words I couldn't before. I feel... brave. Like I'm someone who sings all the time. *(A beat.)* You've moved me Min... Maninder, you've made me feel like I'm flesh and blood and bone and hair. And... and... I know that I'm a right waste of space but I want you to know that... I'd be honoured to take you out. *(A beat.)* If that's at all possible. Ever.

MIN: Where's my mum Elvis?

ELVIS: She went off with them ladies.

MIN: *(She gets up.)* You go home. I'll manage now.

ELVIS: What about what I said?

Silence.

ELVIS: Doesn't it matter?

MIN: No.

ELVIS: Did that vicar bloke warn you... about me?

MIN shakes her head.

ELVIS: Then they must have got you a dreamboat. Someone with qualifications and transport. Bet he smells nice and does exercise... But you know... you won't ever be to him, like you are to me.

MIN: There's no-one.

ELVIS: You never go out.

MIN: I can see out on the telly.

She heads off, ELVIS stops her.

ELVIS: She... she hasn't signed my sheet.

He produces a piece of paper from his pocket. MIN blankly takes it.

MIN: You'll have to wait...

ELVIS thinks for a moment.

ELVIS: *(Sings.)* Precious Lord, take my hand, lead me on, let me stand...

MIN: *(Shouting.)* Shush up! You're home care, you're not supposed to sing.

ELVIS: I didn't mean to offend you.

MIN: I have to... go to the girls' toilets. Then I have to see my mum.

ELVIS: I'll walk with you.

MIN: No.

ELVIS: Why?

MIN: *(Shouts.)* You have no right to address me. You're here for her and look... you're prancing around, in this religious area, saying things. Get out of my way.

After a moment flabbergasted ELVIS shuffles forward so he has his back to her.

MIN: Don't move from here... promise me you won't move...

He nods.

MIN: Stay... and you'll get your sheet signed.

MIN hobbles off. As she walks, we see a terrifying patch of blood staining the back of her clothes.

SCENE THIRTEEN
GURDWARA – BEHZTI (DISHONOUR)

Standing at the workstation, TEETEE and POLLY mechanically wash and wipe kitchen utensils. BALBIR sits nearby, drying stainless steel beakers with a tea towel. POLLY appears flat and distracted and TEETEE's mood is downbeat. BALBIR however is almost unable to contain her excitement.

BALBIR: The deed is surely done by now. And I will be calling upon my dear friends for assistance.

POLLY: Assistance?

BALBIR: Men with glittery turbans must be recruited to make merriment, horses and carriages need to be booked and the cheapest food is to be purchased in the largest quantities. Ladies, our daughter, Maninder is to be wed.

POLLY: The buffalo girl?

BALBIR: Mr Sandhu has chosen her.

POLLY: Her?

BALBIR: To be conjugated with a name on his list.

TEETEE: His famous list...

BALBIR: Can I count on you dear friends?

TEETEE: I hope you are planning a function with all the relevant traditions in place. Without our deep and meaningful customs, the event will be false and flimsy.

BALBIR: I would rather my ears were gnawed off by starving rodents, than risk such desecration.

TEETEE: Are you willing to pay the price?

BALBIR: I can contribute a modest three-figure sum, left by the deceased for this exact purpose. I imagine any further extravagance will be taken care of by whichever capable person emerges from the list.

POLLY: You can't tell people the groom is from a list. It's embarrassing. Shameful.

TEETEE: Best keep your trap shut about that one.

POLLY: They will want to know there has been an introduction...

TEETEE: By the bacholan [matchmaker]...

POLLY: I mean we can't have just anyone betrothed to whatsherface.

TEETEE: And the bacholan will have traditional requirements.

POLLY: Gold earrings. Twenty four carat.

TEETEE: A diamond for the nose is essential.

BALBIR: You will have everything you want...

POLLY: Us?

BALBIR: But I must be able to rely upon your help, your guidance...

TEETEE: Who else is there Bhanji?

BALBIR claps her hands and punches the air with glee.

BALBIR: It will be like the old days. Sitting in a circle, applying mehndi *[henna]*, singing the old bollees *[village chants]*.

TEETEE claps to the gidha beat. The GIANI enters.

TEETEE: Sus meeri thi jumia billa
[My mother-in-law gave birth to a kitten.]
Oh mahnji ah kee gilla gilla
[Ooh missus, what's that wet thing between your legs.]

The women laugh. The GIANI picks up a handful of pakoras and stuffs them in his mouth. POLLY hurries over to him with a stainless steel thali, which he accepts.

POLLY: How are you Gianiji?

GIANI: Comme ci, comme ça.

TEETEE: I understand that earlier you witnessed an insulting happening.

POLLY: We ought not to dwell on that event Teeteeji.

BALBIR: What occurred?

TEETEE: Elvis Singh was misbehaving himself.

POLLY: Best forget it, isn't that right Gianiji?

GIANI: I try my best to forget everything but pictures stay in my head.

POLLY: I hope... that... all is not lost for the wretched individual...

GIANI: Sadly we are all lost.

POLLY: Everyone is permitted to make one mistake, surely?

GIANI: My brother says it only takes one tiny morsel of excrement to attract a hundred flies.

POLLY: Better if we do not ever talk of this again.

GIANI: *(Sad.)* If I am spoken to, I speak back… I have never been much good at exercising control.

He exits. POLLY's face falls.

POLLY: You should not have brought that boy here Bhanji.

Suddenly MIN enters.

MIN: Mother…

BALBIR: Not now ducks, we're talking about you, not to you!

She chuckles. MIN approaches BALBIR.

MIN: Please mother…

TEETEE and POLLY notice MIN's bloodstained shalwar.

MIN: I don't quite know how to speak this…

POLLY: Cursed girls and ladies do not come to God's house at that time of the month!

BALBIR: Oh dear.

MIN: That man… that man…

TEETEE: Maybe it is up to us to teach her Pollyji. For all our sakes.

MIN: But it's not my time.

TEETEE and POLLY drag MIN over so that she has her back to BALBIR, they show her mother the stain.

POLLY: Look at your dishonourable daughter Bhanji.

TEETEE: Importing her dirty monthly blood into the Gurdwara.

The ladies hold MIN firmly by each arm as if she is a criminal.

MIN: I haven't. Honest to God I haven't…

BALBIR: There must be some explanation… perhaps she has the excitement because of the wedding…

MIN: There's something mother… I have to say. Privately.

BALBIR: A bride has no secrets from her bacholan.

MIN: What?

BALBIR: My friends are also your mothers.

TEETEE: There are no excuses for this unwelcome patch of red.

MIN breaks away from the ladies, she's in a state of acute distress.

MIN: Please. I don't know what to do.

TEETEE: You are all muddled up.

MIN: No... I'm not...

TEETEE and POLLY move towards MIN.

BALBIR: Keep your eyes on the medal Maninder. That bronze disc you so merit.

POLLY: Shut up Bhanji. You leave this to us.

MIN moves away from the ladies.

MIN: Stay away from me, you... cows.

POLLY: Such filth is coming out of her mouth.

BALBIR: Do not be hard on her, she does not understand the ways of usual people.

TEETEE: Then it is our duty to explain... what is required of her under this roof.

The ladies move closer to MIN. Frightened, she turns away from them but they carry on a menacing advance towards her. Suddenly she makes a run for it, but POLLY swiftly grabs her. They tussle.

BALBIR: Min... we must realise... it is occasionally necessary to follow a series of twisty side roads before one gets onto the motorway.

TEETEE joins POLLY and they start to beat and kick MIN. She cries out in pain. TEETEE drags her over to BALBIR who is close to tears.

TEETEE: Your turn Bhanji...

BALBIR: It may appear harsh, but there are some ways of the world that you and I have to understand...

BALBIR reluctantly slaps MIN round the face.

BALBIR: And get used to...

There are shouts of gundhee kuthi (dirty bitch) and behsharam (shameless) from the ladies as they continue to beat MIN up. MR SANDHU draws closer. TEETEE takes off her chooni (scarf) and gags MIN with it.

SANDHU: Stop this at once!

TEETEE and POLLY turn to face MR SANDHU.

SANDHU: We are not animals. Please try and maintain some level of decorum.

MIN remains on the floor, gagged, in a heap. MR SANDHU beholds her sadly.

SANDHU: All individuals make unforced errors.

BALBIR: Poor child, she has never recovered from the behzti of her father.

POLLY: And you with your toilet trouble. None of it helps.

SANDHU: I have a suggestion that may put a silver lining on this cloudy business.

MR SANDHU whispers in BALBIR's ear. TEETEE and POLLY bring MIN over to BALBIR and MR SANDHU. MIN stands before them as though she is a pupil who has been sent to see the headmaster.

BALBIR: Dear Maninder, there is something... there is the chance that something useful can emerge...

MIN shakes her head vigorously. BALBIR touches her own leg.

BALBIR: *(Ashamed.)* I'm wet.

POLLY takes BALBIR's arm.

POLLY: I'll clean her up.

POLLY leads BALBIR out. MIN's getting increasingly upset. TEETEE unties the chooni.

MIN: *(Screams.)* I want my mother!

TEETEE: First you have to apologise to Mr Sandhu.

MIN points at MR SANDHU.

MIN: He put himself inside me *(indicates her vagina)* here... and he felt me...

TEETEE: You are expected to say sorry.

MIN: He knows what he did to me. And so do you. And so does God. And you can break every bone in my body and we'll all still know. Because that's what happened. That's the truth.

TEETEE: *(Shouts.)* Just say it!

MR SANDHU starts to cry. MIN attempts to run out, but TEETEE restrains her. There is a struggle which eventually TEETEE wins. She holds MIN around her neck. She drags her back to face MR SANDHU.

TEETEE: Say sorry you buffalo!

MIN: I won't.

TEETEE: Do it!

MIN: Never. I never will.

TEETEE: Does Balbir Bhanji like pain?

MIN: No... you cow... no!

TEETEE: Does she like to be hit and punched and scratched and all her clothes taken off?

TEETEE pulls her hair hard. MIN starts to cry in agony.

TEETEE: Hurry up.

MIN: *(Whispers.)* Sorry...

TEETEE releases MIN, she falls over. TEETEE goes over to SANDHU. Tearful and emotional, she spits on his feet and exits.

SANDHU: Are you hurt?

No response. MIN stares at the floor.

SANDHU: I can't help myself. You know you remind me of him so much. I loved your father. So damn madly. He was always scared of our passion. Embarrassed. And that's why he went the way he did. He broke my heart. *(A beat.)* Would you like a sweetie?

MIN shakes her head.

SANDHU: I just mentioned to your mother... I was wondering if... if... you would like to marry me?

MIN: *(Slowly.)* You lied.

MR SANDHU exits. MIN tries to move about, but her stiff, tired body won't go anywhere or do anything. Exhausted, MIN slumps onto the floor. TEETEE comes back in.

TEETEE: *(Gruff.)* Sometimes buffalo girl, you have to make a sacrifice. For the good of everyone, you realise?

No response.

TEETEE: You want some tea?

No response.

TEETEE: Sweet milky tea helps.

TEETEE goes to get the tea. BALBIR enters and approaches MIN.

BALBIR: Did he pop the question?

MIN nods.

BALBIR: And you are alright?

No response.

BALBIR: Was there something you wanted to tell me?

MIN: There's nothing.

BALBIR: So you are happy to marry him?

TEETEE comes back with a cup of tea for MIN.

BALBIR: I want you to be happy. Besides, he hasn't got much longer on this earth. You'll end up with the sort of bank balance that will attract a fine young specimen.

TEETEE eyes BALBIR coldly.

TEETEE: Quiet now Bhanji.

MIN: You have to sign Elvis' sheet mother.

MIN takes the sheet out of her pocket. She struggles over to BALBIR and gives her the sheet, which BALBIR duly signs.

BALBIR: Yes, we will be alright now. Everything will be alright. You go and get things ready Maninder. I'll wait here.

MIN goes to exit. TEETEE holds out the cup of tea to her.

TEETEE: It's finished.

No response.

TEETEE: You'll be going home soon.

TEETEE reaches out to MIN. But MIN strikes her arm and the tea goes flying. MIN exits.

BALBIR: Forgive her, she has been a boil waiting to erupt.

TEETEE: She's braver than she looks.

BALBIR: Funny how things turn out. I for one was set on the list... but such things do not allow for plain old-fashioned attraction. I didn't know she had it in her... but perhaps she's more of a chip off the old block than I gave her credit for. Don't be perturbed by her demeanour. She's shocked I know, she's come over all strange... all because she can't believe her own bloody bollocks. She came looking for a fish and caught a bloody whale.

TEETEE: *(Flat.)* There is no list.

BALBIR: What?

TEETEE: No list.

BALBIR: Mr Sandhu told me... he talked to me...

TEETEE: Did he ever show it to you?

BALBIR: No.

TEETEE: Did you ever ask to see it?

BALBIR: Stop this.

TEETEE: It doesn't exist.

BALBIR's getting more agitated.

BALBIR: Why would he say there was one when there wasn't? What reason?

TEETEE: Why do you think?

BALBIR is paralysed with shock.

TEETEE: So that girls go up and see him. So he can force them... He likes to do that.

BALBIR: No he wouldn't... he would never do that... you said he is a gentleman...

TEETEE: I didn't.

BALBIR: You know he is... we all know him...

TEETEE: He did it to your girl.

BALBIR: Why are you doing this Teetee? Why are you saying such evilness?

TEETEE: It's true.

BALBIR: How do you know?

TEETEE: *(Flat.)* Because he did it to me.

BALBIR: No... no... this is not... is not feasible... you are trying to trick me...

TEETEE isn't listening. She speaks in a matter of fact fashion.

TEETEE: He was young then so he had better control. Your Mr Sandhu went inside me and took what was human out of my body. My mother wept salty tears when I told her. Afterwards she beat me till I could not feel my arms or legs. Then she turned to me and said, now you are a woman, a lady. Now you are on your own, behsharam *[shameless]*.

BALBIR: But you... you beat her... you said she was at fault...

TEETEE: I do my duty.

BALBIR: You made me hit her.

TEETEE: You did that yourself.

BALBIR lunges at TEETEE. She misses her pathetically and lands on the floor.

BALBIR: *(Fearful.)* It couldn't happen... not before my eyes... like this...

TEETEE: I tried to warn you Bhanji.

BALBIR becomes breathless, it's as if she is having a panic attack.

TEETEE gets up to exit. Distressed BALBIR shouts after her.

BALBIR: Where are you going?

TEETEE: Home. In a little while.

BALBIR: *(Screams vehemently.)* This business isn't finished. You don't do that to my girl... and just go home... you don't... you can't...

TEETEE stands at the exit. BALBIR crumbles.

BALBIR: *(Despairing.)* What will happen to her now?

TEETEE: *(Cold.)* Same as the rest of us...

TEETEE exits. BALBIR breaks down.

SCENE FOURTEEN
GURDWARA – IZZAT (HONOUR)

MR SANDHU is at his desk flicking through the paint pamphlet. POLLY and the GIANI sit in front of him.

SANDHU: Sunwashed stone.

POLLY: I was thinking... possibly... double cream. With a russet leaf ceiling?

SANDHU: Interesting.

GIANI: I like lilac.

SANDHU: What did you say?

GIANI: It is a contemplative colour.

SANDHU: No. Not that.

POLLY: No.

GIANI: I... I find lilac flowers appealing.

SANDHU: Have you been seeing lilac flowers?

GIANI: Occasionally.

SANDHU: And other things?

POLLY: So we're agreed on sunwashed stone. Or double cream.

MR SANDHU gets up and stands over the GIANI.

167

SANDHU: Tell me what things.

GIANI: Please... I really would like lilac to be considered.

SANDHU: Jaswant, have you been sourcing Class A substances?

GIANI: Not since the bedraggled man was in the front room...

SANDHU: *(Interrupts.)* Tell the truth.

GIANI: Meditation and meditative colours help people...

SANDHU: Have you been displaying inappropriate behaviour?

GIANI: ... to feel happy feelings and... escape their demons.

SANDHU: *(Shouts.)* Have you?

No response.

SANDHU: Say thank you.

GIANI: Thank you.

SANDHU: For rescuing me from my demons.

GIANI: For rescuing me from... the one who made my heart beat.

SANDHU: Jaswant!

GIANI: I adored her.

SANDHU: Shut up!

GIANI: I think of her most days. I pray for us... even though I am undeserving of God's care.

SANDHU: She went to prison... to pay for your sins.

GIANI: I am in prison. I beg him to save me.

SANDHU: I saved you.

GIANI: To spare me from the hell in my heart.

SANDHU: I protected you from the filth inside your bones. What did you see?

GIANI: A... lady...

SANDHU: What must one do with the demons one sees?

GIANI: Give them away.

POLLY: The extension Beerji!

SANDHU: What was the lady doing?

GIANI: Snogging... a black boy.

SANDHU: Where is she?

The GIANI gets up slowly.

GIANI: It is a modern, multicultural colour.

After a moment, he points at POLLY. He is on the verge of breaking down.

POLLY: No Gianiji! No!

The GIANI exits.

POLLY: If there is a tone we particularly like, I can enter through the trades entrance...

SANDHU: There is to be an immediate review of the distribution of tasks in the Gurdwara. You will be taking no further part in our plans for the extension.

POLLY: Will I still be able to get the shopping in?

SANDHU: No.

POLLY: What... what will I do then?

SANDHU: That is for God and the committee to decide.

TEETEE enters, MR SANDHU nods at her, acknowledging her presence. POLLY looks away.

SANDHU: *(To POLLY.)* But for now...

MR SANDHU hands POLLY a notepad and pen. He paces about.

SANDHU: In your best handwriting. *(Dictates.)* Dear Gerry, I am writing to verify receipt of the council's correspondence regarding the planned extension of the Westbury Road Gurdwara.

POLLY writes this all down.

SANDHU: I, Mr R. S. Sandhu, as the spokesperson for our committee, am grateful for the points you have made regarding our application. We await the expansion of our religious home, an indication that we form an integral part of our town's thriving coffee-coloured melting pot.

MR SANDHU looks straight at TEETEE.

SANDHU: I can confirm that Mr B.D. Thompson will be charged with the responsibility of carrying out the building works. Mr Thompson has had a long and prosperous business relationship with the committee...

TEETEE: *(Interrupts.)* Pollyji... You said I could have a lift.

POLLY doesn't move.

SANDHU: *(To POLLY.)* I wonder if... I might have a very large cup of chah.

POLLY walks out. MR SANDHU and TEETEE eye each other.

TEETEE: Found a new lackey?

SANDHU: One always comes along. Isn't it Teetee?

TEETEE: And my son?

SANDHU: There will be some other role for your boy.

TEETEE: I explained... this was all I wanted. One little thing...

SANDHU: The future of the Gurdwara is not a little matter...

TEETEE: That you give him one small chance... in return for all you have taken... in return for stealing my body and my soul...

SANDHU: This is not a job for Indians... sometimes we have to defer to the greater authority of our white brothers...

TEETEE: *(Shouts.)* You promised!

SANDHU: I really am very sorry...

TEETEE: I will tell the police. I will tell everyone the truth about you.

SANDHU: Who will believe you Teetee?

TEETEE: You try and stop me!

SANDHU: Witnesses watched as you beat that unfortunate girl. Black and blue. Only when I intervened did you stop. I really ought to have you ejected from the building.

TEETEE lunges forward and pushes him over. He falls onto his desk. TEETEE grabs the kirpan and holds it over him. He whimpers fearfully.

TEETEE: Why does God make us live amongst such dogs?

SANDHU: Forgive me...

TEETEE: In the seventeenth century...

SANDHU: Forgive my sins...

TEETEE: *(Breathes deeply.)* the Emperor Aurang Zeb ordered that all Sikhs be forcibly converted to Islam... his troops used to take our girls and impregnate them to taint their blood... Guru Gobind Singh commanded his followers to fight, so that the souls of the Sikhs were preserved...... and now our glorious mantle is passed on to preserved souls... like you...

BALBIR hobbles in.

SANDHU: Please...

BALBIR: Stop!

BALBIR approaches.

BALBIR: Teetee... you can't...

Shaken TEETEE lowers her arm.

BALBIR: Wait... just wait...

BALBIR approaches TEETEE and takes the Kirpan out of her hand. Lights fade.

SCENE FIFTEEN
GURDWARA – RESURRECTION

MIN stumbles towards ELVIS.

MIN: She's signed it...

MIN's badly hurt and almost out of it, she hands ELVIS his sheet.

ELVIS: Min...

MIN falls into his arms. ELVIS holds her tightly.

MIN: Take me to a tap... I need a wash.

Stunned ELVIS carries her into the men's toilets where GIANI JASWANT is splashing his face in the sink.

ELVIS: I need help...

GIANI: I have already helped you.

MIN gets to her feet. ELVIS shows her into the cubicle.

ELVIS: You go and sort yourself out, I'll be here...

ELVIS closes the door on the cubicle. He approaches GIANI JASWANT.

ELVIS: Something's happened.

GIANI: Those who beat you with fists, do not give them blows...

ELVIS grabs the GIANI and shakes him.

ELVIS: Stop now alright.

GIANI: I saw you... kissing... I saw...

ELVIS: I don't care.

GIANI: The bedraggled man felt love... before... he felt what you feel... God knows...

ELVIS: What are you on about?

GIANI: If only I could serve him adequately. But I cannot... I am unable... I beg you... kill me... please kill me...

ELVIS goes for the GIANI again. MIN emerges.

MIN: Leave him Elvis!

ELVIS lets the GIANI go, he falls to the floor. MIN addresses the GIANI.

MIN: I only came here to say happy birthday and I didn't even manage that. I wish I had sung it then, because right now I don't know about praising. All this lot in here... why do they always have to Say... and Show and Make it known what they are? How good they are... how kind and nice... rich and beautiful and worthy... Cos what if you're not perfect and there's no sign of coloured wings flying in the sky. Seems to me like everyone's pretending the same as each other. I had hopes. They weren't anything special. But they were there. Now I'm beginning to get why people walk around like they do, not ever really looking at each other, because they can't face the sight. And my praising, it's nothing to do with this... Must be difficult, all that pretending... Next time... if I still manage to praise... I'll tell him about you lot, perhaps he'll help... yes... If I can... I'll ask him... for all of us...

She moves closer to the GIANI and speaks gently.

MIN: Vaheguruji kha khalsa... *[God be with you, the members of the Khalsa belong to God...]* Vaheguruji kha khalsa...

The GIANI shakes his head, unable to respond, he remains huddled in a corner. ELVIS approaches MIN.

ELVIS: Tell me.

MIN: No...

ELVIS: I love you Min... even if you don't love me back...

MIN: Oh but I do. I do... with all my heart I do...

ELVIS: Let's get out.

MIN: No.

ELVIS: Why?

MIN: Cos I'm hers. Cos she's all I've got.

ELVIS: There's me now.

MIN: I'm still that thing I was before... that's all I am...

ELVIS: You're more now.

MIN: I don't know all your stuff. Like where you live and where everything goes...

ELVIS: You'll learn... I'll teach you... about life...

MIN: Learning's not for stupids like me.

ELVIS: You ain't givin' yourself a chance.

MIN: Do you know when my birthday was?

ELVIS shakes his head.

MIN: Or what my best telly programme is?

ELVIS: Don't matter.

MIN: Or what I do when she's in bed or when she's eating?

ELVIS: You dance.

MIN: And I'm violent. Often.

ELVIS: But you love me.

MIN: It's not enough Elvis. Not for old stupids. I'm sorry.

ELVIS: *(Ferocious.)* I'm not having that.

ELVIS grasps her hand.

ELVIS: We'll look after each other. And her if we have to. We'll hold hands and wheel her about and we won't care about anything that isn't to do with us.

He holds her to him. He starts dancing with her around the space. At first she moves awkwardly.

ELVIS: And I want to see you dance.

She loosens up.

ELVIS: And dance.

They're flowing now.

ELVIS: And dance till you drop dead.

MIN laughs despite herself. She's half crying, half laughing. She starts to dance by herself.

MIN: Look at me Elvis. Look at me!

MIN moves elegantly around the space.

ELVIS: See... you're free...

MIN: Perhaps I am. Like it's all begun from now.

ELVIS: This second.

Suddenly there is the sound of stainless steel falling to the floor nearby, followed by a deafening scream.

ELVIS runs off in the direction of the scream but is halted by TEETEE. A dazed BALBIR approaches MIN. BALBIR's hands are stained with blood.

MIN: Whose blood is that?

BALBIR: That man... there was so much red... so much red...

TEETEE: *(To ELVIS.)* Take her home.

The scream turns into a wailing chant of satnam, satnam, satnamji, Vaheguru, vaheguru, vaheguruji which continues over the following action.

TEETEE: I will do my duty.

Trembling BALBIR goes to hold MIN's face in her hands.

MIN: *(Distraught.)* No mother... no...

BALBIR: Time now Min... You go. Go.

ELVIS and MIN move towards the exit. Fade to black.

THE END

BEHUD
(BEYOND BELIEF)

'SHAME ON SIKH PLAYWRIGHT
FOR HER CORRUPT IMAGINATION'
Banner at demonstration against *Behzti* December 2004

Behud (Beyond belief) was first performed on 27 March 2010 at the Belgrade Theatre Coventry, in a co-production by Belgrade Theatre Coventry and Soho Theatre, with the following cast:

TARLOCHAN KAUR GREWAL, Chetna Pandya
DCI VINCENT HARRIS/
ANDREW FLEMING, John Hodgkinson
DI GURPAL (GARY) SINGH MANGAT/
KHUSHWANT SINGH BAINS, Avin Shah
SATINDER SHERGILL/GIRL (BABY), Priyanga Burford
MR SIDHU, Ravin J Ganatra
AMRIK/MAN, Shiv Grewal
JOANNE STEVENSON, Lucy Briers

Writer, Gurpreet Kaur Bhatti
Director, Lisa Goldman
Designer, Hannah Clark
Lighting Designer, Richard G Jones
Sound Designer, Matt McKenzie
Movement Director, Ann Yee
Projection Design, Douglas O'Connell

Characters

TARLOCHAN KAUR GREWAL
playwright

DCI VINCENT HARRIS
a man unhinged

DI GURPAL (GARY) SINGH MANGAT
an all too decent individual

SATINDER SHERGILL
a ravenous reporter

MR SIDHU
an overly successful businessman

AMRIK
a man to whom life has not been kind

KHUSHWANT SINGH BAINS
an energised adolescent (performed by actor playing GARY)

ANDREW FLEMING
Artistic Director of the Writers' Theatre (performed by actor
playing VINCE)

JOANNE STEVENSON
Deputy Leader of the local Council

GIRL (BABY)
a cheeky slip of a thing, aged 10
(performed by actor playing SAT)

MAN
just over from the Punjab, 23
(performed by actor playing AMRIK)

Tarlochan's Notes:

Any resemblance to real events is entirely intentional.

Names have been changed to protect the fictional characters.

PROLOGUE

Dawn. The stage is black. The lights go up slowly to reveal an Asian woman, TARLOCHAN, lying on the floor in front of a plain desk and chair in a huge stark white space. There is a red notebook and a filthy old bargain bucket of KFC by her side. At first sight she could be dead but she starts to move and eventually gets up, picks up the notebook and sits at the desk. She's a frumpy, dumpy specimen wearing an oversized hoodie and baggy tracksuit bottoms. TARLOCHAN produces a pen and starts to write in the red notebook. Moments pass. She stops writing and looks towards stage right. DI GURPAL (GARY) SINGH MANGAT, a broad, handsome six-footer with impressionable eyes and a too open face enters from stage right; he is carrying a fat script. It is as though he hasn't seen TARL, like she doesn't exist. GARY sits down at the desk and starts to read the script he is carrying. While he studies it, he scribbles on a pad. TARL gets up and watches him.

GARY: Ugh.

> *DCI VINCENT (VINCE) HARRIS enters carrying a briefcase and a flipchart. VINCE is the Head of the Community Safety Unit and is a wiry, college-educated copper. He sets up the flipchart. Again the characters do not notice/acknowledge TARL. GARY's face becomes further gnarled with distaste.*

GARY: It's making me feel sick.

VINCE: Pull yourself together you skinny homosexual.

TARL: Language!

VINCE: Pull yourself together you bloody blouse.

> *Smartly dressed in a sharp suit, VINCE opens his briefcase and examines some notes.*

GARY: In this scene he takes the kid and… … oh God it's making me feel sick! What's the point of it?

VINCE: They call it drama Gary.

GARY: I reckon her head's contaminated.

VINCE: Contaminated?

GARY: Like when animal rights stick dead mice in tins of beans.

VINCE: You can put it down now.

GARY: It's alright, I'm nearly at the end. *(A beat.)* Wonder what she's like?

TARL: Don't ask that.

GARY: It's alright, I'm nearly at the end.

TARL turns the bargain bucket over. A lone ancient drumstick falls out.

VINCE: I've just spoken to her.

GARY: What did she say?

TARL beholds the drumstick and begins chomping.

VINCE: Wants us to bring her a sandwich and a packet of Monster Munch. Oh shit! Forgot to ask if she's a vegetarian.

GARY: Ring her back.

VINCE: Probably best not to harass her. Do you think she is one?

GARY shrugs.

VINCE: You're not one.

GARY: Doesn't mean she isn't.

VINCE: But it offers an indication.

GARY: Well I don't eat beef.

VINCE: You had a Big Mac on Tuesday.

GARY: I was starving.

VINCE: Better make it cheese and salad.

GARY: Cheese never offended anybody.

VINCE: Unless, she's some sort of raging vegan freak. Sounded like she might be.

GARY: I'll have whatever she doesn't finish.

VINCE: Good man.

VINCE produces a marker pen from his pocket.

VINCE: I'll write this up. Once something's in black and white you always see it more clearly.

During his speech VINCE writes key words on the flipchart like HOME SECRETARY, WALKABOUT, POLEDANCING and FAITHHATE. GARY stands up, folds his arms and observes.

VINCE: Today the city is playing host to the Home Secretary who is meeting community leaders ahead of next week's council elections. This afternoon he'll be licking brown bottoms at the usual ethnic churches. Then there's an 'all you can eat buffet' at our best curryhouse followed by a top secret trip to a poledancing club where CCTV will be temporarily suspended. The strict security necessitated by the Home Secretary's visit means the rank and file will be on full alert in what's being called Operation Walkabout. Which leaves the crème de la crème, that's you and me Gary, in the fortunate position of taking charge of this station's first official faith hate scenario.

GARY: Brilliant.

VINCE: Operation FaithHate centres on the case of Miss Tar-lo-chan Kaur Grewal, a Sikh playwright whose play is due to open this evening at the Writers' Theatre in Pond Street. A venue famous for championing the dissenting voice in society.

GARY: What does that mean?

VINCE: It puts on plays that nobody wants to see.

GARY: How many officers are assigned to FaithHate Sir?

VINCE: Two. *(A beat.)* As you've been reading, her script tells the story of... er...

TARL: Don't say it yet.

VINCE: Set in a... a... whatchamacallit...

GARY: Gurdwara AKA Sikh Temple.

TARL: More entertainment!

Suddenly GARY and VINCE, while remaining in character and in the same positions, do a splendid thirty-second tap dance to showtime music.

TARL: Stop!

They immediately stop.

TARL: Just spell it out.

VINCE: The subject matter and setting have upset some in the local Sikh community with whom the theatre has been in dialogue over the past month. Leaders of the said community have asked for the script to be changed but the writer has refused to comply, which has made them even more angry. Intelligence suggests we need to be alert to threats to Miss Grewal. And that's where you and me come in Gary. Our objective is to keep her safe and ensure tonight's performance goes smoothly. So, what's your assessment?

GARY: I… er… is it… er… what if this whole situation…

VINCE: Yeah?

GARY: … is about reptiles manipulating the masses.

VINCE: Eh?

GARY: The illuminati making innocent individuals wage war against each other to keep the people down. They change their faces from lizard to human to lizard to human to confuse you! They're reptilians Sir, controlling over eighty per cent of the world's wealth. Don't you ever wonder where all the missing children are? And what have they done with David Icke?

TARL: Bin all that.

VINCE: A Great British Institution like the Writer's Theatre won't give in to mob rule. I drove past there just now. Saw some Sikh boys hanging about. There was a sense of rage outside and the air felt heavy… with imminent doom. What I don't understand is, why are they so angry?

GARY: Must have their reasons.

VINCE: We can't have angry ethnic minorities telling the rest of us what to do. I reckon you and me have an opportunity today. By protecting Miss Grewal and making sure the show goes on we'll be giving fair play a leg-up. I mean that's the whole point of living in England isn't it?

TARL: This is shit.

GARY and VINCE stop speaking. TARL tears the first page off the flip chart and screws the paper up into a ball. GARY flicks through the script and VINCE ponders on his marker pen.

TARL: Fucking boring crap shit.

Exasperated, TARL throws the ball of paper hard at GARY and VINCE. Again there is no acknowledgement of TARL.

TARL: I need to scare myself.

The Prodigy's 'Firestarter' plays. A stunning young Asian woman, SATINDER, twenties, enters wearing a killer suit and carrying a designer handbag. Like the other characters, SAT does not notice TARL. She speaks out into space though not directly addressing the audience, and skilfully mimes the first action she describes. TARL stares at SAT. Music fades.

SAT: If you take a screwdriver and press the sharp end gently against your left side, you get a little thrill from the tingle of the pain. Go a bit further and you'll draw a drop of blood. Go further and you see proper scarlet. Any more than that and it's agony but then you can't stop and you're so near an organ you think, why not? All the while you know you shouldn't be… but you do it. Because even though it's terrible it's so kind of…

TARL: … beautiful.

SAT: That's what she's doing. To us. In the newsroom, it's just another story. My colleagues don't realise how much harm she's caused because they've never even noticed the people she's hurt. I'm there ticking the diversity boxes to improve my chances. I'm pretending we're all the same and that there's no racism. I'm doing my job, well. Better than the rest of them put together. And then Tarlochan comes along and spoils it, drawing attention to things that are best left unsaid and no-one knows how to place me any more. It's as if I don't belong because she's made our community look like intolerant fools. Because of her, the news editors are starting to doubt me, which isn't fair.

TARL: What else?

SAT: There've been no recorded incidents of anything resembling what she's written. And to set it in our place of worship is obscene. Tarlochan knows exactly what she's doing. She's abused a part of us that goes so deep. You can't understand it unless you are us. She's brought shame on her culture. She is shame. And the public has a right to challenge her.

SAT takes a Blackberry out of her handbag and begins to compose an email.

SAT: Once I've got the true facts, I can use my imagination to write the story, just like she does. And I want to know why. Did it really happen? Did it happen to her?

TARL: That's enough.

SAT: I'd like to fuck her up.

TARL: You're not what I thought.

SAT: If she made it up, she's one sick bitch.

TARL: You're a big mistake.

SAT: She's a piece of filth.

TARL: No... no I'm not.

SAT notices GARY and walks around him seductively.

SAT: Maybe me and him can play.

TARL: Don't!

SAT: Imagine the headlines – 'On duty Sikh copper caught in ethnic sex act', 'Ploddy Pantsdown' might work or perhaps just 'Brown Shame'. Bound to be some sort of suspension. Any softly softly reaction would lead to accusations of racial favouritism. God I love the press. We're so… ebony and ivory. His parents might even think I'm a good catch.

TARL: I won't let you pretend what you've made up is real.

SAT: My stories make the truth more bearable.

TARL: Go away. Please.

SAT saunters off the stage. TARL turns her attention back to GARY and VINCE. GARY hurriedly flicks through a file.

GARY: Bloody hell.

VINCE: What?

GARY: She only writes for *The* bloody *Bill!* Hey maybe she could get us on, we could show them how it's really done.

VINCE checks his notes.

VINCE: Miss Grewal's currently residing in a flat above the theatre and is adamant she's not moving.

GARY: I don't get it. If it's not safe why's she hanging around?

TARL: I want to watch my play you div. Sorry Gary.

GARY: I don't get it. If it's not safe why's she…

TARL: Maybe you're a bit too divvy.

VINCE and GARY start to pack up and head off.

VINCE: Feels like tonight could be a monumental moment. Humble officers of the law we might be, but we're doing something that actually means something. For our nation.

TARL: Vince doesn't sound right!

They stop.

VINCE: Do you understand what I'm saying?

GARY: Not really Sir.

TARL: You'll have to get rid of him.

VINCE: Better pick up that cheese sandwich, before someone accuses us of religious negligence.

GARY's phone rings.

GARY: They can't do that!

He answers the phone.

VINCE: I was joking DI Mangat. This is England remember.

GARY comes off the phone.

GARY: I'm afraid you're not coming Sir.

VINCE: What? Who says?

GARY: Orders. I'm going on my own.

VINCE: You? But this is England.

GARY: I can't help that. It's the end of the road.

VINCE: Why?

GARY: There seem to be doubts about your performance.
Sorry Sir.

GARY exits.

VINCE: This is outrageous. I'm under orders to deliver a
cheese sandwich. And then I've got to… What is it again?

TARL: Operation FaithHate.

VINCE stands alone, crestfallen.

VINCE: But I'm supposed to be the one in charge.

TARL observes VINCE.

TARL: I'm the one in charge.

VINCE: This is going against nature!

TARL: Face it, you're surplus to requirements.

VINCE: Pissing fuck!

*VINCE walks off. TARL picks up the red notebook she was writing
in and stuffs it in the pocket of her hoodie.*

SCENE ONE

*Early morning. A banner falls forming a huge backdrop. Painted on it
are the words – 'SHAME ON SIKH PLAYWRIGHT FOR HER CORRUPT
IMAGINATION'. A gentle-looking elderly man in a turban, MR SIDHU,
approaches with AMRIK, a serious-looking dropout to whom life has not
been kind. AMRIK is balding and wears a woolly hat and a navy military*

*coat. MR SIDHU wears expensive but mismatched clothes. SIDHU and
AMRIK share an approving smile as they regard the banner. As before
the characters do not see TARL. A turbanned Sikh youth dressed in black
bomber and jeans, KHUSHWANT SINGH BAINS, runs on carrying a black
holdall over his shoulder. KHUSH is a bright, sparky thing, filled with
too much male energy and a fresh, almost delightful buoyancy. SIDHU
warmly pats KHUSH on the back.*

SIDHU: *(Pointing to the banner.)* That's the spirit!

> *KHUSH indicates AMRIK.*

KHUSH: Birji told me what to write.

AMRIK: I gave him the idea, but he put in the hard work.

KHUSH: We'll show those musulmaan…

TARL: … Sulleh's more offensive.

KHUSH: We'll show those sulleh, little bastards coming round
college with their Pakistan zindabad chat. They even had
these flyers printed saying all shit like you Jat boys go on
about defending your religion, what you gonna do about
this? Plenty I said. And they're laughing at us, chatting shit
like if we got one per cent of this disrespect we'd bomb the
heart out of those muthafuckers. We'd bomb the heart out
of that whiteman theatre. You lot sit back…

AMRIK: No-one's sitting back.

KHUSH: That's what I said. But the sulleh are so stupid. They
don't know how to think, only know how to react. That's
why they end up queuing round the block for their dole
money.

AMRIK: Need to control your emotions brother.

KHUSH: I even went on the internet to see about making a
bomb. I mean I wouldn't have really made one. And even
if I had, I wouldn't have used it. But if I could just make
one, I'd take it into college to show those sulleh they're not
the only lot who can do shit.

SIDHU: We are not concerned with such types of disruption.
We are nice, happy folk.

AMRIK: Our niceness is the problem. People think they can say what they like about us.

TARL: Raise the stakes!

AMRIK: If this meeting's our last chance to stop her, how do we play it?

SIDHU: First we tell them we support freedom of speech, as long as the speech is friendly.

AMRIK: Point is we don't operate on a level playing field. I can't go round saying whatever I like about the white institutions because the white institutions won't let me. Tarlochan comes along and the bullshit she spouts about our community intrigues them. They love thinking they're more human than us. Who ever heard of a child...

TARL: Just because no-one's heard, doesn't mean...

SIDHU: Amrik, I am on your side...

TARL: You should be doing something.

The set of a Gurdwara kitchen appears. This comprises a kitchen sink, stainless steel pots and pans, a shelf unit and tea towels.

AMRIK: She's laughing at us and inviting the Goreh theatre people to laugh at us too.

The three characters start washing, wiping and drying the stainless steel utensils and putting them on the shelf unit. This is symbolic of them doing sayva (service in a Gurdwara kitchen).

TARL: All of you working for the benefit of the community. This is good, symbolic.

AMRIK: People who know nothing about Sikhs will start believing her lies. You know what Goreh are like, they only have to start doing Bikram yoga or buy a Madhur Jaffrey cookbook or watch *Slumdog Million*-fucking-*aire* and suddenly they're experts on your culture.

SIDHU: Leave the meeting to me. I know how to handle these people.

KHUSH: Have you read it?

AMRIK: Don't need to. They told us the story. Anyway the title says it all. What kind of dickhead writes a play called *Gund*?

SIDHU: When I first saw her name on the television – such a beautiful Sikh name – I felt so proud that one of our children was writing for *The Bill.* Happy family entertainment.

AMRIK: Her mum and dad chucked her out.

TARL: Only cos the house got repossessed.

KHUSH: Any girl whose parents don't want to know her isn't worth knowing.

TARL: Dad lost my address when he was pissed.

AMRIK: Gora theatre's her new family.

TARL: Coconut.

AMRIK: How many banners?

KHUSH: Twenty more as big as this. One just says 'Crack the Coconut!'

SIDHU: Even though she is torturing me, I feel pity for her. Why is she doing this nonsense?

TARL: Because…

KHUSH: Because she wants to be a celebrity. So she gets in the papers and on chat shows and all that.

TARL: I'm not good with people.

SIDHU: I've never seen her.

TARL: Don't know how to give them the best of myself.

AMRIK: She avoids the attention on purpose.

TARL: And I smell.

AMRIK: Keeping a low profile makes her seem more interesting than she really is.

TARL: Move on now.

KHUSH gets ready to leave.

KHUSH: Better get the leaflets photocopied. I want them to scatter round that theatre like confetti.

AMRIK: Do the copying there.

KHUSH: They won't let me in.

SIDHU: I'll phone one of my friends at the Council, make sure the theatre's office equipment is available to you.

KHUSH: Thanks Uncleji.

SIDHU: You know our first Gurdwara was a room above a laundry? But we worked hard and gathered our money till we built a palace and put our mark on this city. All the name-calling and beating up and laughing at your accent becomes meaningless when you have that mark. Me and your fathers and mothers have been through so much pain. And now this girl, one of our own, hurts us more than we can bear. Doesn't matter whether the Goreh call you Paki or Bin Laden. Their words are nothing compared to the suffering her words are causing.

Suddenly VINCE enters carrying his briefcase and a plastic bag.

VINCE: One ploughman's bap and a packet of Monster Munch.

TARL: What are you doing?

The three Sikh characters behold VINCE, bemused.

VINCE: Thought she might fancy a drink so I got a can of fanta.

SIDHU: Who are you?

VINCE checks his notes.

VINCE: I'm looking for a Miss Tar-lo-chan Kaur…

AMRIK: *(Interrupts.)* Is this a joke?

VINCE: I assure you I'm a very serious character.

KHUSH: Maybe he's one of the gorah theatre lot!

TARL: Will you please leave!

VINCE: I'm trying to do my job.

SIDHU: You're in the wrong place.

VINCE: I see.

Aggrieved VINCE turns and heads out. AMRIK speaks to KHUSH with the dominance of an officer in command.

AMRIK: How many we expecting from the colleges?

KHUSH: Couple of thousand. Gonna be Khalistani flags waving from all directions. The boys are under orders to rush the building like a sea of soldiers. One phone call from me and it's gonna kick off.

SIDHU: Amrik, remember to keep things calm. We must not spoil our chances at the meeting.

AMRIK: You really think you can talk them round Uncle?

SIDHU's phone beeps.

SIDHU: Watch and learn from the master!

SIDHU glances at the text he's just received. He tuts in annoyance.

SIDHU: I order nine tandoori chickens, organic! And twenty kilos of meat samoseh, free range! Now they tell me the Home Secretary is a teetotal vegetarian. His people are asking can we make fish samoseh? Where do they think we come from, Bangladesh?

SIDHU exits. KHUSH goes to follow him.

AMRIK: Do your mum and dad know you're here?

KHUSH stops in his tracks.

KHUSH: They don't understand. Don't even go to Gurdwara any more. Too busy sat on the settee eating Pringles and watching *X Factor*. I hate them.

AMRIK: You know we as a community are our own worst enemies.

KHUSH: How do you mean?

AMRIK: Reading their newspapers, eating their food, sleeping with their women. I tried all that. Learned my lesson. They don't mind us living here but they don't want us taking part. It's easier if you're a woman, like Tarlochan.

The Goreh feel sorry for you. If you're a man, you're the oppressor. Truth is they're frightened of us. And jealous. They crave the power our culture gives to our sex. So they're on a mission to emasculate us.

KHUSH: I reckon Khalistan's the answer. A new country back home, just for us.

TARL: *(To AMRIK.)* Say what you want.

AMRIK: I want to be free of all of it.

TARL: And me. Like it never happened. Like she's going to come through that door and play.

AMRIK: Free of the suspicion that we stink and beat our wives, free of their preconceived ideas that we work hard at school and we'll take whatever shit they throw at us. We'll tell our own stories in our own theatres, learn our history in our universities, have our own political debates. We're not stupid, we still do business with the Goreh but if we live this way we become stronger. Do you agree brother?

KHUSH: Whatever it takes to honour my religion.

AMRIK: As a leader, your followers will need you to go further than they might themselves. Are you willing to go to any lengths?

KHUSH: I am willing.

TARL produces a gun from her pocket. She points it around the stage.

AMRIK: Today's your chance.

TARL puts the gun in AMRIK's hand.

TARL: This is for later, you'll know when.

KHUSH: I promise you Birji, we'll stop this play.

AMRIK: It's not enough.

KHUSH: Why?

AMRIK: Because Tarlochan's polluted mind will do it all over again.

TARL holds the gun in AMRIK's hand and points the weapon at her head.

AMRIK: She's out of control, doesn't care about the damage she's doing. Her thinking is what fuels these Goreh, and that's what needs to be crushed.

KHUSH: I don't understand.

AMRIK: Apparently she can't finish the play.

TARL: I've only just started!

AMRIK: She's written two different endings. Shows she doesn't know what she's doing.

TARL takes the red notebook out of her pocket and flicks through it.

AMRIK: If someone could talk to her and point out the error of her ways, she might change.

KHUSH: That behsharam won't listen to decent folk.

TARL indicates KHUSH's black holdall.

TARL: You open that bag. At the end.

AMRIK: This afternoon she'll be deciding on the ending in the theatre flat. Upstairs from the office where you're copying the leaflets. All you have to do is stay with her till I get there.

KHUSH: But she's got police protection.

AMRIK: My sources say only one officer outside her door. He'll need a piss, eventually. What do you think brother?

KHUSH: I have to be honest Birji, I have got some Goreh mates. And a couple of Kaleh. And one Jewish bloke as well, he's not a close friend, we just sat next to each other in Chemistry and sometimes… he rings me.

AMRIK: You can stay in contact, soon you'll realise they're not friends, they're associates.

KHUSH: And my mum's best mate's called Janet. My dad's is Timothy, Janet's husband.

AMRIK: Your parents are lost, just like Tarlochan.

KHUSH: Didn't realise you knew her so well.

AMRIK: It was in the old days when we made our own theatre. We didn't jump to the Goreh's tune.

KHUSH: What's she like?

AMRIK: Unmemorable, unremarkable. When you find her, you call me, you don't talk to her.

KHUSH: But I want to tell her what I think of her.

AMRIK: There go your emotions again…

KHUSH: Sorry.

AMRIK: You think you can do this? Tell me honestly brother. If not, there are others.

TARL flicks through the red notebook again.

KHUSH: I'll burn her precious play in front of her treacherous eyes!

KHUSH and AMRIK exit. TARL puts the notebook back in her pocket.

SCENE TWO

White sheets on the floor. Solemn Sikh devotional music (singing of Vaheguru) plays low. TARL removes her shoes and covers her head. She walks towards the Guru Granth Sahib – holy book (unseen) and kneels in front of it (placing her forehead on the floor) as is customary in a Gurdwara. A young GIRL wearing a plain beige shalwar kameez enters. The GIRL does not notice TARL but TARL can't take her eyes off her. TARL walks the GIRL towards the book where the GIRL performs the same action as TARL. Holding the GIRL's hand, TARL takes her to sit cross-legged at the side. TARL gently cradles the GIRL in her arms. A young Asian MAN enters and does the same set of actions. The MAN sits down across from the GIRL. The music subsides and the three of them continue the chant of Vaheguru. Moments pass. The MAN and the GIRL stop singing so TARL is left to chant on her own. The MAN stands up and holds his hand out to the GIRL, she takes it and gets up. They go to leave. As TARL watches them both exit, she stops the chant.

SCENE THREE

Morning. Theatre office – a desk, two chairs and a large filing cabinet. Artistic Director of the Writers' Theatre, ANDREW FLEMING, 40s, distant and cool, but easily overwhelmed, enters and sits at the desk. Following him on is Deputy Leader of the Council, JOANNE STEVENSON, also 40s. She's a stout, bullish woman and the smart suit she's dressed in seems to wear her rather than the other way around. Her face is overly made up for the time of day and the flicks in her hair are sprayed to perfection. JOANNE sits opposite ANDREW. Again the characters cannot see TARL who sits at the side.

JOANNE: I'm excited.

ANDREW: Me too.

JOANNE: This whole… atmosphere, it's… compelling. Reminds me of my old university days. I was quite the activist you know.

ANDREW: You?

JOANNE: President of the student union! I used to organise all the demos, write the slogans, lead the chanting. Don't think I was ever happier than when I was togged up in my leggings, my DMs and my Free Nelson Mandela sweatshirt. Oh and I had these marvellous CND earrings. They were huge! Bigger than my head. Can't think where they got to. We were all so passionate. God, we believed so hard. Sometimes we'd be marching… this would really piss me off… some nobody on the pavement would shout 'you'll never change anything you bastard students'. I'd yell back 'I'm changing my day you fat fucker!' Apathy, Andrew, is what's killing this country.

ANDREW: I agree.

JOANNE: You know I admire her, but I can't say I'm a fan. If you ask me, the play's a mess. Too many words that don't go together.

ANDREW: Her work is quite stylised.

JOANNE: Can't call a spade a spade can you?

ANDREW: It's heightened.

JOANNE: I do know what stylised means. I'm not a moron.

ANDREW: Of course not.

JOANNE: Don't patronise me Andrew. I'm allowed not to like it.

ANDREW: There is a knack to reading a new play and knowing whether it's good or not.

JOANNE: So you're a better reader than me?

ANDREW: I wouldn't come to the Council offices and question your choices.

JOANNE: Keep your knickers on Andrew, all I'm saying is it's a matter of taste.

ANDREW: It's not, it's really not. It's like understanding a Chablis or cubism.

JOANNE: I don't believe in elitism. I think the achievement of the common man is to be lauded. I'm a great fan of the heroes of reality television. The winners of Big Brother, the contestants of Driving School and Wife Swap...

ANDREW: Right.

JOANNE: Look, I might not agree with what you say, but I'll defend your right to say it to the death.

ANDREW: Good.

JOANNE: Funny title. *Gund.*

ANDREW: It's actually pronounced 'Gunddd'. The emphasis is on the D. Means dirt, filth.

JOANNE: Very apt. You know council members were wondering why you'd even entered into this dialogue with the Sikhs.

ANDREW: Given the play's setting, we felt it was inappropriate to put the piece on without informing the local community. I know now that wasn't the smartest move. But I thought they'd be okay... er... perhaps talking to them might even boost our audience figures.

JOANNE: God Andrew, you've no fucking idea.

ANDREW: I was taking my lead from Tarlochan.

JOANNE: I think she wanted to provoke them. She wanted to slap them round the face and for them to take the licks.

ANDREW: You'll have to ask her yourself.

JOANNE: Wish I could go round slapping people round the face. Maybe I will one day.

ANDREW: Her play has far more integrity than you're giving it credit for.

TARL: You're too… static.

JOANNE: Bollocks.

TARL: *(Fast.)* Stand up, sit down, stand up, sit down.

ANDREW and JOANNE stand up and sit down obediently.

JOANNE: We're fighting for her right to shamelessly incite decent citizens.

ANDREW: Thought you were on our side.

JOANNE: I'm here aren't I? The other Councillors wanted me to ask you to postpone the production until after the elections.

ANDREW: I had no idea.

JOANNE: Spineless tossers. You know in my game, it's important to take a stand. People remember you then.

ANDREW: That's exactly what my work at the Writers' Theatre is about. You'll see, tonight is going to be a landmark event in the history of British theatre. People in the industry will realise I'm not afraid of courting controversy. I mean can you imagine if the play causes a riot?

JOANNE: The police will deal with it.

ANDREW: A real riot outside stage door! You don't get much more fucking cutting edge than that Joanne. What we're doing is hugely exciting for this theatre and our city. It's going to put us on the international map.

JOANNE: She's fortunate to have your support.

ANDREW: She's going to be an important writer. Many believe she's got great talent.

JOANNE: Who?

ANDREW: Some of our leading theatre practitioners.

JOANNE: Rich unemployed liberals and depressed homosexuals.

ANDREW: You've just expressed a dangerous prejudice.

JOANNE: Freedom of speech! What I mean is you Oxbridge types are hardly representative of the country.

ANDREW: We're masters of theatre.

JOANNE: I wrote an essay on Wordsworth for my O'levels, doesn't make me a poet. She gets to have her say and carry on doing her job. If politicians offend people we're voted out of office.

ANDREW: So your fate will be decided in the polling stations next week?

JOANNE checks her watch.

JOANNE: Did you tell her I've got to get away for the Home Secretary?

ANDREW: Yes. Look, she's under a great deal of stress.

JOANNE: Is she coming or not?

TARL: No.

JOANNE: By the way, the community leaders have asked to use your office equipment before the rally this afternoon. They want to photocopy some literature.

ANDREW: I don't mind them demonstrating in the lobby but I don't want them swarming into the offices.

JOANNE: It'll show you're trying to be transparent and willing. And the press will love you for it.

JOANNE pointedly checks her watch again.

JOANNE: If she's not going to show, there's no point in me hanging around.

ANDREW: Sorry. But you must understand this is a very difficult time for her.

JOANNE: Does she actually exist?

TARL: What?

JOANNE: I mean she's not just a figment of your imagination?

ANDREW: Don't be ridiculous, you've read the play.

JOANNE: Oh yes *Gunddd*! A dyslexic mute could have come up with that twaddle.

TARL: You're getting too big for your boots.

JOANNE: Insubstantial doggerel…

TARL: Right!

Suddenly JOANNE falls over clumsily and bangs her head.

ANDREW: Are you okay?

JOANNE: I think so.

He helps her up.

ANDREW: You know I don't think Tarlochan finds it easy to trust. Perhaps she was let down in the past.

JOANNE: Judging by her self-indulgent play, she obviously relies on her ego.

She falls over again.

ANDREW: Honestly Joanne, have you been drinking?

JOANNE: No!

JOANNE reaches for her bag.

JOANNE: Apparently the Home Secretary's shown a real interest in my relationship with the Writers' Theatre. I'll tell him I met her.

ANDREW: Suppose we could be dealing with someone completely different next week, Councillor.

JOANNE: For your sake, I hope it's someone who's sympathetic to the diabolical mess you've made of your finances.

ANDREW and JOANNE go to exit.

ANDREW: Someone like you?

JOANNE: Naturally.

TARL watches them go.

SCENE FOUR

Noon. A camp bed, a door and an old portable television make up the set for the Theatre flat. Crowd sounds from outside. GARY enters gingerly through the door.

GARY: Hello… Miss… Grewal…

TARL: Try to show some initiative.

GARY immediately checks under the camp bed in SAS fashion. TARL indicates the TV and GARY switches it on. The moving image is projected onto a large screen. ANDREW FLEMING stands on a podium addressing a bustling press conference. TARL and GARY observe.

ANDREW: We must uphold the right of the artist and ensure that writers have the freedom to express whatever they choose.

Loud chanting of 'Off, Off, Off' can be heard in the background.

ANDREW: We at the Writers' Theatre are proud to present Tarlochan Kaur Grewal's *Gund* – a piece of work that is fearless, provocative and contemporary – everything the Writers' Theatre represents.

JOURNO 1: Many local people don't feel they're being listened to. What do you say to those who don't want the play to go on?

ANDREW: Most of them haven't even read it. I believe it's an unrepresentative minority who are objecting to what is clearly an uncompromising satire, packed with dramatic tension and comic…

TARL: Turn it off.

GARY turns the television off. He scans the space again and calls out.

GARY: Miss Grewal?

Loud knocking at the door.

TARL: What's going on?

GARY opens the door to reveal VINCE holding the lunch.

TARL: Oh fucking hell!

VINCE steps into the flat. Again the characters do not notice TARL.

TARL: He's not meant to be here.

GARY: You're not meant to be here.

VINCE: I've got nowhere else to go.

TARL: Should have put you in a uniform Gary, then you could have clubbed him to death with your truncheon.

VINCE: All I know is I'm supposed to deliver this lunch. Feels like I'm in limbo, like I haven't been given a chance.

TARL: Okay stay for a minute while I consider Gary's destiny.

VINCE: Have you had CCTV installed outside the flat?

GARY: Yeah.

VINCE: Been through the hate mail?

GARY: I was just about to.

GARY produces a stack of letters from his pocket.

GARY: *(Opening an envelope.)* Hey someone's sent her a Christmas card!

VINCE: That's nice.

GARY: *(Reads.)* Seasons Greetings. This will be your last Christmas. You are a disgrace to the race. Sending you lots of hate. X.

VINCE: So where is she?

GARY: I think maybe… er… the reptiles have taken her.

TARL: I told you to forget all that!

VINCE: She must be hungry. Maybe if we leave a bit of cheese out she'll show.

GARY: She's not a rodent Sir.

VINCE: If there's no writer then FaithHate is null and void. Fucking hell, there's a tumour forming in my brain Gary! This was supposed to be my big chance.

GARY: I can't help you.

VINCE: Is it because I'm white?

TARL/GARY: No!

The crowd sounds outside get louder.

VINCE: If that many people hated me, I'd kill myself.

TARL/GARY: Oy!

VINCE: Whatever happens I'm sure the show will go on.

GARY: No-one suggested it won't. Did they?

VINCE: Course not. I reckon she's got a right to have her say.

TARLOCHAN turns to GARY.

TARL: What about you?

GARY: I like *The Bill.*

Suddenly there's loud knocking at the door again.

TARL: Fuck.

GARY opens the door and SAT enters. Suited and booted she seems rather demure, exuding a sweet though anxious air.

TARL: Fuck!

SAT: Is she here?

TARL: Get her out!

GARY: Sorry miss but I'm going to have to ask you to leave.

SAT sits down on the camp bed.

SAT: I won't cause any trouble I promise.

TARL drags SAT up from the bed. They struggle. TARL punches her face hard, stunning her. TARL then hurls SAT out of the door. VINCE eyes GARY disdainfully.

VINCE: Do you really think that brown rabble out there will respond to you?

GARY: I don't appreciate that comment!

VINCE: Where is the subject DI Mangat? You can't do your job if she's not here!

TARL: You be quiet!

VINCE: *(Looking around.)* Tar-lo-chan!

VINCE loosens his tie.

VINCE: Tar-lo-chan!

VINCE begins to pant and places his hand on his heart.

GARY: What's happening?

VINCE: I don't feel too good Gary… Gary…

VINCE keels over and reaches out to GARY.

TARL: Leave him.

GARY: Are you alright Sir?

GARY takes his hand.

TARL: I said leave him!

VINCE: I don't want to die.

TARL: Then do what I say.

GARY leads VINCE offstage.

SCENE FIVE

Late morning. White sheets. TARL takes her shoes off, covers her head and goes to pray as before, she then retreats to the side of the stage. A children's version of 'Twinkle Twinkle Little Star' plays. The GIRL enters and goes to sit cross-legged in the middle of the stage. She eats langar (food made in the Gurdwara and presented on a stainless steel thali). The MAN enters and sits next to the GIRL. She carries on eating. He speaks with a strong Punjabi accent.

MAN: Hello Baby.

GIRL: Hello.

MAN: How are you?

GIRL: Very well thank you.

MAN: Ooda, Aada, Eedee... *(The beginning of the Punjabi alphabet.)*

GIRL: A, B, C...

MAN: Ick, Dho, Thin... *[One, two three...]*

GIRL: One, two three...

Suddenly the MAN grabs the girl. It's not clear what he's doing but after a few seconds it's apparent he's tickling her. She laughs hysterically and he laughs with her. She gets away from him and he grabs her again. He tickles her some more and she laughs. This continues until she manages to get away. Then she launches herself at him and starts tickling him. He laughs uproariously. The GIRL cackles and tickles the MAN hard. A comic Hindi version of 'Twinkle Twinkle Little Star' plays.

TARL: This music isn't right.

The music stops. The GIRL and the MAN stop laughing. They come out of character and speak like the actors they are.

GIRL: *(To TARL.)* Is it okay?

TARL recoils, shocked.

TARL: What?

GIRL: The scene, is it okay?

TARL: Er... yeah...

MAN: Good.

TARL watches the GIRL pick up a script.

TARL: I don't... understand... I'm just putting these scenes, your scenes from *Gund* into a new play... you see I'm writing a new play...

Perplexed TARL takes the red notebook out of her pocket and shows them.

GIRL: Have you decided which ending we're doing tonight?

MAN: I mean we've learnt both. Of course.

TARL: Tonight isn't real, I'm just writing...

GIRL: *(Interrupts.)* When will you tell us?

TARL: You're both so vivid. Like you've actually come to life.

MAN: That's down to you.

GIRL: We had some time so we thought we'd go over a few bits.

MAN: Andrew's been so busy with the press.

GIRL: Exciting isn't it?

TARL: So you think this is a real rehearsal?

MAN: *(To GIRL.)* She doesn't like it.

TARL: How come you know I'm here?

GIRL: You're always here.

MAN: You being here helps us to make it more truthful. More real.

TARL: But this… this isn't real.

GIRL: We have to try and make it real don't we? For it to work.

TARL: What?

MAN: Isn't that what you want?

The MAN and the GIRL whisper together.

GIRL: Can we ask you something?

TARL: Yeah.

GIRL: Did it really happen?

TARL: I can't say for sure.

MAN: But the story is based on a real person?

TARL: Yes, I think so.

The GIRL and the MAN exchange an excited look.

GIRL: Who?

TARL: She's dead. I'm positive she's dead.

MAN: So it is real. *(To GIRL.)* Told you. Fancy a coffee?

The GIRL nods and the MAN exits.

TARL: No. No, what's real is something else. That's why I'm writing this new play.

She indicates her red notebook. The GIRL stares at TARL.

GIRL: You must have some idea.

TARL: What?

GIRL: Which ending it is. I mean I need to be clear about my journey.

TARL: In my imagination it's only the first preview.

GIRL: My agent's coming! *(A beat.)* Is it because of the protest?

TARL: What?

GIRL: Suppose you'll choose the soft option, so you don't offend them any further.

TARL: I don't care about that. It's my play.

GIRL: She's my character, I've shaped her. I created her.

TARL: You didn't.

GIRL: She's mine now.

TARL: Wait, this is stupid… you're nobody. You're just someone I'm making up…

GIRL: I guess we can always go on stage and do whichever ending we like.

TARL: Andrew wouldn't allow it. You'd be sacked…

GIRL: I'm only joking. Don't take everything so seriously. You should learn to let go.

The GIRL heads off. Suddenly the comic 'Twinkle Twinkle' music starts up again. It then stops. Confused, TARL retreats to the side of the stage.

SCENE SIX

Afternoon. Boardroom. ANDREW, JOANNE, SIDHU and AMRIK sit around a huge table. Sounds of the demonstration can be heard outside. In particular there is a loud chant of 'Bole So Nihal'.

AMRIK: No actors are getting through that lot. And if they do they might not feel like acting.

JOANNE: You assured us it would be a peaceful protest.

SIDHU: It is peaceful. They are happy, good boys.

AMRIK: We know the play isn't finished.

ANDREW: A new piece of theatre is always being developed during rehearsals, that's simply the creative process.

AMRIK: Don't fob us off. What's she got planned for the end?

ANDREW: I can't inform you of every minute change to the script. You've already had unprecedented access to Tarlochan's work.

SIDHU: You don't care about our feelings Mr Fleming.

ANDREW: I do care Mr Sidhu. That's why we're here, trying to sort things out. This play is a piece of fiction. It's not real, do you at least accept that?

AMRIK: Our taxes pay for your fictions.

ANDREW: Nothing in *Gund* breaks any law. Look, our theatre empowers artists to explore ideas.

AMRIK: And who decides which artists get to explore these ideas?

ANDREW: Someone's got to do it.

AMRIK: Someone who looks like you, someone who thinks like you think.

ANDREW: There's no need to be personal just because you don't agree with my choices.

AMRIK: Everything you present about us is your take on who we are.

ANDREW: I don't write the plays.

AMRIK: Do you accept that you don't understand us?

ANDREW: No. Dramatic themes are universal. And good writing is good writing wherever it comes from.

SIDHU: I wish someone would write a nice play about a nice subject.

JOANNE: We can't control what people write Mr Sidhu.

SIDHU: Is she keeping it set in the Gurdwara?

ANDREW: Yes.

SIDHU: Please, I'm begging you, ask her to change it to a community centre.

TARL: Wait…

The characters start speaking very quickly.

ANDREW: She is aware of your views but she will not compromise the setting.

AMRIK: So what are you going to do?

ANDREW: We hope to go ahead as planned.

AMRIK: Are you prepared to delay the opening?

ANDREW: No.

AMRIK: What's the point of this meeting if you're not going to listen?

TARL: Slow down…

ANDREW: You are being listened to.

JOANNE: I for one am listening.

SIDHU: You have to make some concessions.

ANDREW: We're discussing those issues now.

AMRIK: Tarlochan should be here.

TARL: No, I don't want to…

JOANNE: He does have a point.

ANDREW: It's not appropriate.

TARL: I don't have to be in it.

SIDHU: We can't have this meeting without her!

The dialogue reaches a crescendo.

AMRIK: *(Shouts.)* This is rubbish.

TARL approaches.

AMRIK: All these words, they're rubbish!

TARL: No they're not.

AMRIK: War! This is war.

TARL: *(Shouts.)* No it's not.

The characters stand up and look at TARL, she recoils in shock.

ANDREW: Tarlochan, what are you doing here?

TARL: What?

SIDHU: So this is the girl?

JOANNE: At last!

AMRIK: Long time no see.

TARL: This is wrong.

SIDHU: She's much shabbier than I expected.

JOANNE: So you do exist!

TARL: No... I'm... I'm not in it.

ANDREW: In what?

TARL: I don't know how to be.

ANDREW: Your being here isn't a good idea.

TARL: I know, but this isn't right, you're not saying my words.

The characters look at each other, confused.

JOANNE: What's she on about now?

ANDREW: Best if you come back later.

AMRIK: You look like shit. What happened to you?

TARL: I'm not sure what's going on.

SIDHU: Brain damage.

ANDREW: This is a very stressful time for her.

Frozen to the spot, TARL stares at the characters.

TARL: *(Urgent.)* Stand up, sit down, stand up, sit down...

Nothing happens.

TARL: Stand up, sit down...

ANDREW: What are you saying Tarlochan?

TARL: Stop this now!

ANDREW: I'm sorry but you're going to have to wait outside.

TARL: Outside?

ANDREW: In the corridor.

SIDHU: Please I beg you change it to a community centre.

TARL: What?

SIDHU: Why are you torturing us?

TARL: I don't understand.

AMRIK: She won't talk to you Uncle.

JOANNE: Can we please get on?

The characters sit back down.

ANDREW: Look it's my right to support this writer and to produce her work.

SIDHU: Having the right does not mean it is right. The point is that this young lady is a bad apple.

Stunned TARL observes the characters as the scene continues.

ANDREW: She's an artist, she's going to offend some people. Surely?

SIDHU: So you admit it is offensive! *(A beat.)* How long have you lived in this city Mr Fleming?

ANDREW: Sixteen months.

SIDHU: I have resided here for nearly forty years. This is my home. And to have such pain inflicted on me in my own home is wrong.

AMRIK: We're the lifeblood of this city, it's us you should be entertaining. Why can't I bring my mum and dad and mates into this building to see a show that means something to us?

ANDREW: You can.

AMRIK: You don't want to include us. This time we're not having it, that's what you can't stand.

ANDREW: I admit we need to do better. That's why I'm trying to include you now.

AMRIK: You don't know how to relate to people like me.

ANDREW: Plenty of my staff come from different ethnic backgrounds.

AMRIK: None of them make decisions though and the ones who challenge you always end up leaving.

SIDHU: Please Mr Fleming, realise you are going too far.

ANDREW: Tarlochan is exploring sensitive issues and yes the play might shock some people. That ability to challenge, coupled with decent writing is what constitutes great theatre. And if you don't understand that simple principle…

SIDHU: You think I'm thick!

JOANNE: Let's all calm down.

TARL: Please… this is going wrong…

JOANNE: Will you stop butting in?

ANDREW: I really think you should wait outside.

TARL: Yes, okay. Maybe I'll go and come back… and then things'll be back to normal.

ANDREW: Whatever makes you feel comfortable.

Perplexed TARL half nods. The characters watch her exit.

AMRIK: We are also here to protect Tarlochan. She's still one of us and we've heard certain things.

ANDREW: What things?

SIDHU: Sadly there are a few hotheads amongst our number who are not satisfied by talking.

JOANNE: Then you must deal with them.

AMRIK: Thought you cared about her.

ANDREW's phone rings. He checks the screen.

ANDREW: I'll be back.

AMRIK: Who's left Mr Fleming?

ANDREW: What?

AMRIK: To care about her.

ANDREW exits.

JOANNE: Would anyone like some tea?

SIDHU: No tea.

AMRIK: So what now Joanne?

SIDHU: You think I have fought this hard to make my home here that I will stop fighting just because of what that man says.

JOANNE: What do you mean by fighting?

AMRIK: What do you mean by it?

JOANNE doesn't respond.

AMRIK: With modern communications, ordinary people have the power to become generals of their own armies. Anyone anywhere could receive a call to arms.

JOANNE: That kind of talk might get Andrew all hot and bothered but I'm afraid it doesn't faze me.

SIDHU: All Amrik means is that systems are in place.

AMRIK's phone rings. He takes the call and goes to the side.

SIDHU: You know Joanne I think you are a nice lady.

JOANNE: Thank you.

SIDHU: I have always supported you and I have always urged the residents of your ward to support you. What I have done is like asking people to keep buying the same washing powder, even though there is another cheaper, better washing powder on the shelf. Do you know why I ask them?

JOANNE: Because we share common principles.

SIDHU: No. Because we have an understanding.

JOANNE: Mr Sidhu…

SIDHU: An unspoken, indefinable understanding. Like it is always in the air. Like it is air. How can you expect people to buy a washing powder which stains their clothes?

JOANNE: Mr Sidhu, I think we should keep artistic matters separate from community matters.

SIDHU: That is the exact problem, they have been kept separate. Artistic issues must be monitored, otherwise people can go round making things up.

AMRIK comes off the phone.

AMRIK: Word on the street is the Home Secretary doesn't want his thunder stolen by some stupid play.

JOANNE: The police will ensure things remain calm.

AMRIK: They can't cope with my boys. I reckon the opening will be delayed. Give us time to negotiate, get mobilised.

JOANNE: That isn't going to happen. *(A beat.)* I can see how passionately you both feel but I won't budge. The play's going on without any changes, and that's final.

AMRIK: No-one's listening to us Joanne.

JOANNE: I am. Let the play happen and you will be perceived as the dignified, tolerant community the country knows you to be. By getting all fired-up you're giving Tarlochan and her work even more publicity.

AMRIK: *(To SIDHU.)* She's trying to manipulate you.

JOANNE: I don't believe for one minute she's this brilliant writer. If this *Gund* play is shown, people will see the flaws in the writing and her own work will expose her as the mediocre artist she really is. So in a funny way, you'll be proved right. But to stop her having her say, just isn't possible.

SIDHU: What about our say?

JOANNE: I've been thinking about that. If you write a statement outlining your grievances, I'll make sure the theatre manager reads it out at the start of the play. You'll have a captive audience, taking in your words before they listen to her words. You, the real people will be the voice of reason while the luvvies indulge themselves in her pretentious crap!

SIDHU: I could write something.

AMRIK: It's a token gesture.

SIDHU: I'll teach that girl how to use proper English grammar!

ANDREW comes back in, he's visibly agitated and approaches AMRIK.

ANDREW: Your demonstrators have been threatening my box office staff.

AMRIK: Maybe your customer service isn't up to scratch.

ANDREW: Those workers just about earn the minimum wage. None of this is their fault.

TARL enters and marches up to the middle of the stage.

SIDHU: You should pay your staff more.

ANDREW: I want you out.

TARL: No! Ask them to stay, they're supposed to stay!

Nothing happens. All the characters watch TARL who is becoming increasingly distressed.

ANDREW: Did the police forget your lunch?

TARL: Why aren't you saying what I'm writing?

SIDHU: I told you, she has brain problems.

A fraught TARL goes up to AMRIK and takes the gun out of his pocket.

JOANNE: Shouldn't the police be with her?

TARL assumes a shooting position.

JOANNE: Oh my God.

The characters leap to their feet and shout and scream in fear. ANDREW's arms fly up in surrender. MR SIDHU immediately lies on the floor face down. TARL fires the gun at the characters but only a few sorry clicks sound. In despair, TARL drops the gun. AMRIK quickly retrieves it. The characters breathe a collective sigh of relief. ANDREW angrily turns to TARL.

ANDREW: Have you lost your mind?

TARL: I was just trying something.

ANDREW: *(To AMRIK.)* How dare you bring a firearm into my building.

AMRIK: I didn't even know it was there. She must have planted it on me.

They all turn to look at TARL.

TARL: It's only a pretend one, you can check.

AMRIK checks it and nods.

JOANNE: That was not funny young lady!

SIDHU: We could press charges.

ANDREW: She didn't mean anything by it, did you Tarlochan?

TARL: No.

ANDREW: She's under a great deal of pressure.

AMRIK: Things are going to get a lot worse.

ANDREW: Will you please leave?

SIDHU: Mark my words, this story is not finished yet!

AMRIK and SIDHU head out. A shocked ANDREW turns to TARL.

ANDREW: What the hell were you thinking?

TARL: I don't know.

JOANNE: We can hardly accuse them of intimidating behaviour while you're trying to murder us all.

ANDREW: Quite.

TARL: Sorry.

ANDREW: Anyway, we're fucked.

ANDREW sits down and rubs his eyes. He downs a jug of water.

ANDREW: The police have asked me to delay the opening by an hour.

TARL: No!

JOANNE: *(Shocked.)* What?

ANDREW: They're totally outnumbered, most of their officers are protecting your bloody man.

JOANNE: This is unbelievable.

ANDREW: They can't ensure the safety of the actors. I've no choice. You've got to convince these people Joanne.

JOANNE: They think they can bully me, after everything I've done for them. Well they bloody well can't. *(A beat.)* The Sikhs have asked to read out a statement before the performance.

TARL: But that's giving in.

ANDREW: Might it shut them up?

JOANNE: Be like cutting their tongues out.

TARL: No-one wants to listen to some diatribe, not in the theatre, not at the start of a show.

ANDREW: I'm prepared to do whatever it takes to get your work on. Besides nobody ever remembers the beginning, it's all about the end, eh Tarlochan?

JOANNE: Is there any tea going?

ANDREW: I'll find someone to bring it up.

JOANNE: You make it.

ANDREW: I don't know how to work the urn.

JOANNE: You must have been camping as a boy.

TARL: Is the play still happening?

ANDREW: Of course.

JOANNE: Of course.

ANDREW: We're going up late that's all.

ANDREW's phone rings. He turns it off and starts to head out.

ANDREW: *(To TARL.)* By the way the atmosphere outside is playing havoc with the actors' mental health.

TARL stares at him.

ANDREW: They're losing their focus in the onion scene. Can you come into the studio and offer some moral support?

TARL nods blankly. A shaken TARL watches ANDREW exit.

JOANNE: Try not to worry about the demonstration.

TARL: Am I still me?

JOANNE: Must be hard, I mean for your life to be threatened…

TARL: … or am I writing me?

JOANNE: Rest assured that you have the Council's unequivocal support. I know how you must be feeling. As a woman in politics one is constantly doing battle. One needs tenacity, self-belief, stamina.

TARL: Is my play still happening?

JOANNE: No question. Don't worry about your friendly neighbourhood Sikhs, they'll do as they're told. I mean why shouldn't you attack what's wrong with your culture…

TARL: There's nothing wrong with my culture. No more than with yours.

JOANNE: I blame the parents. Parents across cultures. Do you know that poem – They fuck you up, your mum and dad… *(JOANNE recites the first four lines of Philip Larkin's poem 'This Be the Verse'.)*

TARL: Yes!

JOANNE: What about your family?

TARL: The police are supposed to bring me a sandwich and some crisps.

JOANNE: Well these days your friends are your family.

TARL: There's nobody.

JOANNE: You've caused a proper rumpus with your play.

TARL: I wanted to say something.

JOANNE: Oh very fancy!

TARL: If you make people feel, then they might start thinking.

JOANNE: I think we all think too much.

TARL: And I always felt like planting a bomb.

JOANNE: Andrew said you encouraged his discussions with the Sikhs.

TARL: Maybe I hoped there might be some brown faces in the audience.

JOANNE: You got that one wrong, they're all outside the building. You know, I left my career for politics because I care about people and I want a better society.

TARL: You should have stayed in teaching.

JOANNE: How do you know I was a teacher?

TARL: You look like a drunk with a job.

JOANNE: Are you bipolar?

TARL: Things just sort of come out of me.

JOANNE: There are people outside who want you dead because of what comes out of you.

TARL: I wanted my words to go into their heads. I won't pretend they don't exist. I am of them. And they are of me.

JOANNE: You've lost me now.

TARL: It's not my job to be sensitive and considerate. I hate the quiet softness and tranquillity that people yearn for.

JOANNE: There's a terrible sense of unease about you. Dis-ease. Like Disease.

Sound of police sirens.

TARL: That might be my lunch.

JOANNE: You have my word Tarlochan, I'll fight for you and your play with every breath in my body.

TARL: I'll pray that you keep breathing then.

SCENE SEVEN

Afternoon. White sheets on the floor. TARL approaches and takes her shoes off and covers her head. She goes to pray. The actor playing the GIRL enters.

GIRL: Are you showing me because I'm not doing it properly?

TARL: No… no… you're… perfect.

GIRL: Thanks.

TARL: Are you alright?

GIRL: What?

TARL takes her hand. The GIRL moves away awkwardly. The MAN enters.

GIRL: I'd better get on.

TARL watches as the actors playing the GIRL and the MAN go through the blocking on the set for the next scene they are rehearsing. This includes a stainless steel kitchen unit (same as the one from Scene One), stainless steel cooking utensils, tins of food, bags of onions and packets of flour.

VINCE: Tar-lo-chan!

VINCE waves from the side.

VINCE: Got your Ploughmans!

TARL joins him and blankly starts to chomp on the sandwich from his plastic bag. VINCE holds out a packet of Monster Munch into which she delves ravenously. He grins as he watches the actors.

VINCE: So this is showbusiness!

He eyes her as she takes a bite, it's not pretty.

VINCE: Looks like you're enjoying that.

VINCE gestures towards a window.

VINCE: That lot outside, they're not like us. Don't think the same, don't have the same values. I've said it before, you can't reason with terrorists…

The comic 'Twinkle Twinkle' plays and then stops suddenly.

TARL: *(To VINCE.)* Did you hear that music?

VINCE: Afraid not, the job's stifled most of my creativity.

He nods to the window again.

VINCE: The uniforms out there are a bunch of kids. All the big boys are with the Home Secretary.

TARL: You could have a word with them.

VINCE: We're all different departments, if you speak out of turn health and safety'll come round and make you do ashtanga yoga for six months.

VINCE receives a text. He indicates his phone.

VINCE: He's only gone and locked himself in the Gents! To think the powers that be believed Gary could handle FaithHate on his todd!

He goes to leave.

VINCE: Feels like I'm living the white man's burden all over again. Chin up eh Tar-lo-chan?

He exits. TARL watches as the actors start the scene. The GIRL and the MAN start stacking various items onto the kitchen unit.

MAN: You my friend?

GIRL: Might be.

The MAN lifts up a pot which the GIRL has put on the wrong shelf.

MAN: This one go here Baby.

She giggles.

MAN: Why you laughing?

She giggles uncontrollably and doubles up, almost in pain from the laughter.

GIRL: You talk… you talk like a proper Paki.

MAN: Shut up.

GIRL: *(Imitating him.)* Shut up.

MAN: You a Paki, just like me.

The GIRL stops laughing.

GIRL: No I'm not.

She picks up an onion and sniffs it hard.

GIRL: That's what you smell like.

She pushes the onion into the man's nose.

GIRL: You should have baths.

MAN: I do.

GIRL: I know you don't.

MAN: I have bath.

GIRL: Bathsss you idiot. Bathsss. Make sure you learn English properly before you come and get me from school. And don't show up outside the gates with your smelly Paki friends. You're so stinking well embarrassing.

Suddenly the GIRL comes out of character.

GIRL: Sorry... I've lost it...

ANDREW hops onto the set. The GIRL is quite upset.

GIRL: I don't know what I'm doing any more.

ANDREW: It's okay.

TARL: You don't mean it.

ANDREW: I think she does.

GIRL: How can I play this moment if I don't know how it ends?

ANDREW: She's simply being a child – naughty, precocious, provocative.

TARL: It's not your fault.

ANDREW: *(To the GIRL.)* Less thinking and more being!

ANDREW walks the GIRL round the unit.

ANDREW: So you put a couple of tins onto the shelf, then the pot goes here, laugh... ha ha ha... and say the lines. Then as you take the onion, push it right into his face!

MAN: You never used to be that aggressive.

GIRL: She's a strong character, she has to be forceful.

MAN: Surely the aggression's in the lines?

ANDREW: I like it.

GIRL: For God's sake we're supposed to be opening tonight, which ending is it?

TARL: I'm not sure, you see I've been working on something else.

GIRL/MAN: What?

ANDREW: Tarlochan! You have a duty to the artistic team to make a decision! To finish *Gund*!

GIRL: Do I live or die?

TARL starts walking around the stage manically.

ANDREW: *(To TARL.)* Why don't you go and sit in the Green Room? Have a biscuit.

TARL is running now. She's hitting the scenery, trying to break it down, desperately looking for a way out.

ANDREW: What the hell are you doing?

TARL: Must be a way out somewhere.

ANDREW: *(To the actors.)* Okay, take five.

The puzzled actors exit. TARL follows them out but quickly comes back in.

TARL: Everywhere's just white space.

TARL pummels the flats at the back but can find no exit. She collapses in a heap. The comic 'Twinkle Twinkle' music starts to play. It then stops. TARL tries to compose herself.

TARL: The Twinkle Twinkle music at the end of the first scene, it's not right.

ANDREW: But you suggested it.

TARL: Did I?

ANDREW: In the stage directions.

TARL: I've changed my mind.

ANDREW: You can't keep exerting control like this. Have faith in my interpretation.

TARL springs up.

TARL: We have to do the play!

ANDREW: As soon as the police give the all clear. Anyway the rest of the cast aren't even here, they've been blockaded inside Starbucks.

TARL: Let's perform it in there.

ANDREW: It's not safe for you to leave the theatre.

TARL: That's up to me.

ANDREW: This doesn't just affect you Tarlochan, I have to consider my staff, the actors, the building…

TARL: Please…

ANDREW: *(Irritated.)* Can you for one second think about someone other than yourself? I had other plays I could have programmed you know, some of which had endings! If you hadn't agreed to this dialogue in the first place, we might not be in this mess.

TARL: If my play was on and just your usual blue rinse brigade were seeing it, so what? Nothing would change.

ANDREW: So it's change you're after?

TARL: I've got a right…

ANDREW: Yes.

TARL: If I haven't then I might as well stop breathing.

ANDREW: You must be frightened.

TARL: No I'm desperate. I've waited for this my whole life… And I'm scared if it doesn't happen soon, I'll lose my chance.

ANDREW: If it helps we're in the same boat. I've ploughed a large chunk of the theatre's marketing budget into this production. My reputation's on the line.

TARL: You're certain this is only a delay?

ANDREW: You have to trust me. Oh, I ought to mention… there's been more talk of threats, people wanting you hospitalised and so forth. They seem to hold you personally responsible.

TARL: I am.

ANDREW: I have to make sure that you're aware.

The actors walk back on. TARL retreats to the side with ANDREW. The GIRL and the MAN position themselves on the set.

ANDREW: *(To the actors.)* Okay, go from Baths.

GIRL: Bathsss you idiot. Bathsss. Make sure you learn English properly before you come and get me from school. And don't show up outside the gates with your smelly Paki friends. You're so stinking well embarrassing.

They stare at each other.

GIRL: Do you understand Paki? You'd just better do what I say.

Suddenly the MAN grabs the GIRL and holds her upside down by the ankles. She half-laughs and half-cries. He shakes her hard and releases her. She falls with a thud onto the floor.

GIRL: I'm telling.

She tries to run past the MAN but he blocks her. She turns and runs, the MAN speeds after her and catches her.

TARL: Tell him to stop!

ANDREW: What?

TARL rushes onto the set.

TARL: Stop, leave her alone!

She hurriedly pulls the MAN off the GIRL. The actors jump up defensively.

MAN: What the fuck!

ANDREW: They're trying to play the scene!

TARL: Where are their scripts?

The actors drift off.

ANDREW: They've been off the book for weeks!

TARL: Oh yes… yes… Sorry… I'm sorry.

Loud sounds of chanting from outside.

ANDREW: Tarlochan, hadn't you better decide on the ending?

He indicates a fat script.

TARL: Yes. Yes, you're right. I must.

She sits down at the desk and opens the script, she starts to write. The GIRL comes back on and starts re-stacking the kitchen unit. ANDREW approaches the GIRL.

ANDREW: At some point during rehearsals the writer always becomes surplus to requirements.

TARL stops writing and closes the fat script.

SCENE EIGHT

Late afternoon. KHUSH stands at the photocopier. Hundreds of leaflets are piled high by the machine. TARL enters and watches him do the copying. KHUSH is immediately anxious.

KHUSH: Afternoon. I've got permission. *(Hands her a leaflet.)* Have one.

TARL: *(Reads.)* Don't let the white racist theatre abuse your heritage. Have pride in your religion. Stop Tarlochan Kaur Grewal from spreading her evil lies...

KHUSH: You one of them who work here? *(A beat.)* You look like one of us.

TARL: I'm her.

KHUSH moves away, disturbed.

KHUSH: You? You're not.

TARL: Why?

KHUSH: Thought you'd have better clothes. Thought you'd look more like a Goree.

TARL: Say your name.

KHUSH: Khush.

TARL: Happy.

KHUSH: I hate you.

TARL: But we've only just met. Properly.

TARL suddenly grabs his bag.

KHUSH: What are you doing?

TARL: I have to check something.

She opens it. The bag is full of leaflets.

TARL: So it's not time yet. *(To herself.)* What's going to happen?

KHUSH: What are you on about?

TARL composes herself and takes the fat 'Gund' script out of her pocket.

TARL: Is this what you want, *Gund*?

KHUSH: Come on then, let's have a look.

They walk around the space as though they're playing cat and mouse. TARL shoves the script up her sweatshirt and folds her arms.

KHUSH: *(Shouts.)* You make me sick! I fucking hate you!

TARL approaches him and takes his hand.

TARL: Thank you, Happy.

KHUSH: What?

TARL: For teaching me tolerance. I love you. The most out of all of them.

He pushes her away.

KHUSH: I'm nothing to do with you. Why do you hate your own community so much?

TARL: I'm only a writer.

KHUSH: Then you should write about things in a helpful way.

TARL: I was trying my best.

KHUSH: It's not fair. All those poor people who have to be in hospital and you're walking around free using your arms and legs and your sick brain. *(Quiet.)* Behsharam… kuthee… *[Shameless bitch].*

TARLOCHAN freezes.

TARL: What did you call me?

KHUSH: You heard.

TARL suddenly grabs KHUSH's ear. He falls over and screams in pain.

TARL: You're not my mum or my dad. You don't know me or what goes on in my head. You boys. Getting sent to private school, as if that's going to kickstart your woolly brains. Being spoilt with Nintendo and fat trainers and microwave chips.

She lets him go. He gets his breath back and stands up.

KHUSH: All the girls I know hate you too. And the old ladies and the middle-aged ones as well.

TARL: None of my business what anyone thinks. Whatever I've done is between me and God.

KHUSH: No way is my God your God.

TARL: Where's your God then? In your beard or under your turban?

KHUSH: You don't believe what I believe.

TARL takes off her shoes, pulls her sweatshirt over her head and puts her hands together.

TARL: Ek umkar, satnam, karta purkh… *[One god, named truth, creator…]*

KHUSH: Stop.

TARL continues. KHUSH cups his hands over her mouth. She carries on praying.

KHUSH: I don't want to hear those words coming out of your mouth.

TARL breaks free.

TARL: I want to say them, I need to say them.

They tussle again. TARL falls to the ground.

KHUSH: You're doing this to aggravate me.

TARL: No. Because I have to…

Shattered, they sit on the floor and face each other.

TARL: I'm saying it in my head.

KHUSH: Shut up.

TARL: What are you going to do, crack it open?

KHUSH: I wish you were dead.

TARL: That's a kind religious thought.

KHUSH: My words and actions are the result of your words and actions.

TARL: If you don't want to hear me saying it, you say it, pray for my bad soul.

KHUSH: Why do you want to crush our people?

TARL: Just because we've been through shit, doesn't mean we don't make our own shit.

KHUSH: It's cos you want to be a goree.

TARL: Where do you see me being that?

KHUSH: You just are.

She gets up.

TARL: Your mum and dad have got a shop haven't they?

KHUSH: How do you know?

TARL: They sell beefburgers. And Marlboro lights.

KHUSH: Those two are nothing to do with me.

TARL: So which people are you fighting for?

KHUSH: My principles.

TARL: Is your faith so weak?

KHUSH: Shut up, you're the enemy within.

TARL: Your head's got all mixed up.

KHUSH: How could it not be living in this shithole?

TARL: But you've got a nice shop.

KHUSH: I mean England.

TARL: You want to nick some notes out of the till and buy one of them round the world tickets. Stick a rucksack on your back and see a bit of life.

KHUSH: I'm going home back to the Punjab. Gonna be a farmer, drive a tractor and work the land, our real proper land.

TARL: Like it out there do you?

KHUSH: *(A beat.)* I've never been.

TARL: *(Laughs.)* You won't last five minutes.

KHUSH: I'll be with my brothers and sisters.

TARL: They're all getting visas to come here.

KHUSH: I'll find people there who want to practise my religion with their hearts full of the love of God. I'm sick of the hypocrites here. Like my mum and dad, who go round buying half a ton of gold for the wedding of some nobody they've never met. Get dressed up like a pair of Bollywood pimps and sit in the Gurdwara wishing the time away till they can get merry. I hate it when they bring the book, our holy book, to some three-star hotel where men are dancing with bottles of Johnny Walker on their heads.

TARL: I used to hate all that.

KHUSH: No-one's bothered. Everyone just wants and wants and wants.

TARL: They can't help it, their souls have been infected. You know you should read *Gund…*

KHUSH: Never. You're worse than all of them, you've gone somewhere you'll never come back from.

TARL: Do you reckon that lot out there are like you?

KHUSH: Yeah.

TARL: Those boys couldn't care less. They're here to feel the beats of the dhol, tell off a behsharam like me and get high on the party atmosphere. And there's no way out, except to get on a plane and drive a tractor.

KHUSH: There are women outside as well.

TARL: Someone has to keep you alive. You're just as different from them as I am. You're the one that's most like me.

KHUSH: Fuck off.

TARL: How are you getting on with Amrik?

KHUSH: He's like my older brother.

TARL: Do you think he believes?

KHUSH: Of course.

TARL: When Amrik was a boy, his mum used to send him to learn Gurmukhi at the Gurdwara. But he got confused by the lamah so the Gianis beat him. One day one of them stuck a hot iron on his hand, left a dark red mark. Have you seen it?

KHUSH shakes his head.

TARL: Take a look sometime. He called it his warrior mark. If anyone asked him about it, he'd say 'Got into a fight with a pig at a demo'.

KHUSH: Shut up.

TARL: Aren't you supposed to tell him you've got me?

KHUSH quickly searches for his phone.

TARL: Why do you believe so hard?

KHUSH: I just do.

TARL: Perhaps because there's not much else going on.

Fury consumes KHUSH.

KHUSH: You're no Sikh, you fake. No-one gives a shit about you or your pretend faith. Give me that piece of shit you call a script and I'll burn it. I'll burn this whole motherfucking theatre down.

Suddenly TARLOCHAN throws him the 'Gund' script which he catches. She turns to go.

TARL: Go on then brother. Light up.

KHUSH attempts to stop her, TARL brushes him off.

TARL: Don't get your kuchee in a twist.

KHUSH: You don't know what I'm gonna do.

TARL: I'm pretending to be a brave Sikh, like you are.

KHUSH: I'm telling you I'm setting it on fire!

He takes out a lighter. TARL continues out.

TARL: If it's still here when I get back, we'll both know there's a God.

She exits.

SCENE NINE

The GIRL sits on a wooden stool in front of the stainless steel kitchen unit. Her hands and feet are tied up with pieces from a white sheet. She's only wearing her vest and pants and her shalwar kameez lies in a pile on the floor. The MAN stands next to her, he's tearing up a white sheet.

GIRL: *(Screams.)* Help!

MAN: No-one can hear you Baby.

GIRL: Sorry for what I said.

MAN: Sure?

GIRL: I'm just a stupid little girl. I'm sorry, I'm sorry, I'm sorry…

MAN: Too late.

The MAN opens a packet of flour and throws it over the GIRL. She starts to cry.

GIRL: I'm telling my dad. Everything.

MAN: I told him already. He's coming to see you now.

The MAN takes one of the strips he's torn from the white sheet and gags the GIRL with it.

MAN: Can't hear you Baby, talk louder.

Muffled sounds from the GIRL's mouth. The MAN pulls the gag even tighter. The GIRL is extremely distressed.

MAN: Come on Baby, talk louder. Louder!

SCENE TEN

Early evening. The Stage. The GIRL remains gagged on the stool, she is dimly lit. Loud sounds of chanting and unrest can be heard from outside. (VINCE/GARY/TARL and AMRIK/SIDHU/JOANNE do not acknowledge one another or the GIRL as their respective dialogue proceeds.) MR SIDHU is sitting down, writing on a piece of paper. He looks up.

SIDHU: Just because this girl has a Sikh name does not mean she is a Sikh... I for one have never seen her at the Gurdwara...

VINCE and GARY enter running towards a neon Ladies sign. They stop.

VINCE: *(Shouts.)* Tar-lo-chan! Did you confiscate her belt and shoelaces?

GARY: She's not the type to top herself.

VINCE: That rabble have got to her.

GARY: Don't suppose you've ever considered why they're so angry?

VINCE: Tar-lo-chan, we're the bearers of glad tidings!

GARY: I'm asking you to listen.

VINCE: That is exactly why the Great's gone out of Great Britain. Every asylum-seeking economic illegal migrant thinks he's got the right to have his say. Whatever happened to keeping quiet and suffering?

A triumphant AMRIK enters. SIDHU gets up.

SIDHU: The statement is complete!

AMRIK: Who cares about that? My boys have ringfenced the theatre. They won't rest till they've brought this city to its knees!

SIDHU: I don't want to pick up the pieces of your mess.

AMRIK receives a text.

AMRIK: My mess will bring about the result you can't. Maybe if you and your lot had fought harder we wouldn't be here.

He glances at his phone.

AMRIK: Khush has got the girl.

SIDHU: Our aim is to stop the play, we are not kidnappers.

AMRIK: You wait, she'll tell the press she got it all wrong. Then she'll thank me for making her see sense.

SIDHU: You will set the whole community back.

AMRIK: Isn't that your favourite bit? After the mayhem on the streets… it's over to you, having Marks and Spencer sandwiches with the councillors and the cops. All of you going on about how bad it is and how you'll make the peace. And you do, in your elastoplast way until the next time, and then you go back for more sandwiches.

SIDHU: Why are you talking like this?

AMRIK: You're partly to blame for the way the goreh portray us, you make them feel as if they know us.

SIDHU: You think influence comes without sacrifice? The goreh like me, they listen to me…

AMRIK: Our people have changed. They want to listen to a new song.

SIDHU: We have Sikhism.

AMRIK: Come on Uncle, if you were a man of God, you'd let her have her say.

SIDHU: You disrespect me just like she disrespects me.

GARY: *(To VINCE.)* You don't know anything about me or my culture. I might as well be a white bloke.

VINCE: That's what you want isn't it? To be accepted like everyone else.

GARY: We can't have a conversation without you knowing best or taking the piss.

VINCE: I am in charge DI Mangat.

GARY: You came back and took over.

VINCE: This is how it's supposed to be. In England.

AMRIK: Why did you bring us to this fucking country?

SIDHU: For a better life.

AMRIK: Well here we are.

AMRIK goes to leave.

SIDHU: Amrik!

AMRIK ignores him and exits. TARL emerges from the Exit sign.

VINCE: You're alive Tar-lo-chan! Brilliant.

VINCE's phone rings, he goes to the side to answer it.

GARY: Starbucks has been liberated. The actors are out.

TARL: So the play's on?

GARY: Yeah.

VINCE comes off the phone. Agitated JOANNE runs on.

VINCE: Some woman's waiting for you in the foyer. A Miss Satinder Shergill.

TARL: The journalist?

VINCE: From the Mail, yeah.

TARL: I can't meet her.

VINCE: I've taken the call now. You have to go.

TARL: But you're supposed to keep me safe.

The GIRL's dead body falls from the stool.

VINCE: Don't worry, Gary's going to escort you.

GARY starts dragging TARL offstage.

JOANNE: *(To SIDHU.)* The police are having to bring officers in from the neighbouring constabulary!

SIDHU: You must stop this play.

JOANNE: I can't. Look, your grievances have been aired to a national audience, it's time to call the protest off.

SIDHU: What did the Home Secretary's people say?

JOANNE: Please Mr Sidhu…

SIDHU: If this play goes on blood will be shed.

JOANNE: I've been thinking, the next time there's the slightest whiff of offensive material we'll come down on them like a sledgehammer to a brittle bone.

SIDHU: The police cannot cope and the Home Secretary will not set the army on civilians because of the bloody theatre. You are going to end up with no play and a nightmare in our city. You have created this Joanne, so it's up to you to use your imagination and find a way out.

TARL: No... please... I don't want to see her.

VINCE: We'll rendezvous back at the flat DI Mangat. I expect a thorough progress report on FaithHate.

VINCE exits as TARL struggles with GARY.

SIDHU: You expect us to put our exes in your boxes.

JOANNE: I'm very grateful...

SIDHU: *(Shouts.)* Then show us some respect! You think Britannia still rules the bloody waves? Because you come and eat a few chappatis at the Gurdwara you are the bloody Queen?

JOANNE: No...

SIDHU: Then pay attention and start representing your community.

TARL: If she gets hold of me it'll be over.

GARY: He says I have to.

TARL: You want to be in charge remember.

GARY roughly pushes her away. JOANNE and SIDHU exit.

GARY: No I don't! I just want to do my job. I joined the police because I wanted to make a difference. I had high hopes...

TARL: You can make a difference by not taking me. Please Gary, I'm begging you.

GARY: I don't understand what's going on.

TARL: Is your natural instinct to take orders or help others?

GARY slowly backs off.

TARL: Problem is your intentions are confused. You need more work.

GARY: But I've got a job… I'm a police officer.

TARL: What else are you?

GARY: I'm… er… a police officer. And… a Sikh.

TARL: Brown skin shows the uniform off better but it doesn't change anything, so your journey is to learn that you're just part of the system.

GARY: Same as you.

TARL: You won't understand this Gary, but I'm slightly different to you.

GARY: How?

TARL: I'm really real. And you're pretend.

GARY: Eh?

TARL: Like an illusion.

TARL takes GARY's hand and runs it all over her face, her body.

TARL: What do I feel like to you?

GARY: Fat and squashy…

TARL: Real?

GARY: Course…

He touches her arm.

GARY: This bit's sort of like a… lizard.

He pulls away quickly.

GARY: Careful the reptiles don't chew you up.

TARL exits.

SCENE ELEVEN

Early evening. The MAN enters. Standing by the kitchen unit, he starts wrapping the GIRL's body up in the white sheets, pieces of which are now stained with blood. JOANNE stands opposite ANDREW on the set which represents his office – desk, filing cabinet and chairs. It's as if the two different sets have become integrated but JOANNE and ANDREW do not acknowledge the MAN, nor he them.

ANDREW: This directive's coming from the Home Secretary's people isn't it? *(Shouts.)* Isn't it?

JOANNE: Listen to yourself Andrew, you sound like a paranoid schizophrenic.

ANDREW: Don't tempt me Joanne, I've got a pen knife in my pocket.

JOANNE: Think it through.

The MAN exits. The GIRL's corpse remains on the integrated set.

ANDREW: There's nothing to think about.

JOANNE: Do you ever bother looking out of the window from your ivory tower? Coachloads of youths are arriving from all over the country. Forget the riot, we're facing a potential atrocity.

ANDREW: Let the army deal with it.

JOANNE: They need authorisation from the Home Secretary. He won't, I've checked.

ANDREW: Then any blood that's shed is on his hands.

JOANNE: This is no longer about presenting anal rape and foul language to the converted few. We're risking lives.

ANDREW: Honestly Joanne, this is one of your pathetic ploys isn't it? Atrocity my arse.

JOANNE: Why do you care so much?

ANDREW: Because I'm an artist.

JOANNE: Without this building there are no artists. If this play goes ahead and there's bloodshed, do you suppose anyone in this region's going to support you? In a year your funding will be hacked away and this place will die.

ANDREW: You're putting me in a fucking impossible position!

JOANNE: I'll fight for you. I can build a bridge between you and them, repair the damage.

ANDREW: You promised me.

JOANNE: You've brought the world's media to our city. You've shown that theatre provokes and causes uproar, that it's relevant.

TARLOCHAN enters and observes the kitchen unit. She picks up a tin and reads the label.

TARL: These have got Arabic writing on them. You can't put these in a Gurdwara.

ANDREW: It's just a bit of dressing.

TARL throws the tins and flour onto the floor.

TARL: You should have asked.

ANDREW: Is it really that big a deal?

TARL: This is why they won't believe anything you say, because you never try and understand what you don't know.

JOANNE: Some of us have bigger preoccupations at the moment.

TARL kicks the tins and packets around the space. The red notebook falls out of her pocket.

ANDREW: Stop that Tarlochan.

TARL: I'm begging you, please get it right.

JOANNE: She encouraged this ridiculous dialogue. Why?

TARL: I thought they might listen...

JOANNE: Why would anybody listen to you?

TARL exits. JOANNE pointedly turns to ANDREW.

JOANNE: Face it, she hasn't considered your plight for one second.

ANDREW: I don't know what to do.

JOANNE: She'll write other plays, if she's a proper writer she will. In a few months we'll do some juggling with the kitty money and you can take this *Gund* thing on tour.

ANDREW: What will people think of me?

JOANNE: No-one's backing you. Not the police, not the council. If you're going to survive, you and I need to maintain a united front.

ANDREW: You might not even get in next week.

JOANNE: If I don't, you really are fucked. You're dying Andrew, you and your Oxbridge friends. No-one's interested in what you lot think or say any more.

ANDREW: Are you saying that I don't have a point? That I won't stand up for what you know is the right thing to do?

JOANNE: What's stopping you? Go and do it then!

As she exits, JOANNE picks up the red notebook.

SCENE TWELVE

Lights change. It's as if there is no set and this moment cannot be located.

The corpse of the GIRL remains on the floor wrapped in the bloody white sheets. TARL enters and picks the GIRL up as though she is very precious. She regards her lovingly and carries her off.

SCENE THIRTEEN

Evening. The integrated set. KHUSH is slumped down reading the 'Gund' script. After a few moments TARL enters.

TARL: Why didn't you burn it, action man?

She grabs the 'Gund' script from him and he jumps up.

TARL: It's okay, I knew you weren't capable.

AMRIK enters. TARL puts the script in her pocket.

AMRIK: Good to see you.

TARL: *(In Punjabi.)* I'm ready for you now. How are your mum and dad?

AMRIK doesn't respond.

TARL: No ear for his own language.

AMRIK: You look terrible.

TARL: I eat shit.

AMRIK: Have you finished your script?

TARL: What do you want?

AMRIK: For us to talk. You're not the only one who's got the right to be heard.

TARL turns to KHUSH.

TARL: Back in the day, in the real world, Amrik used to fancy me.

AMRIK: Oh… please…

TARL: I wasn't always this bad looking. We were in youth theatre together. He was in his own way very talented. And kind. But I think that's gone now.

AMRIK: I might not like what you're doing but I care what happens to you.

TARL: Really?

AMRIK: You enjoying your moment in the limelight? Everyone talking about you, saying how concerned they are about your welfare. Won't last much longer. Fleming and his lot might defend your rights and tell you how brave you are but they don't get what you're about. Not like I do.

TARL: They like my writing.

AMRIK: They make you believe you'll rise and shine. But to them you're like a puppy at Christmas and once they've had their fun you'll be back out on the streets again. A little mongrel looking for a new owner. And they'll go in search of a new pet. You won't ever, can't ever be anything more than the exotic ethnic who makes them feel multicultural.

TARL: My play's what matters.

AMRIK: You think putting it on will set you free?

TARL: Yes.

AMRIK: It's destroying you.

TARL: What if you're right? What do I do?

AMRIK: Come back to your people, where you belong.

TARL: What about what's in my head?

AMRIK: You'll be looked after. The filth in your head will go away, won't be any need to write it.

TARL: So... so it will be like it never happened?

AMRIK: Exactly.

TARL: What if I just feel like writing shameful things?

AMRIK: That'll stop and you'll write something worthwhile.

TARL: But don't I need to be free?

AMRIK: No, you need to feel secure. Why don't you let me have a look at the script? We can work on changing it, together.

TARL takes her 'Gund' script out.

TARL: And after that, I'll belong again? You'll take me back?

AMRIK: Yes.

TARL: I think... I think... I'd rather give Nick Griffin a blow job.

AMRIK: What are you Tarlochan? What has your life become?

TARL: I like it.

AMRIK: Give me the script.

TARL: The play's going on.

KHUSH: Birji...

TARL: Shut up shit! Hurt people hurt people don't they Amrik? *(To KHUSH.)* Have you met his daughter?

AMRIK: Fuck off.

TARL: *(To KHUSH.)* Do you ever wonder why he's not married? Are you a Gaylord Amrik?

AMRIK: I am getting married. To a girl from India.

TARL: That is... so... you are so predictable. After all the years of fighting talk you end up with a virgin from the village.

TARL's phone rings. She glances at the number and turns it off.

TARL: I have to go.

AMRIK: I'm warning you…

TARL stands right in front of him.

TARL: Thing is I know you're not a bad man…

She goes to leave.

TARL: See you lot after the show.

She exits. Embarrassed silence.

AMRIK: Did you speak to her?

KHUSH: No. I only walked in a minute before you.

KHUSH glances at a mark on AMRIK's hand.

KHUSH: What's that mark Birji?

AMRIK: My warrior mark. Got into a fight with a pig at a demo.

MR SIDHU enters. He does a triumphant little dance.

SIDHU: I did it! I only bloody well did it! Joanne says they may even ask me onto the theatre board. The play is stopped. I stopped it the old-fashioned way. I told your boys and they are retreating.

AMRIK rushes to look outside. He turns to KHUSH.

AMRIK: Get on the phone, tell them to come back.

KHUSH: But the play isn't happening.

AMRIK: The protest will go on.

KHUSH: I reckon she needs help.

SIDHU: And a good hard chapair *[slap]*!

AMRIK: You don't know her, she's dangerous. What did she say to you back there?

KHUSH: Nothing.

AMRIK: Do you feel the same as you did this morning?

KHUSH: Don't know.

AMRIK: Then she's done a good job. She's persuaded you to doubt everything you truly value. I'm instructing you to carry out my orders, even if you don't feel like it. If you still feel the same way this time tomorrow then do whatever you like. Trust me, brother.

KHUSH: Okay.

AMRIK: Get outside and organise your troops. Hurry! Then I want you back here.

KHUSH: But you don't need me any more.

AMRIK: There's something I want you to observe.

KHUSH runs out.

SIDHU: You are a graceless man Amrik. What has happened to make you so mangled?

AMRIK: I've watched and learned from the Master Uncleji.

MR SIDHU goes to exit.

AMRIK: Where are you going?

SIDHU: To pick up seven kilos of salt cod. The fish samoseh appear to be more of a reality than ever.

AMRIK: They're all laughing at you. Joanne, Fleming, the Home Secretary…

SIDHU: Let them laugh. As long as I get what I want, let them laugh.

SCENE FOURTEEN

Showtime. ANDREW's office on the integrated set. JOANNE and ANDREW solemnly stand before a shaking TARLOCHAN, she is having a panic attack.

ANDREW: *(Alarmed.)* What's going on?

JOANNE: Panic attack. Teachers have them all the time.

JOANNE reaches for a jug of water on the desk and throws it over TARLOCHAN.

JOANNE: Old trick from the staff room.

TARL: I don't understand.

JOANNE: Circumstances have changed.

ANDREW: It would be irresponsible of me to place the theatre in further jeopardy so I'm afraid the decision has been made for me.

TARL: Is this real?

JOANNE: No writer has the right to frighten a community.

TARL: Has this really happened?

She grabs JOANNE and feels her body all over.

JOANNE: *(Angry.)* Get off me!

TARL: Stand up, sit down, stand up, sit down…

JOANNE: She's lost the plot now.

TARL: So is what's in my head stronger than what's real?

ANDREW: What?

TARL: Or is it the other way around?

JOANNE and ANDREW exchange a weary look.

JOANNE: Maybe it's some sort of bipolar code.

TARL: Please… I need to know…

ANDREW: Just because we can't put *Gund* on at the moment doesn't mean there's no future for the play.

TARL: There's no future.

ANDREW: In a few months, there's a strong possibility of mounting a co-production with a prime London venue, you couldn't hope for better exposure …

TARL: Is it because you didn't like the ending?

ANDREW sighs.

TARL: Maybe I can come up with something else.

ANDREW: Oh, Denis Edwards wants to talk to you. Did you see his last play here?

TARL shakes her head.

ANDREW: He's keen on writing a fact-based drama about what's happening to you right now. Apparently there's interest from Radio 4.

TARL: You're a coward.

ANDREW: I'm as much a victim of this situation as you are. I have to consider the welfare of my staff as well as the damage being done to our bricks and mortar by those morons outside.

TARL: Don't call them that.

ANDREW: You call them worse in your play.

TARL: What will you do now? Put on those Enid Blyton Asian plays where everyone loves each other in the end? Get the curry smells wafting through the auditorium while the audience are mesmerised by the singing of wafer thin red and gold dancers. We're not all like that. My life isn't like that.

JOANNE: Perhaps you should ask yourself why it isn't.

ANDREW: I sincerely hope we'll work together again.

ANDREW turns to go.

ANDREW: The press are waiting.

TARL: What do you do Andrew? I can write, what can you do?

He exits.

JOANNE: Has it ever struck you that no-one is particularly interested in what you do?

TARL: Why are all those people outside then?

JOANNE: It's what surrounds what you do that is of interest. Creators have been overtaken by commentators. No-one reads books any more, they read about them, no-one even has any real opinions, they just like to hear them being discussed. It's people who don't actually do anything who set the agenda.

TARL: But if I didn't write the play, no agenda would exist.

JOANNE: The time for writing is over.

JOANNE opens her bag and takes out a hand mirror, she checks her make-up. TARLOCHAN approaches a portable television and turns it on. As before the image is projected onto a screen. ANDREW FLEMING stands on a podium and addresses a bustling press conference.

JOANNE: Don't watch this.

ANDREW: Everyone connected to the Writers' Theatre is very disappointed that the performance is cancelled. But matters have been taken out of my hands. I have personally spoken to Tarlochan and she has specifically requested that the play be pulled. The police have informed her of an increase in threats to her personal safety. The theatre appreciates Tarlochan's fear in these circumstances and we support her right to protect herself. We abhor the violence which has caused damage to the front of the Writers' Theatre building and hope that once the situation in the city has calmed down we can look to producing *Gund…*

TARLOCHAN abruptly turns the television off and the screens go dead. Devastated, she turns to JOANNE.

TARL: Why… why did he say that?

JOANNE: He had to say something.

TARL starts to crumble and shake.

TARL: What am I supposed to do now?

JOANNE: Perhaps you'll use this experience to write a new play.

TARL checks her pocket, it's empty. She starts frantically searching all over the set.

JOANNE: What are you doing?

TARL: I've lost my script.

JOANNE: Don't you get it? No-one's bothered.

TARL: I have to find it.

She rummages around and opens the filing cabinet. The corpse of the girl wrapped in the bloody sheets falls out on top of her. TARL screams in horror.

JOANNE: No-one's listening.

TARL breaks down. JOANNE eyes her coldly.

JOANNE: I was waiting for you to break. You need to be a lot stronger than this, young lady. *(A beat.)* Maybe it's some sort of bipolar code… He had to say something… The time for writing is over…

Aghast TARL stares at JOANNE. JOANNE opens her bag as if to take out her mirror. She instead takes out the red notebook, it falls to the floor. TARL picks it up.

JOANNE: Panic attack. Teachers have them all the time. I was waiting for you to break. You need to be a lot stronger than this, young lady… No writer has the right to frighten a community.

SCENE FIFTEEN

TARLOCHAN and SAT are seated in chairs on the integrated set. TARL clutches her red notebook. SAT holds a pad. She flicks through some pages and reads.

SAT: You say you were about four years old. It was the summer holidays and you and your older sister were watching television with your Uncle who had recently arrived from India. You think he was an illegal immigrant. Your sister made fun of the way he walked and spoke. Your Uncle took swigs from a bottle of Johnny Walker Black label. He didn't understand what your sister was saying but after a while he realised she was laughing at him and he punched her. She continued to laugh so he struck her again. He was very angry and he dragged her out of the room, up the stairs. He was shouting and she was screaming. You wanted to go to the toilet but when you tried to open the door you couldn't. He'd locked it. Later that day you remember the house being cleaned by various family members. You never saw your sister again. Your mother was away in India at the time and your family moved out of the area shortly after this incident. From that day on nobody in the family mentioned your sister. Your Uncle now runs a successful minicab business in Vancouver. What was your sister's name?

TARL: Can't remember.

SAT: This would be easier if I put your words on a disc.

TARL: No. No recording.

SAT: You subsequently retreated to a world of fantasy. You excelled academically, developed a form of obsessive compulsive disorder. One notable psychotic episode at University after which you were allotted a CPN. Father alcoholic. Absent mother. Sexually deviant behaviour from your teens onwards. Worked in a hospital laundry and a butcher's shop. You read cookery books in your spare time and enjoy watching darts.

TARL: That's it.

SAT: Why not go to the police about your sister?

TARL: I said I'd talk. Not answer questions.

SAT: What about the play?

TARLOCHAN gets up to go.

SAT: Why give me an exclusive?

TARL: Feels like I'm dead.

SAT: But you're not.

TARL: You'll burn me alive regardless.

SAT: I don't get it.

TARL: You're the one I hate the most. I want you to have me.

SAT: Have you been telling the truth?

TARL: Does it matter?

SAT: *(A beat.)* Everything that's happened, it's a shame.

TARLOCHAN stops.

TARL: You know the most terrible things need the most love. But they never get it.

SAT fades out. TARL opens the red notebook.

SCENE SIXTEEN

TARL is furiously writing on the last page of her notebook. The GIRL's corpse lies in the middle of the stage. TARL reads out the beginning of Scene 16 to the audience. As she reads the characters do what she says.

TARL: Scene Sixteen. Evening. AMRIK is leaning over the photocopier on the integrated set. KHUSH enters.

KHUSH: Tried to get them back, but they didn't want to stay.

TARL: TARLOCHAN enters with the red notebook. They all look at each other.

TARL stands and they all look at each other.

TARL: This is for you. It's my new script.

She chucks the notebook to AMRIK who catches it. AMRIK takes out a lighter. KHUSH panics.

KHUSH: Don't! There's no need.

AMRIK: I want you to watch me.

KHUSH: I read *Gund*.

AMRIK: All the more reason.

KHUSH: It's not what we thought.

AMRIK lights up a flame.

KHUSH: At least read it first Birji!

AMRIK opens the notebook and looks at the first page.

AMRIK: *(Reads.)* Behud…

KHUSH: Beyond Belief…

AMRIK sets fire to the notebook. KHUSH tries to put the fire out.

TARL: *(To KHUSH.)* Leave him!

The paper burns until it is ash.

TARL: I found a great ending.

AMRIK: Shut up!

TARL: You don't understand Amrik, it's perfect.

AMRIK suddenly fires the gun at TARL but it just sounds a sorry click. AMRIK keeps trying to shoot TARL but keeps failing. TARL lies down next to the GIRL's corpse and puts her arm around the dead body. Suddenly the photocopier starts going and sheets of typed paper come out of it and are blown around the set. KHUSH collects pieces of paper together. AMRIK fades out. As the paper continues to come out of the photocopier, it seems like the stage is transforming into a sea of scripts. KHUSH reads the script.

KHUSH: *(Reads.)* Prologue. Dawn. The stage is black.
The lights go up slowly to reveal an Asian woman,
TARLOCHAN, lying on the floor in front of a plain desk and
chair in a huge stark white space.

KHUSH fades out. TARL slowly gets up just as she does at the start of the play. She goes to sit at the desk, picks up a red notebook and starts to write.

THE END

FOURTEEN

Fourteen was first performed at Watford Palace Theatre on 21st May 2014 with the following cast:

TINA, Yasmin Wilde

Writer, Gurpreet Kaur Bhatti
Director, Brigid Larmour
Designer, Ruari Murchison
Lighting Designer, Prema Mehta
Movement Director, Kate Flatt

Characters

TINA

Act One

April 1983. Sunday, early evening. At the side of the stage is a cheap divan single bed covered with a flowery pastel coloured duvet. An old fashioned radio cassette recorder is plugged in next to it and a frail dark wood single wardrobe is at the back. A block of stairs (six steps) is at the opposite side. Culture Club's 'Church of the poison mind' plays on the radio. It's nearly the end of the song. TINA, a fourteen year old Asian girl, ungainly, dumpy, rushes up the stairs and runs in. She's wearing an old shalwar kameez. She hurriedly finds a tape, puts it in the recorder. Presses play and record. The song finishes early and the DJ, Tommy Vance, announces the next song in the charts – Style Council's 'Speak like a Child'. TINA, stops the tape, takes the cassette out. She aggressively turns the radio off, approaches the stairs, holds up the cassette and calls out.

TINA: Too late! And she's mad about the harmonica bit. Mad about it! I'll have to wait till next Sunday now! And it's heading down the charts so there's no chance it'll be on Top of the Pops… She'll have to wait seven days! I hate you!… I'm not going back there next week!… I don't even believe in it… I hate God alright!… He's… he's useless…

She switches the radio back on. TINA listens to the Style Council for a moment, turns it off.

TINA: I miss The Jam.

She goes to the wardrobe and changes from her shalwar kameez into tracksuit bottoms and a sweatshirt. She puts the cassette back into the recorder – the last few bars of the song play and Tommy Vance's voice is heard. Cassette stops.

TINA: Promised Sharon I'd tape it for her. I was going to place it in her hand after the bell, on the way to the chemistry lab. We usually have a chat while we put on our white coats and safety glasses. Sharon's painted 'Choose Life' on the back of hers. I haven't. I always feel sad on Sunday night. If I ever decide to kill myself it'll be on a Sunday night. The world feels so small, like there's nothing in it. Songs of Praise makes it worse. *(Sings.)* 'In the bleak midwinter, frosty wind made moan!' No wonder all the Christians in Northern Ireland want to kill each other.

She finds her school bag by the wardrobe. Sound of shouting and screaming downstairs. TINA moves to the stairs and calls out.

TINA: Sorry for shouting before. Didn't mean it. Just because I'm agnostic doesn't mean he's useless. Sorry Dad.

She turns to the front. Sits on the bed with her school bag.

TINA: Sharon says the harmonica bit makes her feel all dreamy, she hums it and then she does dances like the drunks do on Vicarage Road precinct. I'll explain. It's not even that far, Durban Road... but we all have to get involved with the clearing up don't we? Every Sunday. At the end, he folds the white sheets, and me and Manjit Nagra get stuck with drying the cups. She sits in a corner whispering with Harvinder's mum and then has a fight with the ladies who make the tea. Too much cardamom, not enough clove. They're screaming by the time the Church Warden comes for the keys. If one of them could drive to the Gurdwara, this problem wouldn't have arisen. But he's too scared and she's... well... she's not scared. I do know it's wrong to lose my temper and I try not to. Still they don't seem to hear me if I do shout. I saw a mouse on the stairs once and I screamed so loud Miss Hitchcock knocked the front door. But they didn't hear. She was cleaning the Kenwood Chef, apparently, and Dad was watching World in Action.

She looks through her school books.

Did most of my homework Friday lunchtime. I can't be giving in shoddy work. I've been encouraging Sharon with her Latin. She's actually good but she refuses to memorise declensions or gerundives. Says she can't be arsed. Everything she shines at she seems to mess up. I mean she can get through a page of quadratic equations quicker than me, but then she goes 'I'm never gonna factorise a sack of potatoes am I?' 'And how's a Venn Diagram gonna change my world?'

Shouting and screaming downstairs. TINA gets up and goes to the top of the stairs.

Stop!

Shouting continues.

Shut up!

Shouting continues.

Will you listen to me! Somebody!

Shouting reaches a crescendo and then the front door slams. Quiet.

That's him gone up the precinct for sweet and sour pork balls. Better save me some.

She looks around the room, absorbs the silence.

I can still remember when we had a full house. My mum, my dad, me, my dad's mum Beji, my two illegal immigrant cousins Jaggy and Bal, Mr Aluwalia, my dad's friend, who slept in the dining room whenever his wife kicked him out and a young married couple who lived in a corner of the cellar. But then Beji got TB during the Montreal Olympics. And Dad helped Jaggy and Bal buy houses behind the football ground. And Mr Aluwalia left his wife and moved in with an Italian bloke who looked like John Travolta. I think the young couple got a council flat on the Meriden Estate. That summer when Beji died was so hot. I was on a Fab and a can of Lilt a day. While everyone was crying and wailing in the front room, I'd go up to the rose trees in our garden and pick the petals – red, yellow, white and pink, put them in a jam jar, mix with water and make perfume. Smelt like that Tweed off the adverts. One day I came home from school all excited but my dad had got in before me and had pulled all the rose trees out. Him and my two illegal immigrant cousins were planting rows and rows of mustard greens. Like they were making their own little corner of the Punjab in West Watford. I'd tell him about all the adverts on the telly that said Save Water. I'd try and make him understand that the white people would like us more if he didn't hose the grass and mustard greens twice a day but he'd just nod and say 'Hmmm' while he attached the hosepipe to the tap. I tried to say the neighbours would join the National Front if he didn't Save Water but he… he just kept on watering and smiled and said I was a good girl. It was the same summer Jaggy and Bal bought matching flares and joined the Anti-Nazi League. They don't come round any more. Not since she called Bal's mum a useless prostitute. Don't blame them.

Finds exercise book and pen. Comes back and sits on the bed.

Right then, Mr John Keats. *(Reads.)* 'Where are the songs of Spring? Ay, where are they? Think not of them, thou hast thy music too… ' *(Reads to herself.)* You know what, I reckon this poem could do with another verse. *(Scribbles frantically as she chants.)* 'I hate everybody, I hate everybody, I hate everybody, I hate everybody, I hate everybody, I hate everybody, except the body that is Sharon Esmerelda Collins!' Yeah. That's better.

She puts her pen down.

Dad said they spent ages trying to have me. Years. And when I came out, I cried all day and all night. Understandable how that might get on your nerves. She thought if she could have another go, the next one might be a bit more jolly. You know, the way they look in the Mothercare catalogue. But there were no more after me. Doctor said she was too old, Dad said he was relieved. He thinks she's dissatisfied. That's why she goes on at him. Poor Dad. Not his fault. She's always complaining that he's not taken the butter dish out on time. Or that there's a few crumbs of toast left in the grill pan. Once he left the toilet seat up and she threatened to stab him with a fork. It's not easy. And they didn't choose each other.

Sharon's made her choice.

First rays of sunshine in Cassiobury Park and she's trying to get a tan. Wants to make a good impression on Asif's mum. But she won't. I've told her strawberry blond won't go black. Not properly black.

And blue eyes can't turn brown overnight. Says she likes him though. Really likes him. And he's there day after day at the school gates, parked up behind the Radlett coach in his Datsun, waiting for her to walk up Lady's Close.

Sharon gets a glimpse of him and she stops dead. Transforms her navy A line into a mini. She saunters past and he winds his window down. I watch and wait. Hoping I won't miss *Blockbusters*. Sometimes she gets in the car but she never lets Asif drive off.

I sit on the wall. If I see the skinheads coming I knock the car window. But they're usually hanging out in the graveyard, trying to chat up one of the South Oxhey girls from Upper Five D.

Asif's mates show up at some point. Once I tried to make conversation about the problematic hygiene issues at Greenham Common, but the fat one laughed and the one with the moustache ignored me. If Mum saw me talking to them she'd go mad. 'Where are their women?' she always asks. 'Why don't they let them out, work down the factories, serve in their shops?' I dunno do I? I dunno what she's on about. Silly cow. But she doesn't like Asif and his lot. Calls them the Moghals. Apparently they did some unspeakable things to our ancestors, but that was then wasn't it? We've crossed continents since the sixteenth century.

If the skinheads turn up, Sharon's in trouble. They saw me and her walking through the subway on Exchange Road one time. Started their usual. 'Paki lover. Paki lover. Paki lover.' Sharon got her satchel and went to swipe one of them. She missed and they started laughing. I pointed out I was born in Shrodells and my parents are from North India. And just because me and Sharon sit next to each other in the majority of lessons... Well, they're wrong on all fronts.

She eyes her exercise book.

(Reads.) Keats brings the idea of Autumn's potential and qualities into the everyday world. He makes the season real in his poem.

He suggests that he is able to accept that the seasons change and that there is a cycle of life. Death, birth and death and birth.

I flipping hope there's more than that to look forward to. *(Looks up.)* I read the Ode out in class last week.

Mrs Taylor said my command of assonance was beautiful, even though Debbie Clark and her cronies laughed when I said bosom.

She gets up, inspects her body.

Sometimes I wonder what sex is like. I mean why would you want… that… that part of a man's body… anywhere near you. I get kissing and love and all that, I mean I think I do because it's on the telly and all that… but actually putting it inside… no thank you very much. Maybe you get used to it. I can't imagine my mum and my dad… probably was just the once.

Sits back down on the bed.

Sharon says she hasn't with Asif. I know she's come close but she's positive she won't. Not yet. Wonder what her mum'd say. Might even approve. She's dead excited about Greenham, and she's broadminded. I mean Sharon and her sisters all have different Dads. Sharon doesn't know her one. Must be handsome though, probably like that Richard thingy from *An Officer and a Gentleman.* Yeah, Richard thingy could be her Dad. And because he's not around, there are no arguments. They're so flipping happy.

Her Mum and my Dad were having a discussion about Arthur Scargill on Founder's Day. Dad reckons he could do with a haircut. And Sharon's Mum had to concede he's not as attractive as Dr David Owen. School finished early and we were all at a loss. Luckily Dad handles these situations with proficiency. He suggested the Golden Egg, and the four of us piled in. While her Mum was ordering her second knickerbocker glory, Sharon said Dad talked her through her options. He's kind like that. Helps people when they can't help themselves. She's doing the same as me now. Three sciences. History, Latin and French.

Picks up her exercise book.

(Writes.) Autumn matures all fruits with the friendly help of the sun. Taking the stanzas as a whole, the prime note of the poem is one of optimism. It is my view that John Keats was a victim of Pollyanna syndrome. *(Stops writing.)* Mrs Taylor said I could probably do my English A' level now. Says I'd get an A. That's stupid. I mean I'm only fourteen. Keeps telling me the world's my oyster.

The arguing starts again. TINA moves to the top of the stairs.

Why do people pray to God every Sunday, then come home and be like this?

If he cares about children, like they say, then why doesn't he stop it? God doesn't love me, or anyone, because he doesn't exist. When I'm old enough, I'll go to the doctor on my own and I'll say I can't sleep and he'll have to give me tablets. I'll crush them up and put them in her Ovaltine. She won't be in the mood for shouting then.

TINA climbs down the stairs. Jumps off one step, then two, then three, then four. She goes back to the top, looks down.

When I was little, jumping off the stairs felt like flying. Every year on my birthday I'd go a bit higher. I'd always fall badly and bruise my arms and knees. But I didn't mind. Actually I quite like the hurting.

She jumps off the fifth step, lands badly. Is hurt. Gets up, goes back up the stairs.

Nobody knows.

Screaming and shouting from downstairs. The telly is turned on.

Better go and have my roti. Pork ball if I'm lucky. *The Professionals*'ll be on soon.

Theme tune from 'The Professionals' plays. She heads downstairs. Lights dim.

SCENE TWO

Days later. TINA walks in. She's wearing her school uniform. She seems in a daze. Her schoolbag is on her bed. Paces around in a circle.

TINA: They shouldn't have done that. Not fair. Four Goliaths against one David. He's not young or strong like them. Wait till I tell Sharon. She'll know what to do.

Looks down at her hands.

I'm shaking.

She grabs her bag. Finds a club biscuit at the bottom. Gobbles it up.

Think he needs a cuddle. Mum's no use. Hasn't said a word. Too busy chopping onions for the palak paneer. And he's… he's in a heap.

Said he went to Sainsburys. Got me a mandarin trifle like I asked. And he bought the usual. You know, the stuff she writes down on her flipping list. And a tray of twenty four eggs. Because I said I wanted to make fairy cakes on Saturday. He bought them for me. He was pulling the trolley behind him and he's very gentle so he was holding the tray, balancing it on his arm. He walked through the high street, you know, past Chelsea Girl and Top Shop and Charter Place. Right at the sweet shop that smells of humbugs and smoky pipes. Past St Mary's Church and then he got to the graveyard. Ambling along like he does. And the skinheads came over and stood in front of him. Asked if they could count his eggs. He tried to carry on, but he couldn't get through. They took the tray out of his hand and started smashing the eggs on his face, on his head, on his checked jacket. There's yolk and white and shell all on the fluff now. He hasn't got another jacket, not like that. He said they were laughing at him. People walked past and didn't say a word. He came in all shouty and upset. I found a tea towel. Wiped him down.

She looks down at herself.

It's all on me.

She picks up her pillow, wipes herself down. Holds the pillow.

He's sitting on the floor in the front room crying in front of Nationwide. Kept saying 'Am I a good father? Am I a good father?' Course you are I told him. Put my arm round him. And I told him, it'll be okay. It will. But he just pushed me off. It won't, he said. It bloody won't.

Perhaps I should ring Sharon. They always have good conversations those two.

Checks her watch.

She'll be having her tea. English people have tea you see. Knowing my Mum, dinner won't be in front of the telly till the end of *Dallas*.

Dunno why the skinheads hate us so much. I know a couple of them. Russell Cooper and Keith Nelson were the year before me in the Juniors. Keith got called fleabag because his Mum never wiped his nose and Russell was good at rounders. He sang 'We plough the fields and scatter' at the Harvest Festival one year. Voice wasn't bad but it didn't merit a solo in my opinion. If I'd known he'd end up shaving his head and strutting around in a Harrington, I'd have chucked a couple of tins for the old people at him.

If the skinheads talked to my Dad they'd realise he's normal, there's nothing to hate. He likes a sausage sandwich and Dave Allen and Man United. He doesn't deserve egg all over his hair, down his checked jacket. I used to feel sorry for Keith, the boys used to push him about and sing 'Skinny white legs and knobbly knees, doodah, doodah'.

Wish they'd done it to me. I find things easy to bear. Lock them up in a compartment and forget. Takes Dad a long time to get over things. He had a migraine for eight weeks once. Can't stand seeing him sad. You know what I want, what I'd like to do… I need, I need…

She finds a tennis racket from her wardrobe and puts something unseen into her pocket.

This. *(She acts out the following action.)*

She runs down the stairs.

Right. *(Runs on the spot.)* Up Vicarage Road. Into the subway. Hold my nose so I don't smell the wee.

Past the tramp and Hayley Morton snogging whatsisname from the Boys' school. Into the graveyard. I don't care that it's getting dark. I don't care that I'm on my own and that I haven't got a coat or a door key. *(Stops.)* All I care about is finding a gang of bastard white boys. Hopefully it's Russell and Keith and that lot, but if it isn't, anyone'll do.

She produces scissors from her pocket. Brandishes them with menace.

Get them to kneel. Why not? Makes your blood flow having someone in front of you, head bowed. Imagine how fantastic God feels on a Sunday in St Michael's Church Hall, Durban Road. And then…

She lifts the tennis racket above her head. Starts methodically hitting at imagined kneeling young men. She whacks the racket hard, repeatedly, until she is breathless.

You crack their heads open. Leaves a right mess. Just like a tray of eggs.

She drops the racket.

Wish I could do something. But I can't.

Sits on the bed, composes herself. Checks the time.

Coronation Street might cheer him up.

Opens her school bag.

(Reads.) The Parent Teacher Association invites you to the Annual Barn Dance. They go every year. He has a pineapple juice and she takes a thermos. They sit and

smile politely and nod while they watch the other parents
kissing and cuddling from too much Cinzano Bianco.
Can't imagine them dancing. She's been known to clap
her hands at a wedding, but you'd need a forklift truck to
move her feet. Bet he'd like to though. I could show him...
I mean it's just country dancing for old people isn't it?

Gets up, does a choreographed series of country dancing steps.

We could sit next to each other in the main hall, it's all
dark and they stick those disco traffic lights in the corners.
I could do introductions. Marion Hart's Dad writes
columns in a newspaper and Esther Allywood's parents
run their own business, stuffing envelopes. I'm sure they'd
find common ground. All dad needs is to come out of his
shell. If she wasn't in the picture, things'd be different.
Me and him could've watched *The Maltese Falcon* the other
night instead of *Name That Tune.* We could buy chicken pies
from Bejam, I mean I learned all about mashed potatoes in
Home Economics. We're perfectly capable of fending for
ourselves. It'd be... picture perfect. If there was just a way
of her going...

*Suddenly TINA keels over in pain. She finds a packet of sanitary
towels in her bag, goes behind the bed and puts one in her pants
– unseen.*

Never realised it would hurt so much. She moans that now
I'm getting older I'm expensive.

Puts the packet away.

She says back home they washed a towel by hand.

She comes to lie down on the bed.

And she says I eat too much. Can't help it.

Finds another club biscuit at the bottom of her bag.

Feel better if I feel full.

Eats the biscuit.

He escapes at night. After the news. I followed him once.
He walked round the block. Had a wee down an alley.

Then I watched him go home. That's his night out. Having a wee. I sat on the front wall for ages. Thought I saw Asif's Datsun crawling up the road, but I could have been wrong.

I stared at the streetlights and thought this must be what Keats and that lot go on about when they look at sunsets and nature.

Every summer holiday Mrs Taylor asks us to write about where we've been. Alice and Elizabeth are always complaining about how France and Spain are too hot. And Sharon goes camping in a van with her mad mum.

I don't have the heart to say we go shopping up Southall Broadway, so I say we always visit a special spot in the West Country which isn't exactly a lie. At least when you're out there's life around you. Even if it's not yours. Suppose that's why he gets his coat ready after nine o'clock. Though he might not tonight. Maybe we should call the police, about the eggs. Maybe I'll tell Mrs Taylor as well as Sharon. Tell the whole school. Make them announce it in assembly and say it's wrong and that he doesn't deserve it and I don't and it's not fair. Or maybe it's best to forget it.

She gets up, approaches the stairs.

Pretend it never happened.

She jumps and hurts herself. She climbs back to the top of the stairs. And prepares to jump again. Lights dim.

SCENE THREE

Beginning of May. Nino Roto's 'Romeo and Juliet' theme plays in the background to Simon Bates' 'Our Tune'. He finishes talking and 'Our Tune' fuses into Dusty Springfield's 'You Don't Have to Say You Love Me'. Fades out. TINA kneels in front of a mirror, she's backcombing her hair.

TINA: We're not meant to go out at lunchtime. She's asked me before and I've always said no. Rules are there for a reason. Sharon dares me. I don't do dares I tell her. Not since that pushbike ran over my foot on Wiggenhall Road.

She started getting angry. Said how can we be best friends if we never go out? Didn't know what to say. She knows I'm not allowed out except to school or the doctors. Said she didn't want to go on her own. Said she needed to meet Asif and it was important. What's wrong with after school I asked. Said she was busy. I told her there was a debate on in the common room. I'm second speaker in 'This house believes that an oxo cube has a greater function than Princess Diana.' Mrs Taylor helped me formulate my arguments. The other speakers are from the Lower Sixth but she reckons I'm more than a match. I can't just… not… show up. Then Sharon said she'd ask Debbie Clark. 'But she called you a tart' I reminded her. 'After hockey when you were wearing that black bra'.

Sharon said she didn't care. Least Debbie was a laugh. Least she was brave. Least she had a life. I blinked so she wouldn't see the tears. I mean everyone's got a life haven't they? If you're breathing, you must have. Sharon was about to walk off and I stopped her. What about if I walked up the high street with her? Say just up to McDonalds? I could eat my sandwiches on the way. And wear my plimsoles so I could run back, after all Karen Elgin's First Speaker and she's not exactly famed for her brevity. Sharon grinned. She has got great teeth!

Finishes her hair. Starts applying make-up.

By the time we got to McDonalds I was starving. Ate my sandwiches at recess because all she'd left for breakfast was half a rich tea biscuit. I was sure I had an orange club at the bottom of my bag but when I checked – nothing. Asif met her outside. I was about to turn and go when he asked if I fancied a spot of lunch. Don't eat beef do I? Suddenly a voice pipes up 'How about a filet of fish? Or a chicken burger?' It was the moustachioed one. 'She likes chocolate milkshake' says Sharon. 'Bet she does' says old moustachio. And he opens the door to McDonalds. I looked in and I saw this bloke smiling. Looked like Luther Blissett, thought

I might get an autograph. Mrs Taylor said she expected to the common room to be packed. Why wouldn't it be?

Everyone was looking forward to a battle between two icons of our time – Princess Di and a beef oxo cube. My stomach rumbled when I thought of the oxo cube and I wondered how Karen Elgin might cope on her own.

Sharon took my arm and we walked in. Me and her sat by the window while Asif and moustachio queued up for the food. 'Told you this'd be fun' says Sharon.

I didn't say anything. I had a closer look and it wasn't Luther Blissett. Wasn't even a bloke! Sharon and Asif went to sit at another table, I was about to go with them when Moustachio came back. He'd got me a chicken burger and a filet of fish and two large fries so I couldn't complain. Then he said he needed the loo. Took ages. I'd finished eating by the time he got back. Didn't realise the chicken burger was for him did I? Got a bit moody with me when I asked if I could have an apple pie but he still went up and got in the queue. Was getting a bit heated on Sharon's table. Asif started shouting at her. Got her by the scruff of her neck. She pushed him away and came over. We're going she says. I told her I was waiting for pudding when she pulls me up and starts walking back. Chucked him she goes. Wouldn't tell me why? Even though I was asking and asking. We get to Exchange Road and go under the subway. I always hold my nose and run, I mean it's like inhaling a toilet down there, but suddenly she stops, looks at me and goes 'You're a good friend Tina. Whatever happens, you're my good friend.' What does she mean 'whatever happens'. What's she on about? Seems brighter though. Even linked her arm in mine.

She inspects her make-up. Starts messing up the eyeliner round her eyes so it looks as though she has black eyes. Takes a hand mirror, holds it up to her face.

We got back late. Walked straight into double English. We're reading 'I am David'. He's on his way to Salonica. They were all quiet when we walked in. Mrs Taylor stared.

Her face was red. She asked me what happened. Couldn't speak. Sharon sat down and opened her book. Mrs Taylor starts shouting. Apparently I've let the team down. Says she'd invited the Head of English from the Boys School. People have expectations. In this school, we expect them to be met. What did I have to say for myself? Couldn't move. Needed the toilet. She goes 'You think you're very clever don't you'. I don't actually. She's the one who's always going on about it. 'Well you're not,' she barks. You're pathetic and stupid.' Debbie and Alice and Elizabeth and the rest started to laugh. I think they were more shocked than being horrible. Never seen Mrs Taylor like this before. Her voice is usually soft and gentle, you know like the deodorant. She's like mums are supposed to be, you know on adverts. Said my behaviour had changed her opinion of me. Said she was giving me a detention. I sat down and turned to page 59, where we'd left off. Mrs Taylor told Alice to start reading even though it wasn't her turn. I was going to get up to go but I knew she'd tell me to sit down so I didn't bother getting up. Rachel Cooper noticed first. She sits behind me. Copies my notes sometimes even though I've asked her not to. Rachel jumps up, makes a face. 'Silly cow has pissed herself' she goes. I'm trying to concentrate on the next paragraph, but what was hot and wet a minute ago is cold and damp now. And now they are all laughing.

Really having a good old laugh. I look at Sharon, but she won't look back at me. Bitchface Taylor shouts at me to go and get myself cleaned up. So I go.

Her make-up is all over her face by now. She looks a real mess. Finds her school uniform and scissors. Starts cutting it up.

Haven't been back. I wrote a note and got her to sign it. Inflammation around the tonsils can be hard to shift. She says I'm developing too quickly. That I'm not to open the door to the milkman or the postman.

Being at home's not so bad. Crown court and Heinz tomato. And she's at work. There's plenty of activity in a hospital laundry.

So, I'm missing character analysis in *Jane Eyre* and a quiz on the periodic table. Think I'll live. Sharon's been asking for me. Dad says he saw her mum on the way home from the Junction. Sharon's phoned as well. Didn't know she even had the number. Suppose I should be pleased.

I want to see how this shoplifting case ends now, you know on Crown Court. Dad asks me if I'm alright. Bought me a packet of Tunes the day after it happened. But I can tell he's sad. Still hasn't got over the eggs. Goes out earlier now, before Nationwide. He's always back for his roti. Suppose you build up an appetite walking. They haven't spoken for eleven weeks.

It's the May Fair down Cassiobury this weekend. He keeps saying we'll go but I won't. The fair's a dream. Like Willy Wonka and The Wizard of Oz mixed up.

When I was in infants, Dad took me and two girls from my class. We wore frilly dresses and he bought us candy floss and toffee apples. Someone won a cuddly dinosaur. Me and my friends wanted to go on the Big Wheel, Dad said no at first, said we were too young, but we screamed and begged and the blokes on it didn't care so we went on. We all started crying before we got to the top. He was right, we were too little. He held onto us though and we were okay. We all got separated in the Hall of Mirrors. Everywhere I looked my body was different shapes and my face wasn't my face. I kept looking and looking and eventually… luckily we found each other and my Dad was… he was there. Thank you God. He was there. He held our hands and we had hotdogs on the bridge over the river. Think we went to Whippendell Wood later. I can't remember. But I'm sure… I'm sure it was the best day of my life. What were their names? … Jane… Lisa… I think Jane went to Bushey and Lisa… I don't know…

Her uniform is now in smithereens. Beholds the scissors.

Dad says we're a warrior race.

She holds up the uniform.

Don't suppose I'll need this again.

SCENE FOUR

TINA is wearing navy tracksuit bottoms and an Aertex PE top. She smashes a hockey ball with a hockey stick across the stage. Her eyes trace the arc of the ball's flight.

TINA: When it lands in the middle, when you get it right, it's so... perfect... like the most perfect moment... and that's why you keep trying again and again... to make it feel like that, to feel like... like... Bjorn Borg.

She goes to find the ball, contemplates it as she puts the stick down.

I'm more used to getting hit by the ball. Recently though I've been helping Louise Willis practise. She's goalie for the fourth year. She's going blind in one eye. Says it makes her look harder out of the other one. Keeps her extra vigilant, so she doesn't miss a trick. Tells me not to worry where the ball goes, just to whack it as hard as I can.

Picks up the stick. Swings it.

I smashed her kneecap last Wednesday. She took it quite well. Says she's getting used to the plaster. Says it gives her more support than she imagined. Doubts she'll ever get it removed. Me and her go down the pitch most lunchtimes.

We were on our way the other day when Sharon stopped me by the Science block. Asked if I fancied chips after school. I didn't. Have to get straight back these days. My mum's stopped cooking. Keeps crying all the time. I found her sat by the mop bucket the other day clutching a bottle of dettol like the drunks hold onto their beer cans down the precinct. Anyway the dinner's my responsibility now. And I need to start boiling potatoes for my mash straight after *Blockbusters*, so I can't do chips with Sharon can I? Then Louise calls me to get a move on. So I start walking off… 'Wait,' says Sharon… ' but I couldn't listen… so I just said 'I have to go' and got myself to the pitch.

When I walked back into the classroom for the first time, it was like everyone had forgotten, except me. Mrs Taylor smiled nervously when I got to my desk. Said she knows I'm a winner and winners don't drop the ball. Silly cow. We've finished *I Am David*, so it's onto the *Moonstone* now. Agatha Christie without Hercule Poirot.

I can't get excited. And that picture of Wilkie Collins on the cover's making me very conscious of my facial hair. Sharon sits on her own most days, like she's in another world. I'm next to Cheryl, who's fourth in line to Debbie Clark.

My dad's out with his leaflets straight after work. Says he's never met a man who stimulates him as much as Dr David Owen. He reckons he's our saviour and the only way forward for the country is the middle way, especially after the Falklands'. I was helping him attach safety pins to rosettes the other day when I told him what I was predicted, Mrs Taylor's already going on about University and entrance exams and colleges built by mediaeval folk. I told Dad I'm working really hard. That I'll give him something to be proud of when that results letter comes. I'll make our fortune with my brains and then we can be free. He carried on folding leaflets and said he thought Dr Owen's plan to replace Polaris with Trident was a good one and that Michael Foot should never have worn that donkey jacket. I stood there and stared while he got his bag and walked out. It's not like him to not listen. I'm sure it's not. I'm sure once the election's out the way, he'll be back to normal.

She's losing weight. She ate a few baked beans last night but she won't touch my potato. Should have taught me how to make roti. I see her take a few mouthfuls of cornflakes in the morning but it's not enough. I'll buy some Gold top milk. And I'll check the side effects of those tablets.

TINA finds a tracksuit top, puts it on. Sits on the bed.

I don't always go straight home. And not because I'm going to Sainsburys or Bejam. I just walk around town. Looking at stuff and seeing what it makes me feel. Like John Keats. Sometimes I see old Moustachio. His name's Farrukh.

The first time he was sitting on a bench outside C&A when he called me over. I had a few of Dad's leaflets with me so I took the opportunity to explain the value of a strong public sector alongside a vibrant market economy. He asked if I wanted a Benson and Hedges. I didn't. He's at college apparently. Says he wants to be a sound engineer. Fat chance. Not after he failed all his CSEs. I asked about Asif and he went quiet. Wouldn't say what happened between him and Sharon. Even though I kept asking. I still think about her all the time. Close my eyes and I see her mousy hair and shiny teeth. Moustachio says if I ever want a milkshake to tell him. He's always about.

When I think about it. I am hungry and I am thirsty.

She gets up uneasily.

And I'm getting sick of mashed potato. She should have taught me. She's picking up a prescription so she won't realise. Doesn't even realise who I am. She called me Nina the other day. It's Tina not Nina. She named me, she should know. He's canvassing voters round Tolpits Lane. Better not get his head kicked in.

She starts to walk.

Up Vicarage road. Down the subway. Hold my nose. Through the graveyard. There's the High Street. I can see Moustachio. Hanging out with his mates, but not Asif. He looks at me hard, like he's confused, but then he smiles like Ronald MacDonald and we go inside. He gets me a Quarterpounder. I tell him I don't eat beef. But he thinks I should try it. So I do.

She sits down. Produces a tray of MacDonalds food from under the wardrobe, finishes off eating it.

And I like it. So much. I want the same again. So he gets it for me. I am bloody starving.

Gets up.

Ready to go now. Thanks. It was tasty. What's the big deal about a cow? They're not dirty like pigs are they? Or are pigs clean. I don't know. Anyway thanks. We're walking out and I feel ill. I'm not stupid. I know he's gonna try something. We get to Timothy Whites and he grabs my elbow and sort of lurches his lips at me in the doorway. I say no thanks. Sorry but no. And he looks at me. And at my top and he tells me to lift it up. Says he won't touch. I don't want to. I don't. But he has paid and I haven't got any money. We never have any money. So I…

She half lifts her top.

He's paid and so he must deserve something. Mrs Isaac taught us about quid pro quo in Latin and I'm only… it's only cos he bought me so much and it's not cheap and he'll never be a sound engineer cos he's so thick. I show him for a minute and then I turn and…

Starts running, gets breathless.

And I get to Perrings and suddenly Asif's there. I don't know what he's doing cos I haven't seen him for ages and he tells me to stop. And I don't know why I do. Cos I'm stupid. Cos he's telling me to. Cos I've got a stitch. I didn't really want the second milkshake or that apple pie. Asif says he wants to talk to me. I'm no good at talking I tell him. I just want him to leave me alone but he looks at me and… and… his face creases up and he says he loves her. He still loves her. I don't get it… And then he shouts… ' She broke my heart! The bitch broke my heart'. Begs me to tell her to take him back. He's pleading, nearly crying by now. So I put my hand on his shoulder and then I hear a scream, it's coming from Market Street. And I look up and it's my… it's her. On the way back from the surgery with a trolleyful of tablets. And then she's on me. Pulling my hair, punching my stomach. 'Kuthee, haramjadee'

[Bitch/whore]... I try and tell her I haven't done anything but I can't speak cos she keeps kicking my face. I crawl around and stagger up and Asif's gone and I tell her it's not my fault she couldn't have another baby.

A better one than me. And I start running. I don't stop... until I get to green trees and the No Cycling sign that I used to cycle over when my Dad taught me to ride my Tomahawk. And I'm safe cos I'm in Cassiobury, cos it's still open and even though it's getting dark a few people are about with their dogs and their roller skates. And I stop and... I breathe. Properly breathe. Fresh air. It's lovely. Then suddenly in one second I stop breathing. I see... I see... I spot the leaflets first. In his carrier bag that he always carries. He's not wearing his rosette though. He's sitting on a bench. Next to Sharon. With his brown hands on her white skin. Touching her, kissing her...

I close my eyes. Wishing for blindness like Louise Willis. And I walk home with my eyes like that, hoping that something runs me over before I make it to the front door.

SCENE FIVE

June 9. Election Day. TINA walks into her bedroom. She's wearing her school uniform and carrying her school bag. She sits on the floor, opens her bag, takes out an exercise book.

TINA: Mrs Taylor reckons I'm in danger. Started off with that A minus. Then a B plus. Then another A minus and now a B. She says my standards are slipping. I think Benvolio was a homosexual, she disagrees and suddenly I've got a B. Silly cow. She doesn't know all of Romeo's secrets. Nobody does. Not even pissing Juliet. And who cares?

Discards the exercise book.

Who cares anyway? What's the point? Whatever happens, nothing happens. Teachers don't know shit. Nothing the rest of us can't copy out of books. He's folding leaflets downstairs. She's down the Gurdwara most days. Even stays overnight sometimes. He'll be up the polling station later. Tonight's his big night.

She produces a packet of Benson and Hedges from her bag. Takes a cigarette. Lights it and starts to smoke.

We were looking at frogspawn and there weren't enough microscopes. Me and Sharon had to share. She started crying when I told her I'd seen them. I asked her why and she said he gives her stuff. 'But you've got everything,' I said. She just looked at me and started laughing. She was still crying but smiling and I dunno, it was weird. I asked if he made her… and she didn't say anything… I got angry, got her pretty face in my hand and asked her again. 'Did he make you?'… She sort of nodded…

TINA moves to the stairs, calls out.

Dad!…

'Are you saying he… he… forced you'. No answer…

(Calls.) Can you come here a minute? Dad!… .

She moved my hands off her face. And I'm like… I have to know!

(Calls.) I wanna ask you something.

You have to tell me Sharon!… .Then she looked at me hard, right through me and she goes…' But you know Tina, you must already know.' And she walks off.

She looks down the stairs.

(Calls.) You could still win Dad. No matter what the papers say. The war's over.

And he walks up the stairs. It's over.

Puts out her cigarette.

And I put my arms round him, hold him tight, like he must have held me when I was a baby. And we smile at each other and then I push him and he tumbles. And he tumbles.

And I can't believe I've done it but I have and then I…

She walks down the stairs. Stops, stares.

He keeps moaning 'Why'… 'Why'… And I just… *(Shrugs.)*
And then I see him getting up, ever so slowly… So I open
the front door… And now… I don't know what it is…
except it's now.

Lights down.

Act Two

2014. A weekday. TINA's flat. A teenager's single bed at the back. Posters of Jake Bugg and a couple of decent bands on a wall. A table and chairs at the front. A kitchen unit which is cupboard/drawers cum work surface at the side. The place is clean and comfortable. It's an Ikea job through and through. There's a bright rug on the floor and everything's nice, spick and span. TINA enters carrying shopping bags and post. She's dressed in casual oversized Primark. Cheap trainers. She looks tired, older than her 44 years. She's gained weight. TINA chucks the post on the table and sits down. Takes a packet of posh biscuits out of a carrier bag. Hurriedly opens the biscuits. Stuffs one in her mouth. She savours every mouthful.

TINA: Oh yeah… Oh yeah.

She takes another one. Eats. Tastes orgasmic.

TINA: I needed that. Apparently Ocado deliver round the clock, so there's always some van driver ringing Miranda's bell. I've had these biscuits three weeks in a row now. Says she over-orders. Says the boys hack her computer to find out her password, she keeps changing it but they're too quick. A crate of Diamond White and five boxes of Krispy Kremes arrived last Friday. That can't be right, I mean Jasper's only nine. I tell her to hide her credit card but she says it's easier said than done. They chuck out half of what they buy. I should know, I'm the one emptying the bins. Anyway I protest but she insists. Says I should consider it a tip. Says I deserve extras. And… I am grateful.

She gets up, starts unpacking the shopping. Removes a large birthday cake, regards it, convinces herself it's worthy of admiration.

TINA: Yeah, it's good. It's alright. Jam and buttercream. Marzipan on the inside of the icing. She'll like it, she will. I didn't want it to be too… y'know… and it's not, it's fine. Fine.

Puts it on the table.

TINA: I showed Miranda. Her daughter Isobel's birthday is the week after. Same age as well would you believe? Miranda's organised a day spa for a load of Isobel's friends and then a DJ in a hall. She invited Amber... but I told her... Amber won't want to miss *X-Factor*.

She gets a text. Reads it, chucks the phone down. She's visibly shaken but composes herself. Goes back to the shopping.

TINA: Miranda asked me if I think manicures and pedicures are enough. Be fine I told her. She wondered if she should choose a package that includes a hair removal option. If you like I said. But what do you think Tina, she goes. You know how much I value your opinion. I dunno do I? If they're a hairy lot, then yeah maybe. I mean I was at that age. Still am. Nothing wrong with a tube of Veet. Fraction of the price of a day spa and you can stick it on in front of *Dragon's Den*. Miranda's never heard of Veet. Went all wide-eyed and called me a 'mine of information' before she added it to her Ocado list.

I used to address her as Mrs Sheldon. But she wasn't having it. Says she feels we have a connection. All this dropping of Mister, missus, miss, they used to do it at Amber's primary school and I hate it, blurs things. I mean they're where they are and you're... just... you're you. Then she asks me what I'm doing for Amber's big day. Pissing Miranda! I told her I'm keeping things simple. Might do a day spa and a DJ when she's 16 but not now. I mean fourteen's not... in my view it lacks significance... and my daughter's never been one for mass gatherings... she's more of a one-to-one type. We both are. She's got a group. Good girls, Martha and Lottie and Nasreen. They'll play their terrible music while I listen to Sister Sledge on my headphones. I might even set them a quiz. Oh and, I've got that pizza flyer somewhere, saved it for Saturday.

Rummages around in her bag. Finds one. Beams.

Any pizza any size. Nine ninety nine. Shit... only on Tuesdays.

Text again.

(Sharp.) Leave me alone.

She grabs her phone, doesn't read text, turns it to silent.

TINA: Pissing Jaggy!

Paces about.

I can't go into West Watford now can I? I've just got in. It's two buses or a minicab so I can't. And with the one-way system I might not even make it till… tomorrow. Cab costs too much. I'm saving a cab for his funeral. Suppose I could walk. Been walking all day. I mean I pay for his pendant alarm. Jaggy knows I pay. Direct debit. I've kept it going for two years. I'll go tomorrow. Yeah, tomorrow. I was planning to visit anyway and drop off his incontinence pads. Besides, the carers'll be in soon. Jaggy's with him. And Bal might pass round. Anyway he's had a charmed life. No major health problems. Doctor says he's just old. And weak. Plus he's only fallen out of bed. Not that far to the floor. Carpet's at least two-ply with underlay. *(Checks phone.)* He's fine. Good at surviving falls. Sitting up and eating chips now. It's two buses and Amber'll be home from school soon. I don't want her coming back to an empty house today. She always comes back to an empty house and I only have one day a week when I can sit down and listen. Properly listen. She knows I'm not one to turn down work. I'm not having her going without.

I left home straight after I did the pregnancy test. Mum and Dad didn't even notice. They stopped asking me questions after my O'level results.

Doesn't matter what Jaggy or Bal think. 'Don't you care Tina'… 'He's so lonely Tina'… 'He's your bloody Dad'… 'You could make an effort, you lazy kuthee *[bitch]*.' Well, I'm trying my best. He's never short of pads. He's lucky he's got decent carers. Not like those ones on *Panorama* who slap you round the face and call you names. Nobody deserves that. Not even him.

I looked into doing it, you know home care. But… round here they want you to have a car cos the buses are so shit. They want you to do all that wiping and washing and being kind and loving someone like your own for seven pound fifty an hour. Think I'd enjoy it actually but I'd never see Amber because of the shifts and I'd lose my housing benefit. Besides I'm getting at least a tenner an hour off Miranda and she's recommended me to some of her mates. Cash in hand. It's only cooking and cleaning but they're so appreciative. It's like they never learned how to do the basics and now they're too scared to chop an onion or sweep a floor.

TINA gets up, takes off her coat. Puts on her slippers.

TINA: She passed my number to her friend Deborah Montague. Lives in a detached on the Cassiobury Estate. Not as big as Miranda's but impressive enough. The husband's something to do with computers. She's training in Reiki. Two lovely kids and a nanny six days a week. Miranda explained she was desperate for help.

TINA finds a couple of onions, starts chopping them on the table.

Deborah opened the door and our eyes locked across the sizeable porch. Could tell she wasn't sure but I recognised her straight away. Debbie Clark. Used to be in my class. Never had that much to do with each other but we hovered around the same corridors and dungeons like you did at our school. I remember once coming out of Miss Kennedy's office, she'd just informed me I'd won the second year prize for achievement and Debbie was waiting on a bench in the foyer. She'd been told off for wearing eyeliner and had called the form prefect a slag. She was on her third detention that week so Mrs Taylor sent her to see the Headmistress. She'd been crying and I felt sorry for her. I mean at that moment… she had nothing and I had everything. I tried to catch her eye, give her a smile, tell her it'd be alright. That she could change her ways and be different… that there was hope… but I never got the chance cos she never looked up. Even though she must have known I was there.

Still chopping. Stops.

Deborah Montague smiled and showed me in. She was about to give me the tour when I stopped her and said… I was just passing to say that I couldn't help her out… that I was sorry but I was booked up. Cooking and cleaning round the clock and plus I needed to help Amber with her homework now and again. She looked disappointed and said if a space came up… I said of course. I'd let her know. Promised I would. Even though I won't. She shut the door and I decided to go and sign on a bit early.

Composes a reply to text.

'Fish in butter sauce in freezer. Tell him will be round Tom for ready meal delivery. Tell him am thinking of him.' *(Thinks.)* That's a lie. *(Deletes.)* Delete. No need for untruths. Best to focus on the practicalities.

Pushes the chopped food to one side. Starts opening the post.

Miranda reckons I'm overqualified. Stupid cow. I told her I've only got one A'level. English Lit Grade A. She says it's not that, it's my spirit, my inquiring mind. I'm not bothered. I like working on my own. And it's amazing how much satisfaction you get from applying Mr Muscle to caked on mould. She once said if her PA, Jill, ever left, there'd be an opening for me. But then I'm sure Jill had that shingles scare last year and Miranda went and got a temp in.

Anyway I'm not slagging her off. She's been good to me and she's got a lot on her plate. Running the business. Board of governors at the school. And she's got her hands full with that Jasper. He's getting worse. Out of control.

Opens a letter. Tuts.

TINA: I've told the school already. No! I help out where I can. Hotdog stall at the Summer Fair and I'm happy. Don't mind verifying the answers for the Quiz Night or mopping up the parents' sick after the Christmas disco but… pissing hell, Sponsored Strictly, no thanks. Not with my coordination. I was heading for the top deck of the bus the other day. We were pulling out of the Junction and I fell over my Bag For Life and tumbled down the stairs. Nobody said anything. Bumped my knee. Didn't mind. Used to it. I was always falling down stairs when I was young. Still got the scars. Warrior marks. Who used to say we're a warrior race? *(Thinks for a minute.)* Someone. Martha mentioned that her Dad, Clive, might offer himself up for the paso doble. He's on his own as well. Amber was egging her on. I know what they're up to. But I'm not interested. Once was enough with Amber's Dad. I keep Martha sweet for Amber's sake. But her Dad… .Reminds me of Lofty from *EastEnders*. Not what you'd call one of life's natural winners. Best if we stay away from each other.

Finds a pen. Takes the letter. Reads and ticks as she reads.

Sponsored Strictly. No… Christmas show. Yes… Can I donate… No… Do I want to receive further emails… .No, not really. But I'll say yes for my daughter's sake… Cake sale. Yes… Do I have any old, unwanted clothes?

Thinks for a minute. Looks down at her shabby attire.

I'm wearing them.

She tears the slip off.

Truth is I do know a few moves. Me and my mate Karen used to go to salsa one night a week. There were never enough men, so I obliged and I got reasonably mediocre at the samba. Karen was desperate to meet someone. Think she did, some bloke outside the toilets. I don't bother calling her any more. Not now we've got Freeview.

She gets up, opens the food cupboard. Takes out a tin.

Kidney bean Bolognese. Again. Banana and a jammy dodger for pudding. Fantastic. When you watch the news, makes you realise me and Amber are extremely fortunate. I see all that suffering in Syria and Turkey and everywhere… and it makes me cry.

She looks around the room.

Least we've got the flat. And food. And the telly. She has meat at school so… you don't need meat every day do you? She gets free dinners. But she doesn't know, so I pretend to pay. Don't want her feeling… unusual. That's how I used to feel. I'm not messing it up for her. I might be finished, but she's just about to start.

TINA starts opening the tin.

She'll need a good meal when she gets in.

SCENE TWO

Saturday afternoon. 'Don't You Want Me Baby' by the Human League blares out of an ancient ghetto blaster. Blown-up balloons float around the flat. TINA is dressed up in black trousers and a sparkly Primark top. She fusses around tidying the already tidy flat up – altering the angles of chairs and arranging party poppers on the table. Occasionally TINA gets into the music and breaks out into a few steps of the paso doble. Intermittently she puts up expensive-looking decorations above Amber's bed. Music fades. TINA starts sticking balloons up on the wall.

TINA: Wasn't planning to decorate. But then Miranda had all this stuff left over from Isobel's Do. Went well by all accounts, except for that minor incident. She handed out iTunes gift cards instead of party bags. Each to their own. Amber's too old for party bags IMHO. When she told me what happened, I wasn't surprised. He's very… sensitive is Jasper. Wants his Mum's undivided. You can't though can you? Give them everything. Anyway Miranda was alloting the caterers their key tasks when Jasper wee-ed all over the DJ's speakers. She's paying for new ones of course, the money's not a problem, it's the fact that he took it out and pissed on the stage in front of everybody. Miranda's sister-in-law thinks he wants sectioning. I'm not so sure.

She moves over to put balloons up on the other side of the flat. As she moves over she does a few paso doble moves.

TINA: Oh no, shit, that's the man's bit. Keep thinking I'm the Matador instead of the Bull. Knew this would happen.

Hope they don't throw eggs. I've never been au fait
with stilettos so Clive said I can wear my trainers. Can't
risk breaking my ankle, not in my line of work. Amber
convinced me in the end. Said I should get involved. Said I
might make friends with some of the other mums. I smiled
and agreed that might be nice.

Her face darkens. She's suddenly angry.

Why would I wanna be mates with those bitches? They
never even look at me, never mind talk to me. It's like I'm
empty space. Just because I don't go to Zumba and I'm
not a project manager. I'm still human. Miranda and her
private school mates have got too much money to give
a shit but the middle middles, they like to let you know
they're better, so they can feel like they're somebody.
Sorry… *(Suddenly remembers herself.)* … I don't mean to be
bitchy. I'm sure they're decent people, just like to keep
myself to myself, that's all.

Does a couple more moves.

One, two. One, two, three, four… Clive's not so bad. He
is boring. And stupid. Not as tall as Lofty. And he's never
gonna enter Mr Universe. But then I'm no understudy for
Angelina.

Puts up some more decorations. Contemplates the room.

She's gonna love this. I've always made a point of marking
her moments. Never really had friends round when I was
her age. Maybe if I had we wouldn't have lost touch. You
can find people now though can't you? On the internet. Or
they turn up on *Deal or no Deal.* Try to avoid all that.

*She goes over to the kitchen unit. Finds pizza dough in a bowl, under
a tea towel. TINA begins kneading the dough.*

Thought I'd part bake the bases and then they can choose
their toppings. I went to Aldi, got proper mozzarella. And
I gave her a tenner, sent her down the Harlequin. They're
probably ogling grips and scrunchies in Claire's right now.

Stretches the dough out.

My mum never used to bother about birthdays. But my Dad, he'd buy an angel cake from Mr Knighton's and stick the same candle in it for me, year after year. Can't stomach angel cake. *(A beat.)* Jaggy said he had another fall. Nothing serious, but he wants to be more careful. Apparently he'd like to give Amber a fiver for her birthday. Don't know why I was surprised he remembered. He's good at remembering. Told him, she doesn't need a fiver. And it isn't like he's got money to spare, not with the cost of vests and cup a soup.

Finds a rolling pin, starts rolling out the dough.

Amber keeps going on about visiting him. I blame the telly. Too many adverts. She thinks he's gonna tell her a story about the war and open a bag of Werther's Originals. Fat chance. I mean he slurs his speech now and he's mainly on purees though he can suck a chip. Miranda's got Sky so they fast forward the bits they don't want. Me and Amber have to sit there. Taking all the lies in.

She's seen him a few times. Once in Charter Place and that day at the bus stop. When she was seven I told her he'd had a bad accident. Fell down the stairs when I was at school. He got up and seemed fine. But from that day on, things were never quite right. I told her he caught a disease which means he can't touch people. So if she ever sees him, around town, without me, she's not to touch him. I added that he doesn't realise he's got it cos his brain's not right, so sometimes he tries to touch people when he shouldn't. She cried when I told her. Made him a card out of a packet of Coco Pops saying 'Get Well Soon Grandad'. Was easier when she was younger. They trust every word that comes out of your mouth. Recently she's been asking about his illness. Wants to google it, see if there's a cure. I've insisted there isn't, but she keeps bringing it up.

Puts a round pizza base to one side. Breaks off more dough. Starts rolling.

Family's very important to her. Especially since she doesn't know her Dad. She's determined to track him down one day. I've advised her it won't be easy. I explained he's

French, so he lives in France. Holiday romance. We were madly in love, he's a musician. Writes and plays and busks outside cafes where philosophers argue about the origin of the species. Told her he must be the reason she's so artistic. No Facebook in those days and I lost the beermat he wrote his number on so couldn't tell him I was pregnant. She was sad about that, but she understood. Don't even know his surname. Just Jean-Michel.

Puts a round pizza base to one side. Breaks off more dough. Starts rolling.

His real name's Keith. Or Ken. Went back to his one night after too much tequila at The Game Bird. Was over before it started.

Keith had nice hazel eyes. Builds lofts I think.

Something that requires a van. I saw him in town a couple of years ago handing out leaflets for the EDL. He didn't notice me. Lives in Carpenders Park. Doubt he'll recall much about that evening.

Puts a round pizza base to one side. Breaks off more dough. Starts rolling.

Miranda asked if I needed any help with the catering. Dunno what she was thinking of. I mean she can barely brush her own teeth. I said I'd manage. She's started taking tablets. Anti-depressants. Think it's all getting to be too much. Feel sorry for her. He's only nine.

Puts a round pizza base to one side. Breaks off more dough. Starts rolling.

Keep trying to get her to see the funny side. Imagine the tales she'll be able to tell at his wedding. He's a boy, a normal, boisterous boy. I made her a camomile tea and I sent her upstairs to lie down on her yoga mat. She smiled and hugged me. Stinks of that Jo Malone. The weird one with the basil. Anyway she goes 'What would I do without you Tina.' 'Live in filth.' I said. Then she laughed. 'You're so funny.'... 'You should write down all the funny things you say. Pissing Miranda! When have I got time to write shit down?

Puts the last pizza base to one side. Washes her hands. Tidies again. Does paso doble moves.

One, two, one, two… Pissing Clive, he's too tall. Wish we'd stuck to doing the moves from *Tiger Feet*. That was my suggestion but he was fixated on the paso doble. Truth is Latin's beyond us both. We had the option of the American Smooth but Clive was worried about bending backwards cos of his neck. Some sob story about a herniated disc. So the paso doble it was. We haven't got a hope in hell of winning. Not when Melanie Fisher's hips are representing the Rumba. Claims she's had half the Dads in Year 8, but she hasn't.

Does some more steps and moves over to the kitchen unit. Finds a make-up bag. Takes out a powder compact. Applies it.

Want to do her proud tonight. I know I'm old and I look like shit, but you can always try to paper over the cracks. Look at that lot on *Loose Women*. Very happy to flaunt what they haven't got. They're an inspiration. Your mum's important when you're a girl. When she started Year 1, some kid told her I was fat and ugly. Since then, I've tried to make an effort.

Applies lipstick.

You wouldn't have caught my mother with an eyeshadow palette. She wasn't one for personal grooming. When Amber asks after her, I just tell her that her Grandmother was complex. Good word. Least it makes her sound interesting to Amber. She would like to have met her, but Mum dropped dead when I was seven months pregnant. Jaggy and Bal reckoned it was the shock. It was her time, that's all. Missed her more than I thought I would. Doesn't matter any more.

Finishes doing her make-up.

We're looking to the future now. Both of us. Starting tonight.

Lights fade.

SCENE THREE

Lights up. The room is decorated perfectly. Marilyn Manson's 'Tainted Love' starts to play loudly. Suddenly TINA enters, she's dressed as before in her party gear. She runs around chaotically, popping balloons and ripping down decorations. Effectively trashes the place until it looks as if a bomb has hit it. She runs off the stage. Music fades.

SCENE FOUR

Next day. TINA enters wearing plain tracksuit bottoms and a T-shirt. She contemplates the room. Takes out a black bin bag from the kitchen unit. Starts filling it with the array of burst balloons and decorations. She clears up for a bit, then slowly comes to sit on Amber's bed.

TINA: She says I've ruined her life. What cos the pizza dough was a bit soggy? No, she says. Fuck your cheap pizzas she goes. Nasreen's mum saw you down the Job Centre. I'm allowed to look surely? Said she knows I sign on. So, isn't a crime is it? I just… I didn't… I mean… I got all the balloons and decorations and cake didn't I? What does it matter? You lied, she goes. You're a liar. You say you work, but you don't. The girls are calling you a scrounger. Said I do my best. Work seven days a week sometimes. Most weeks. Do her homework with her, don't I? Helped her with that *Merchant of Venice* assignment. Head of Year even wrote a note of congratulations cos of her mature insight into Shylock's motivation.

Gets up, puts the bag to one side. Finds another, starts to fill it.

I've frozen the pizzas. Was a bit of a squeeze getting them in that freezer compartment but I managed it. Her friends said they weren't hungry. Didn't even hang around that long. Hugged her at the door and gave me evils as they pressed the button for the lift. Then it was just me and her. Same as usual. Said she didn't feel like cake. Showed her the playlist I'd put together. She just sat there in silence so I put that Jessie J one on she likes… you know… *(Sings.)* 'Ain't about the ch… ch… ch… ching… .ain't about the bl… bl… bl… bling… ' . Anyway she turns it off, starts screaming that she hates that shit. That she's not five years old and then I dunno…

Sits down at the table.

Says she's ashamed of me. What else have I been lying about? Nothing I says. Made a mistake but I don't want her to be upset. Want her to concentrate on her birthday. Let's watch the telly. I'll open a bottle of Sprite. What homework's she got? I can help. I remind her she's got promise. They tell me she's brilliant. World's her oyster. Don't want her to piss all that talent up the wall. That's what Mrs Taylor said I did. You, she shouts. Can't imagine you ever having any talent, you useless cow. You're a cleaner. You clean other people's shit up. That's all. You're nothing. And then… and then… Can't remember the rest.

Starts clearing the table.

I've spoilt her. Apparently you do when there's just one. Then one day they get dethroned. Felt like slapping her round the face but I just sat there. Told her I'm proud of my work. Might be nothing but I like it. Miranda and her mates say they couldn't possibly function without me. And after everything… she won't understand this… but after everything… I'm happy to be breathing in and out.

I stared at the pizza bases. All the toppings were in the fridge. My stomach was rumbling, so I broke a bit off one. I mean she'd gone, wasn't coming back. Stuffed it in my mouth. Suddenly Amber's in a pile on the floor. Crying all these angry tears. She's so angry… and I… I remember feeling angry, like that. You lied she goes. You've betrayed me. You've broken my heart Mum. The dough was only part baked. Tasted a bit weird but I still ate it. Told her I was sorry.

Finds a dustpan and brush. Begins to sweep the rug. Suddenly stops.

Please can I see him Mum? He is my Granddad. I told her, I've told her… But she kept going on. She wants to know somebody's her family. What about Jaggy and Bal? No, not them. Them and their kids, they eat too many takeaways and play computer games all day. I want to know him. Because he's like us. He must be someone like us.

Sweeps again.

Well he's not. I mean your family's never like you. That's why we have friends. She'd stopped crying by now. Was starting to get insistent. Then Miranda sent me a text. She can't cope. School are sending Jasper for an assessment. Something's not right. And she's not on top of the business. Says she's feeling deeply anxious, keeps forgetting to take the anti-depressants. Can I come round for a chat next week? She needs to talk to someone.

Walks over to the bed. It's crumpled up. She starts to make it lovingly, as though she is putting her daughter to bed.

I am sorry. I will never… ever lie again. You are… so precious… Says all she wants is to see him. Begs me. Makes me promise to take her one day next week.

She's clearly disturbed by the prospect. Finishes making the bed. Sits.

Jaggy says he's deteriorating. The carers write 'meal not touched' on the food sheet most days and and he needs help with his spoon now. I'll go round before Miranda's. Make roast chicken and carrots and cabbage and potatoes. Stick it all in the blender and force him if I have to.

TINA gets up. The place is almost as it was. She continues to tidy.

Clive turned up after. Martha spends Saturday nights with her Mum. He's sourced some costumes. Mine's gold. Gave him Lottie's pizza and we watched the *X Factor* on ITV plus one. He thinks we need more practice. I told him this is as good as I'm going to get. He kept moaning so I let him stick the practice music on…

Paso doble music begins to play. She gently starts to dance.

… And for once he was right. Does calm you down. If you ask me, Melanie Fisher's a shoe in for first prize. But Clive reckons we're in with a chance.

SCENE FIVE

Two weeks later. Friday. TINA is wearing badly fitted leggings and a jumper. She and Amber have just had dinner and TINA is clearing up plates and putting stuff in the kitchen area. A vulgar gold lame dress hangs at the back in Amber's bedroom. TINA talks as she clears.

So, I arrive. Ring the bell four times, it's that Vivaldi's *Four Seasons.* Goes on and on. No answer. Use my key in the end and there she is sat on the decking sipping a camomile tea. Why didn't she answer the door? Sorry she goes, Vivaldi's inaudible out the back. But you asked me to come Miranda, and it's early and it's Sunday. You said it was an emergency. I've had to stick my daughter in front of Andrew Marr. Then she starts crying, says she doesn't know how to work the washing machine. Apparently her husband's had to take the kids to soft play. She can't be around people, nobody except me. I leave her staring at those agapanthus she had potted by that lesbian gardener and I go inside. Place looks like shit so I scrape the breakfast bowls and load the dishwasher. Spray some Flash on the surfaces and stick the kettle on. I've told her before to go and see a counsellor. But she says they're too unfriendly and anyway I'm better value for money.

Finishes clearing up. Goes to get the gold dress.

I'm about to get my coat when she wanders in. He's been getting drunk at work. I knew that, but last week he got caught taking crystal meth in the toilets with one of the security guards. And now... now they've sacked him. She's going to have to sell the business to pay the mortgage and the school fees. Wasn't the script she'd written for herself. Nothing's what you think it is Miranda. Nothing and nobody. It'll be alright I tell her. Then she chucks her camomile tea mug against the wall and it smashes everywhere. I'm not clearing that up Miranda. No, I know, she goes. And next she explains that they can't afford me any more. She's sorry, says she's devastated to leave me in the lurch and she starts crying again. I tell her, I'll be fine. I will survive. Even though loads of them have cut back their hours.

After this series of *Bake Off,* seems like they're all learning to cook and clean for themselves. Not a problem, I'll find another gang at another private single sex. There are always women who need somebody. Then she asks me to sit down.

TINA sits, faces the audience.

Jasper's had his assessment. It's not good. He's been hurting children in the playground and the toilets. They describe his preoccupations as unusual. They're not keen on Special Needs at that school so they've asked him to leave. I tell her to fight but Miranda reminds me she doesn't like conflict. Says she's ashamed. Why isn't he normal? What's she done wrong? Probably nothing I tell her. Just… just put him somewhere decent, make sure he's with teachers who care. Promises she will and then she says she wishes she was dead.

And then I told her about this friend I had, whose life changed in one moment. She was young, about Amber and Isobel's age, she had all this promise and then something bad happened, something truly terrible and suddenly, in a second all her promise was gone. Point is, my mate didn't jump in front of a train at Watford High Street, she just… she just kept going.

And I look at pissing Miranda sitting on her John Lewis dining chair and I tell her. This'll be the making of you.

You love that boy with all your heart, till you've got no love left for anybody but him and it'll be the making of you.

She blows her nose and thanks me. It'll be okay I tell her. It'll be okay I tell myself. What will you do Tina, she asks. None of your pissing business Miranda, but I smile and say I'll see.

Will you have to go to a food bank? I can see the excitement in her eyes. No, I won't, you pissing bitch. I'll never do that. Still got the voucher my doctor gave me that time…

Takes the voucher out of her purse.

… but I'll never ever do that.

Screws it up, puts it back in her bag.

If you go, she says, will you tell me what it's like?

I get up. *(Gets up.)* I'd better head off now. Find my coat.

She takes her gold dress. Removes her leggings and jumper.

She's very grateful I came on a Sunday. Let's have coffee soon. Now she's got all this time on her hands we'll have to get together more often and maybe Amber can come over and revise with Isobel. I get my bag. Show her how to set a spin cycle and then I say bye. We both know I won't be seeing her again.

TINA puts on her gold dress. Beholds herself in a mirror.

Mutton dressed as Mutton. Still don't look as bad as Clive. I'm sure real matadors don't wear shiny waistcoats from TK Maxx.

Finds an old vanity case. Starts applying make-up.

Amber's meeting me there. Her and Martha and Lottie and Nasreen are serving the non-alcoholic cocktails. And I've told Clive I'm practised out. Best that he stays away. I mean a groom's not supposed to see his bride is he? Clive agrees we don't want to peak too soon. Keep it fresh. Honestly, he gets on my pissing nerves.

Receives a text. Reads it. Stops.

Amber wants me to bring the fiver he gave her.

Goes to a drawer, opens it, takes out the fiver. She sits down, regards it.

We went last Wednesday, after school. I made marmite sandwiches and bought a value pack of hula hoops for the two buses. I've got a water bottle I fill up with tap water and my weekly pass. So we're going along, looking out

of the window at our town. Beautiful ugly Watford, all
concrete and cars and flashes of green and people never
looking at each other because they're too busy or scared
or thinking about whether there'll be a 3 for 2 offer at the
Harlequin, or whether their kid's gonna pass the entrance
exam or whether their wife still loves them and what ready
meal they're gonna eat in front of Nigella.

She gets up, moves to the side, acts out following actions.

Get off the bus in town. See the schoolgirls piling out from
Lady's Close, same as me and Sharon used to. We walk
down Vicarage Road, through the precinct, wind our way
through the roads. I've still got my key I've had since I was
fourteen. I open the door and for the first time in her life
my daughter, aged fourteen walks into that house.

Our dining room's his bedroom now. We walk in and the
place smells of cod in parsley and wee and old man. I stick
her in the front room and I check on him. He's sleeping.
I'm glad. I show her. Right, you've seen him now, let's be
off. But she wants to stay. And then... he wakes up...

She stops for a second, then imagines herself again with her Dad.

I walk over to his bed and he's so happy to see me, he
starts with the tears. I fluff up his pillows and pass him a
tissue. He asks if I'm gonna give him his dinner. No, Dad
I can't, the carer's gonna do it. He takes my hand and
cos he's so weak I can pull it away after a few seconds. I
turn round to get her but she's already there, standing at
the door. She's crying, making her way towards the bed.
'Hello Granddad.' Remember not to touch him Amber.
'I'm Amber, I made you a card', she bought this one
from a shop and she's written some long stupid message
in it about blood and family and being descended from
Ludhiana and France and how he's a piece of her jigsaw
and she's determined to be a part of his life and take care
of him.

And Thank God there's a key in the door and it's the
carer and I tell Amber we have to leave, right now. But

she won't. Then luckily she sees his commode, he needs a wee and it freaks her out and she remembers I'm her mum and so she does what I say and we turn to go. Just as she's saying goodbye he interrupts her. 'Five pounds' he mumbles. And so I get it from the drawer where his pants are while the carer turns the microwave on. 'Thanks Granddad, I love you' and finally I get her out onto the road.

She stops. Pours a glass of water, drinks it.

Keeps asking when she can go back. I've told her he's not up to visitors. Doesn't like people, hates children and treads on insects. She wouldn't listen. Started going on and on, so I had to tell her to shut up. I need to concentrate on my steps.

TINA puts the empty glass on the table. Then finds an iPod in AMBER's room.

Lottie's mum mentioned that Melanie Fisher started tap when she was four. Jazz and latin not long after. Clive reckons it's the taking part isn't it. Still, no excuse not to strive is it? I've always attempted to strive, no matter what everyone thinks.

Plugs in the iPod. Queen's 'Bohemian Rhapsody' starts to play. TINA starts doing her paso doble moves in spirited fashion. Her mobile goes, music stops. She answers the phone.

TINA: Hello… yes… Oh, no… you've got the wrong number… Yes, I am his daughter… but my cousins deal with his carers… Jaggy Dhillon and Bal Dhillon… But I can't… I'm on my way out… Oh…

She sits down.

Yes, I'm his only daughter… But then… then shouldn't he be in hospital? Right… if that's the case… I think he would prefer to… to be at home… So my cousins are coming at some point?… Yeah, I can understand that he wants me to be there… I'll… I'll… er… see what I can do…

Comes off the phone. Stares at it for a long time. Chucks it across the room. Looks down at her dress, gets distressed.

What was I thinking? I can't do this… I'm not this… And him… I should have known… he always destroyed anything good…

'Bohemian Rhapsody' plays again. She smashes the glass of water on the floor in front of her. She does the paso doble perfectly but in a frenzied fashion upon the smashed glass. TINA rips her dress so the train of it comes off. Her hair goes everywhere and she smudges her make-up as she dances. It's an arresting sight. She dances and dances until she falls in a heap on the floor. Lights dim.

SCENE SIX

Later that night. TINA enters. She's barefoot and her dress is ripped. She's carrying a gold handbag over her shoulder and a pair of gold shoes in her hand. Stops suddenly.

TINA: Forgot to give the driver a tip. *(Breathes deeply.)* Too late.

Walks over to AMBER's bed. Sits and strokes the pillow lovingly.

Amber did well. I was proud. But I'm glad she's staying over at Nasreen's. I don't want to keep pretending that I'm sad. I am but not in the way… anyway, I am. We sat together, next to his bed. Jaggy and Bal hovered with cans of coke. Their crying made Amber cry so in the end… in the end I let her hold his old bony fingers.

His brown skin had gone yellow. He managed to thank me for coming and asked if I was going to a wedding. Said I looked like a fairy. No Dad, it's something I'm doing at Amber's school, but it doesn't matter. It matters Tina, he says. You go. You go and get married. I'm not getting married Dad. You go Tina. Hurry up, I'll be alright with the boys. And Jaggy and Bal nodded.

And so me and my girl stood up and left that house. Jaggy booked a cab, so we got in. As the driver stuck the postcode in the satnav, I stared at my old front door. The door that I'd walked in and out of my whole life and I remembered how I'd look out of the window, counting the seconds till my Dad came back to that front door from the precinct, hoping he'd bought me prawn crackers and extra sweet and sour sauce. Amber taps my arm. 'I forgive you Mum,' she goes. Yeah, I said. I know.

TINA heads to the kitchen area, finds a plate. Opens the cupboard, searches for food, there's none. Remembers something, opens her bag, finds her purse, opens it, searches for something, finds the food bank voucher she screwed up.

TINA: Voucher's expired.

She chucks it on the floor. Puts the empty plate on the table, observes it. Checks the coins in her purse.

I'll buy some self-raising flour in the morning.

TINA puts her shoes on. Does a Paso Doble move.

Clive was texting all evening so by the time we got to the school I knew they were running late. We walk into the main hall and I see him. I'm sorry, he says. Why, have we missed our turn?

No, because of your Dad… When are we on?… Tina, he goes… When are we pissing on Clive?… It's supposed to be now and they're waiting… but… don't you want to?… Suddenly I grab his fat hands and I pull him into the middle of the dancefloor. And one of the Dads from Year 9, dressed up as Freddie Mercury, starts singing. And me and pissing Clive look at each other, like we love each other and we dance and we dance, like we've never danced before. When we stop I see tears in his eyes and I hold him tight while the judges turn their score cards over. Everyone claps and I catch Melanie Fisher smiling. She knows we can't touch her. Me and Clive stop for a large chicken fried rice on the way home. While we wait, he explains fracking to me. He's not as thick as I thought.

TINA takes a small trophy out of her bag.

Clive and the girls were delighted with second place. Mrs Taylor wouldn't have found it acceptable. But maybe, this time, it's alright.

(Dances paso doble. Stops.) Later Clive asks me if… now that it's all over… if I'd like to learn a new dance. So I tell him. I tell him… I just might.

She dances. Lights fade.

THE END

KHANDAN

KHANDAN was commissioned by Birmingham Repertory Theatre and was first performed at The Studio, Birmingham Repertory Theatre on 22 May 2014 with the following cast:

JEETO, Sudha Bhuchar
LIZ, Lauren Crace
MAJOR, Neil D'Souza
REEMA, Preeya Kalidas
PAL, Rez Kempton
COOKIE, Zita Sattar

Writer, Gurpreet Kaur Bhatti
Director, Roxana Silbert
Designer, Jamie Vartan
Lighting Designer, Chahine Yavroyan
Sound Designer, Giles Thomas
Visual & Projection Designer, Nathan Jones
Casting Director, Julia Horan CDG
Assistant Director, Erin Gilley
Voice & Dialect Coach, Zabarjad Salam
Design Assistant, Gayatri Jani
Stage Manager, Ruth Morgan
Deputy Stage Manager, Juliette Taylor
Assistant Stage Manager, Hannan Finnegan

Characters

JEETO GILL
60s, a portly, kind looking, forceful widow with
dangerous eyes, mother of PAL and COOKIE

LIZ GILL
early 30s, white, loud, big hearted and exuding
cheap glamour, wife of PAL

PAL GILL
early 30s, powerfully built leonine alpha male,
ridden with ambition

COOKIE SAMRA
early 40s, ferocious, rough, successful, sister to
PAL, married to MAJOR

MAJOR SAMRA
mid 40s, overweight, greying, quiet, nervy,
husband to COOKIE

REEMA GILL
late 20s, elegant, serious, rejected wife of JITI –
PAL and COOKIE's cousin in India

Location
Suburb of a city

Setting
The Gill family living room

ACT ONE

SCENE ONE

A few weeks before Christmas. A large bright nouveau riche living room space in neutral colours opens out into a modern well-equipped country style kitchen fitted with a breakfast bar. The atmosphere is regal, comfortable, vast, blank. Huge stainless steel pans sit on the hob. A mahogany sideboard, dining table and chairs occupy part of the living room area and a DFS leather extendable armchair is plonked in the middle. Small, decorative tables are scattered around. Family photographs in gold frames adorn the walls alongside images of the Golden Temple and assorted Sikh Gurus. There is a plush burgundy carpet and a large plasma screen in one corner.

JEETO, 60s, a portly, kind-looking woman with dangerous eyes walks into her home. She wears a bright blue tabard on top of an old flowery shalwar kameez. Carrying a leather handbag over her shoulder, she absent-mindedly holds a wad of letters which she has just picked up. JEETO sings/hums 'Challa', a famous Punjabi folk song, this morphs into the 'Oh na na na' chorus from Rihanna's 'What's My Name'. She goes to the kitchen and calls.

JEETO: *(Shouts.)* Pal!

> *Fills a pan with cold water.*

> *(Shouts.)* Chah peeneeyeh? *[Do you want a cup of tea?]*

> *Puts the pan on the hob. Chucks a couple of teabags, green cardamom, black cardamom and a cinnamon stick into the pan.*

> *(Shouts.)* Pal!

> *She takes off her tabard and goes to seat her significant bottom on the DFS chair. Puts the post down on a small table next to her. She reaches for her bag and takes out a framed black and white photograph of a handsome, distinguished male. She looks at it with long hard love. Then puts it on the table next to her. Stares at it.*

JEETO: *(To the photo.)* Chah peeneeyeh? *[Do you want a cup of tea?] (A beat.)* Only joking. Stupid. Stupid man.

LIZ, 30s, white, loud, big hearted and exuding cheap glamour breezes in. She's wearing fashionable too tight clothes and struggles with a load of shopping bags and an advent calendar. She puts everything on the floor and addresses JEETO as she admires the calendar.

LIZ: The kids made me an advent calendar out of toilet rolls and cornflakes packets. Nice innit? They stuck a smartie with sellotape in all the windows. *(Thinks/A beat.)* You lot'll have to have 'em.

She heads out.

JEETO: Nee Koorih! *[Hey you girl!]*

LIZ stops, sighs, covers her head with a scarf and goes over to touch JEETO's feet [in the way a Punjabi daughter-in-law would touch her mother-in-law's feet].

JEETO: Chah!

LIZ: In a minute.

LIZ nips back out. JEETO picks up the photo, looks longingly at it again. Puts it back in the bag. LIZ returns holding a few more supermarket carriers.

JEETO: And put plenty milk. You never put enough milk.

LIZ: Cos it's dairy innit.

JEETO: Oh choop khar. *[Be quiet].*

LIZ: I'm not supposed to have dairy. Remember? Stops the egg sticking to the womb lining.

JEETO: Kee ponkee jundiah? *[What's she going on about?]*

LIZ: Or something.

LIZ opens a packet of fancy biscuits and considers them.

LIZ: Boasters were on special offer. *(Takes one.)* One boaster never killed anyone did it? *(She eats.)*

JEETO: Eat kurreeh eat. You need more flesh on that white body of yours. Do you want my grandson to break your bones when he comes out of you?

LIZ: You have the rest *(Passes biscuits to JEETO.).*

JEETO: Don't worry they can fix bones these days. Not like back home, when my Nanaji broke his toe, the doctors amputated his foot. You are lucky that won't happen to you.

LIZ starts putting the shopping away.

JEETO: Pal?

LIZ: Cash and Carry.

JEETO: Stock should be there from the morning.

LIZ: He was too busy in the morning.

JEETO: Busy? What is this busy? These days everyone is always moaning, groaning they are bastard busy. You have to find time if you are running a business. Pal's daddy would have been to the Cash and Carry before Pal and Cookie put on school uniforms.

LIZ puts the shopping away. JEETO takes her shoes and socks off.

JEETO: Chillumchee *[Basin].*

LIZ fills a basin with water and squeezes some soap into it.

LIZ: I gooned the atta *[kneaded the dough]* before I went to work.

JEETO: I'll make the rotis.

LIZ brings the basin over, JEETO rolls up her shalwar.

LIZ: I'll make 'em, yours are too fat.

JEETO points to the calendar and puts her feet to soak in the basin.

JEETO: Show me.

LIZ takes it to her. JEETO has a good look.

JEETO: Very colourful.

LIZ goes to get a load of toddlers' pictures. JEETO opens a day on the calendar and eats a smartie.

LIZ: The parents don't want these ones. They say they run out of wall space. Say after a while they all look the same.

JEETO: I like this one with the sheep.

LIZ: That's supposed to be me.

JEETO hands the pictures back. LIZ contemplates them.

LIZ: You know if your grandson or granddaughter does come, I'll never leave him. You know like at nursery.

LIZ pours milk and half a bag of sugar into the pan. Turns the hob off. Pours two cups of tea out.

JEETO: You won't need to, while he is small I am here.

LIZ: Oh yeah… course.

LIZ hands her a cup of tea. JEETO looks down at the cup.

JEETO: Next time put more milk.

LIZ: One small cup can't hurt. *(She drinks.)*

JEETO: You girls these days have it easy. If I'd given my mother-in-law tea like this, she would have beaten me with an iron bar. And if my mother-in-law had given her mother-in-law tea like this, her mother-in-law would have poisoned her.

LIZ takes the Advent calendar from JEETO.

LIZ: *(Tuts annoyed.)* You've eaten Christmas Eve!

JEETO: Oh choop kar *[be quiet]*. What is this Christmas anyway? Everyone just spending more and more bastard pesah *[money]*.

LIZ: It's not just money, it's for the kids innit? And for everyone to have fun with their families.

JEETO: Fun?

LIZ: There's more to life than the shop Mum.

JEETO: We always stay open on Christmas Day. The only shop in town. Customers come from miles.

LIZ: Pal's… closing this year.

JEETO: Closing?

LIZ: That's what he said.

JEETO: Acha. We will see. You people shouldn't be afraid of hard work.

LIZ: He's not.

JEETO: Shop work is hard but it's better than cleaning toilets. Did you know I cleaned toilets when I first came to this country?

LIZ: You mention it most days.

JEETO: When Pal's father got the keys to the shop, he took my hand and he said.

LIZ and JEETO: Jeeto, you'll never clean after another gorah *[white man]* again…

LIZ: Come on Mum, you must have to do some cleaning in the hospital.

JEETO: Wiping the tea trolley is different from putting my hand where *[white]* goreh bottoms have been.

She reaches for the post and hands it to LIZ who starts going through it.

LIZ: My phone bill, your phone bill, Pal's phone bill. Electric. This one's for you.

She hands JEETO a blue airmail letter. JEETO studies it.

LIZ: Who's it from?

LIZ grabs another Boaster. Hops onto the Breakfast Bar where she perches cross-legged.

JEETO: Chacha.

LIZ: Oh right. Hang on, hang on a minute, I know this one… that's Pal's dad's older brother.

JEETO: Younger brother stupid!

LIZ: I hope no one's died.

JEETO: No one back home left to die. Chacha needs money. Like the rest of this bastard world.

LIZ holds up another child's picture.

LIZ: This one's the Virgin Mary, holding baby Jesus.

JEETO: You think your Mary was a virgin?

LIZ: Maybe.

JEETO: Is this why I have no grandson? What is wrong with you people? Uncross your legs Kurreeh!

Suddenly all the lights go out. JEETO and LIZ gasp. A glow stick becomes visible, it spells out I LUV U in LIZ's direction.

LIZ: *(Screeches with joy.)* Ah, that is wicked!

PAL, mid 30s, turns the lights on as LIZ giggles with glee. He's a powerfully built leonine alpha male. Buoyant, lively and slightly drunk, he wears a high street suit.

PAL: Harj had a box left over from fireworks, he was selling 'em in the pub.

JEETO: You had a box left over from fireworks in the shop.

PAL: Can't I buy my wife a present now?

LIZ: Course you can babes.

JEETO: Fer Pub gaya? *[So you went to the pub?]*

LIZ gets PAL a cup of tea.

PAL: Satwant's birthday, I had to go for one.

LIZ: Don't say you did karaoke.

PAL: I had to.

LIZ: Without me? Pal!

PAL: It was his birthday.

LIZ: Let's do it now. Go on you and me.

PAL: Not now.

JEETO: Cash and Carry nee gaya?

PAL: I'll go in the morning.

LIZ: Go on.

PAL: I haven't had me chah!

LIZ: Pal!

PAL sighs, plonks down his tea and wearily slicks back his hair. He sings reluctantly while LIZ does the 'Oh oh ohs' between each line.

PAL: *(Sings.)* When you smile the world is brighter. You touch my hand and I'm a king. *(Touches LIZ's hand.)* Your kiss to me is worth a fortune. Your love for me is everything. I guess I'll never know the reason why you love me like you do.

LIZ joins in the chorus. They do the affected Elvis mannerisms and sing well and in tune.

BOTH: That's the wonder… the wonder of you… Ooooh… ooohh…

They kiss.

JEETO: Is any cunjar *[whore]* ever going to hoover this carpet?

LIZ: I did it yesterday.

LIZ starts making rotis. PAL loosens his tie and takes off his shirt. He finds a casual top hanging off a door and puts it on.

JEETO: *(Pointing at the carpet.)* This colour shows every crumb and fluff. If you got the patterned one like I said you would only need to hoover once a month.

PAL: I keep saying get a cleaner.

JEETO: And throw more peseh down the toilet?

PAL: It's not that expensive.

JEETO: I don't want some kurreeh *[girl]* looking through my bin, telling the world how many times I blow my nose.

LIZ opens a shopping bag.

LIZ: There were loads of offers in Asda. What do you think of this for Cookie?

She holds up a sparkly top.

PAL: Alright.

She produces a man's jumper.

LIZ: I know this is a bit… boring but Major'll like it. I mean he'll wear it.

JEETO: Have you got figures for November?

PAL: Not yet.

LIZ: The girls want Ann Summers vouchers…

PAL: But Simmy's only eleven.

LIZ: I told her Cookie'll go mad. Anyway I've got them a couple of DVDs and sparkly hair bobbles.

JEETO: Mark my words, figures for November will be down.

PAL: They won't be. And if they are, I'll make it up in December.

JEETO: Daddy always opened Christmas Day.

PAL: Yeah, well, it's up to me now.

JEETO: You should listen to people who have the experience. If you stay open you increase profits. Work hard and one day you might even open another shop. Daddy always dreamed of you having your own business.

PAL: And I will, just might not be a shop.

JEETO: Kee? *[What?]*

LIZ: Pal's working on a new idea Mum. You should hear it.

JEETO: Cookie had a good November.

PAL: You get tips in a salon.

JEETO picks up her letter. PAL observes her.

PAL: Chacha?

JEETO nods.

PAL: *(To JEETO.)* How much is he asking for this time?

JEETO: Chacha is looking after your land.

PAL: I've told you I don't want it.

JEETO: And the kauthee *[house]* for when I retire. He's building me my own bathroom remember?

PAL: You've got an ensuite upstairs!

JEETO: Did I mention he is painting the verandah? In a few years I will be sitting outside on the old munjah. Breathing in the smell of fresh saag and mackee dhi roti cooking on the choolah. Watching the Pappar man go past on his bicycle while I read letters from my grandson.

LIZ: He'll probably Skype you.

JEETO: Stupid! You think there are computers in the pind
[village]?

PAL: Mum! India's the technology centre of the world. With
the amount of money we send him, Chacha could open an
Apple Store in the pind.

JEETO: Hah, hah, hah *[yes, yes, yes]*, you know everything.
(Opens letter.)

PAL: What's the point anyway? You're not going.

JEETO: *(Reads.)* Dear Bhanji, Every time I pick up the phone,
tears flow from my eyes. So I am writing you this letter,
bearing a terrible pain, one which only a parent can
understand.

PAL and LIZ gather round.

JEETO: *(Reading.)* I told you many times that my son was
mixing with a wrong crowd. And now, Jiti has left the
kauthee *[house]* for good. He said he doesn't want to be
a farmer any more. He said he wants to be a hero in
Bollywood.

PAL: He'll be back in a few days.

JEETO: *(Reads.)* I have repaid all his debts, but his bad history
in this area means the men will not let him enter the
village, ever again. Reema is here with me and is a great
comfort. Still, everyone is blaming the poor girl. They
say she should have looked after her husband better. The
neighbours are calling her names, they say they always
knew she was bad news.

LIZ: Why?

JEETO: She's from Jullundhar. *(Reads.)* I beg you Bhanji, please
send her a ticket to come to UK.

PAL: What?

JEETO: *(Reads.)* My daughter-in-law has no future here in
Punjab. And you must realise for everyone's sake, it is
best that she leaves. Reema is a good girl Bhanji, she is

more my child than my son ever was. I beg you, show pity on her and give her this chance. Yours most respectfully, Jasdev Singh Gill.

She puts the letter down, looks at PAL.

PAL: No... no way... If she leaves the pind, who's gonna make Chacha's roti? Who'll wash his kachees *[underwear]* and cut his toenails?

JEETO: We have three empty bedrooms.

LIZ: It's not easy being a daughter-in-law.

PAL: Mum!

JEETO: Kee? *[What?]*

PAL: Did you know about this?

JEETO: How could I know?

PAL: She can't just turn up here.

JEETO: That girl is our responsibility.

PAL: And what happens after she arrives? I'm the one who'll have to buy her a bus pass, teach her how to use a till, take her up Primark...

LIZ: Maybe she can come for a bit.

PAL and JEETO eye one another gravely.

PAL: She's not planning a city break Liz.

JEETO: Your Chacha is old. It's not safe for a woman without her husband on that farm. If you don't care what happens to her, at least care about our honour.

PAL: She's Jiti's wife, he should be looking after her.

JEETO: You think we should leave her to rot in that house? Watching your Chacha cry into his lassi?

PAL: We can't afford it.

JEETO: If you open Christmas Day you could pay for a ticket.

LIZ: Come and have your roti.

PAL goes to sit at the table. LIZ presents him with a range of dishes and a pile of chapattis. He eats hungrily.

JEETO: Cookie is opening Christmas Eve till 9 p.m.

PAL: Perhaps Cookie can buy a ticket then.

LIZ brings JEETO her food on a tray.

LIZ: You'll have to put the tree up soon Pal. I'll ask if the girls want to come over and help.

JEETO: Daddy would have done it already.

PAL pushes his plate away, half slams the table. Gets up.

PAL: Oh yeah. He'd have stuck some ragged old tinsel on that wonky silver tree we've had since 1985.

JEETO stands up, her feet are still in the basin.

JEETO: You show your daddy some respect!

PAL opens the fridge, gets a beer, holds it up.

PAL: This is what Daddy respected.

He puts the beer down hard on the table.

JEETO: Cookie walked before she was one years old. Do you know that? She would cry because her feet felt cold on the lino in that stinking kamarah *[room]* we shared with Uncle Nagra. We lived on roti *[bread]* and dayhee *[yoghurt]* for a month because Daddy wanted his daughter to feel carpet under her feet. And when we brought you back from the hospital he held you up in that stinking kamarah and smiled and he said 'This is your country son. You show those haramzadeh *[bastards]* who call me Paki and spit at my back. You show them!'

PAL takes a swig of the beer and goes back to his food.

JEETO: He did everything for you children. And you cannot help your chacha.

JEETO sits down. LIZ starts clearing up.

PAL: You expect me to provide for her, just like that?

LIZ gets a text.

LIZ: Cookie hasn't cooked so they're coming over.

She gets her coat.

LIZ: I'll need more butter to chopurr the rotis. *(To PAL.)* Have you got any change?

JEETO: Biscuit jar.

LIZ takes a large glass jar out of a cupboard. It's full of cash. She takes some money and heads out. JEETO puts her food to one side. Starts drying her feet.

PAL: How are your feet?

JEETO: Swollen.

PAL: I want you to pack the hospital in.

JEETO: These hands need to work. *(Eyes PAL.)* Daddy promised Chacha he would look after him. You have to be Daddy now.

PAL: I'm doing my best.

JEETO: I want that girl here.

PAL: *(A beat.)* We'll see.

PAL picks up the beer, opens it, takes a swig. Mariah Carey's 'All I want for Christmas' plays into the next scene.

SCENE TWO

New Year's Eve. The same living room is lavishly adorned with Christmas decorations, crammed full with cards and a lit up B&Q tree looms at the back. COOKIE SAMRA, early 40s, ferocious, rough, hard-faced and immaculately made up, sits at the table, texting avidly on her iPhone. COOKIE drips with gold, and wears an expensive, ultra fashionable shalwar kameez. She puts the phone down, wanders over to the kitchen area, opens the fridge, stares into it. She has a quick look around and carefully removes a bottle of white wine. COOKIE hurriedly unscrews it, takes a long swig and puts it back.

COOKIE walks back to the table, opens her designer handbag, takes out Gold Spot mouth freshener, sprays it into her mouth and retouches her lipstick. Her phone rings, she scans the caller's name, takes a deep breath, sits back on the dining chair, answers the phone, talks quietly.

COOKIE: At my mum's… They're picking up my cousin's wife from the airport… I dunno, might be five minutes, might be five hours, you know what they're like… I can't can I?… I'm sorry…

Person on the other end puts the phone down. COOKIE chucks her phone down onto the table. Seconds later it rings again.

COOKIE: What d'you do that for?… I can't can I? We're all supposed to be going to this party at Inderjit's house… No… I told you…

LIZ enters, she's glammed up too in a shalwar kameez, but carries a broom and cleaning materials. COOKIE's getting angrier.

COOKIE: I said… What?… Fuck off then!

She suddenly notices LIZ staring at her. Composes herself.

COOKIE: *(Into phone.)* I mean… er… I'm sorry… the salon's closed until the second of January. If you ring back then, you can make an appointment.

She turns her phone off. Eyes LIZ uneasily.

COOKIE: One of my regulars… she… er… wants… her… moustache waxed for this evening.

LIZ: Bit late now innit?

COOKIE: That's what I said. I mean I can't drop everything, just cos she's got a bit of regrowth.

LIZ starts sweeping the floor.

LIZ: New Year's Eve innit, everyone wants to look their best.

COOKIE: What you doing?

LIZ: Making it nice for her when she arrives. So she feels comfortable.

COOKIE: She's gonna be living for free in a five bedroom house, you don't get more comfortable than that.

LIZ: Might be hard for her, getting used to the pace of life y'know.

COOKIE: Stick some Indian films on for her. That'll keep her happy. Oh and get some cream cakes, they like cream cakes for some reason. If there's any in the shop past the sell-by date she can have them. *(Fiddles with her phone.)* Thought they'd be back by now.

LIZ: Mum says she'll be helping round the house when I'm at work and when the little one comes along.

COOKIE: Have you got some news?

LIZ: Not this month.

COOKIE: I wouldn't worry about it. You're not missing much.

COOKIE checks her Rolex. She's getting annoyed.

COOKIE: Where are they? I can't be dealing with this Indian timing.

LIZ: Traffic innit.

COOKIE: Suppose she'll wanna go sightseeing at the weekend. Buckingham Palace and all that shit.

LIZ: Dunno.

COOKIE: They all wanna go there. And Madame Tussauds. Five quid for a diet coke it was when that Jiti came. I can't be dealing with it. I told Mum I'm not taking her. You lot'll have to do it.

LIZ: I don't mind.

COOKIE: Suppose Major could go.

LIZ: So you closed tomorrow?

COOKIE: Yeah. You can't do a Brazilian with a hangover. Couple of girls are going round to clients' houses.

LIZ: You could do with a day off. Be nice for Simmy and Jasmin.

COOKIE: They're not bothered.

LIZ: Thought they'd be coming to Inderjit's.

COOKIE: No, they're going round some schoolfriend's. Major's dropping them.

Sound of front door opening outside.

COOKIE: At last. What's her name again?

LIZ: Reema.

MAJOR enters. He's mid-40s, overweight, greying, badly dressed in an ill-fitting suit, quiet, nervy.

LIZ: Alright Major.

MAJOR: Alright.

He takes off his jacket to reveal a bright shirt patterned with aeroplanes.

COOKIE tuts in shock.

COOKIE: What the hell are you wearing?

MAJOR: What's wrong?

COOKIE: Looks like one of them crimplene shirt sets you got for our wedding.

LIZ: Do you want chah?

MAJOR: Yeah, go on.

LIZ puts the tea on.

COOKIE: You're supposed to wear that Paul Smith one I bought you for Christmas.

MAJOR: I thought this was it.

COOKIE: I left it on the bed. *(Tuts.)* You have to embarrass me don't you?

MAJOR: Nobody cares what I'm wearing.

COOKIE: Course they do. You know what Inderjit and them lot are like. They'll be laughing their heads off, saying we can't afford designer.

MAJOR: They won't.

COOKIE: Why not just get one off that eBay and kill me now? You'll have to go home and change.

MAJOR: I'm not going home.

COOKIE: You are.

MAJOR: Liz is making chah now.

COOKIE: You're going home.

He comes to sit down. Checks his watch. LIZ gives him his tea.

MAJOR: They still not back?

LIZ: Maybe the plane was late.

COOKIE: He could have texted, I could have gone to meet Tracey and them lot. They were going up TGIs for cocktails. *(Tuts.)* Bloody Indian Timing.

LIZ: *(To MAJOR.)* Are the girls excited about New Year's Eve?

MAJOR: *(Beams.)* Oh yeah. There's a load of them round Nina's house having a sleepover. They're all in their pyjamas and they're gonna watch that new Disney film…

COOKIE: So they say.

MAJOR: They've got about ten boxes of Krispy Kremes. And Nina's mum's making them hot chocolate with marshmallows.

COOKIE: They'll probably do drugs later.

MAJOR: What d'you have to say that for?

COOKIE: They're teenagers innit. That's what they do.

LIZ: Not Simmy and Jasmin.

MAJOR: You're bad-minded you are.

COOKIE: I'm joking! I don't want either of them turning into a smackhead do I? Like some sullah.

MAJOR: Do you have to use that word?

COOKIE: Who are you? Ofsted or something? I'm only having a laugh. It's New Year's Eve innit.

MAJOR walks round to get more tea. COOKIE eyes his shirt, makes a face.

COOKIE: You look like Thomas the tank engine.

MAJOR: They're aeroplanes not trains!

LIZ: Shall I get you one of Pal's? He won't mind.

MAJOR: Go on then.

LIZ exits. Silence. COOKIE's phone pings as she receives another text.

MAJOR: Who's that?

COOKIE: Tracey. Letting me know what time they're meeting.

MAJOR: Thought you told her you can't make it.

COOKIE: She's just letting me know.

They contemplate one another awkwardly.

MAJOR: Let's try and have a nice time tonight.

COOKIE: Okay.

LIZ comes back holding an aubergine designer shirt. MAJOR puts it on. They watch him, it's ridiculously tight.

LIZ: Er… how is it?

MAJOR: *(Optimistic.)* Alright, yeah. Bit tight under the arms.

COOKIE: What do you expect? *(To LIZ.)* Do you know what he eats for lunch?

MAJOR: Don't start!

COOKIE: Domino's on Monday. McDonald's on Tuesday and Wednesday.

MAJOR: Only the filet of fish.

COOKIE: With fries and milkshake! Then Nando's on Thursday.

MAJOR: Not every Thursday.

COOKIE: Then Domino's again on Friday.

MAJOR: I don't have any breakfast. I never have breakfast.

COOKIE: It's a wonder he can walk to the car.

Sound of the front door opening. LIZ jumps up.

LIZ: They're here!

COOKIE and MAJOR turn to face the entrance. PAL, JEETO and REEMA walk in. REEMA is elegant, serious-looking and dressed in a tasteful shalwar kameez and shawl.

JEETO: Reema, this is Cookie.

REEMA: Hello Bhanji.

COOKIE: Call me Cookie.

JEETO: And Major.

MAJOR: *(Hands together.)* Helloji.

REEMA: Hello.

PAL: This is Liz, my wife.

LIZ: Sat siri akal.

REEMA: Hello.

JEETO: Sit.

She indicates the armchair to REEMA who sits down. LIZ starts making tea.

JEETO: *(To REEMA.)* Chah peeneeyeh?

REEMA: Just a glass of water please.

LIZ: You must need chah, it's freezing out!

REEMA: I'm fine really.

LIZ gets her a glass of water.

JEETO: Meh pushaab karkihoneehyeh. *[I'm just going for a wee.]*

She exits. PAL notices MAJOR's shirt, his face falls.

PAL: What you wearing that for?

MAJOR: Liz said you wouldn't mind.

PAL: Brand new that is. I got it for tonight.

MAJOR: I was just trying it on.

PAL: And you've ripped it!

MAJOR: Only the seam, no one'll notice!

He starts taking it off.

PAL: Leave it! I can't wear it now can I?

They compose themselves and all turn to smile awkwardly at REEMA.

COOKIE: So... er... how's Chacha?

REEMA: He's... coping.

COOKIE: He's proper nice isn't he? I went back to the pind
[village] when I was a kid and he taught me how to milk
the mudge.

REEMA: That's nice.

COOKIE: Yeah. So... er... how is the mudge?

REEMA: Papaji doesn't keep buffaloes any more.

COOKIE: That's a shame. Oh he made sure we had a right
good time. I remember he took me and Daddy up Chaura
Bazaar and I managed to get a whole Golguppa in my
mouth, in one go. Massive it was. Jiti was well impressed.

Awkward silence.

MAJOR: Has... er... Jiti been in touch?

REEMA: No.

*Awkward silence. REEMA opens her bag, takes a few items out – book,
purse, papers, she puts them on a side table.*

COOKIE: Probably busy isn't he? I mean everyone's rushed off
their feet in Bollywood.

REEMA: I have some presents for you. Bhanji, Liz.

*She hands COOKIE and LIZ each a small wrapped package. They
open them to reveal small carved animals.*

LIZ: I've always wanted an elephant!

COOKIE: Mine stinks!

REEMA: They're hand carved. From Sandalwood.

LIZ: Ah, they're lovely. You shouldn't have!

COOKIE: *(Sniffs.)* Smells like that Britney Spears' Fantasy.

MAJOR: *(To REEMA.)* Flight teekseeh? *[How was the flight?]*

REEMA: Fine.

LIZ: I've made dhal and bhindi, when you're ready.

REEMA: Actually I had dinner on the plane.

LIZ: Oh. So what do you think of it so far? You know, England?

REEMA: Well, it's very dark outside…

LIZ: Course. Er… do you like the street lamps?

REEMA: *(Nods.)* Er… yes… You have a very beautiful house.

JEETO returns.

JEETO: Come Reema, I'll show you your room. Liz bring my chah. *(To PAL.)* Suitcase.

PAL: Major'll get it.

He chucks his car keys to MAJOR who catches them, sighs and follows REEMA and JEETO out. LIZ makes JEETO's tea.

LIZ: Very refined isn't she? Proper sophisticated.

COOKIE: She's a teacher innit. Probably speaks better English than you.

PAL: And you.

LIZ: You'll never guess what Pal. Some woman just rang Cookie up asking her to wax her moustache tonight.

PAL: Bit late innit.

LIZ exits with the tea. PAL beholds his sister's upper lip. COOKIE is texting.

PAL: You wanna get the council in to mow yours.

COOKIE: Shut up.

COOKIE gets another text.

PAL: *(Indicating the phone.)* Better not be that fucking Tariq.

COOKIE: It's my mate Tracey.

PAL: Is that what you call him nowadays?

COOKIE: Get lost.

PAL: You got no sharam, you know that?

COOKIE: You're the one who married the goreeh.

PAL: She makes better roti than you, and she hasn't got a tache. Anyway least I had the guts to come clean.

COOKIE: You could have come home with an Albanian crack whore, Mum'd still ask how many biscuits you want with your chah.

PAL: You see him though don't you?

COOKIE: Only cos he lives in the area. I don't see him, see him.

PAL starts fiddling with his iPad.

PAL: You still talk to him though?

COOKIE: Why shouldn't I? You talk to the girls you were at school with.

PAL: That's different.

COOKIE observes PAL on his iPad.

COOKIE: When did you get that?

PAL: Christmas present.

COOKIE: From Liz?

PAL: From me.

COOKIE: You're supposed to give to others at Christmas, not yourself.

PAL: Tax deductible. *(Admiring an app.)* Here, look, this App tells me how much money's going through the till. Updates every five minutes!

COOKIE: You wanna spend your time making money, not counting it.

LIZ comes back in. COOKIE looks over PAL's shoulder.

COOKIE: *(Reads.)* Initial specification for Apna Ghar Nursing Home… Oy, you're not sticking Mum in there!

PAL: Course not. Me and Harj are writing a business plan for a new project.

LIZ: There's a lot of money in nursing homes Cookie.

COOKIE: What do you know about business plans?

PAL: Enough.

COOKIE's phone rings.

COOKIE: Hello… Yeah, hang on a minute…

She exits. PAL plays with his iPad. LIZ clears up in the kitchen.

LIZ: You looking forward to Inderjit's?

PAL: Chicken tikka for starters. Roti, dhal, meat and chol after that. Apna Punjab playing while I neck me second bottle of Johnny Walker. Course I am!

LIZ: Perhaps this'll be our year.

PAL: Definitely.

LIZ: And… perhaps it'll happen.

PAL: Yeah, why not?

LIZ: Cos we've been trying for ages. Years.

PAL: One of them things. Tests came back normal.

LIZ: Yeah…

PAL: Just gonna take time.

LIZ: I don't understand why, that's all.

PAL: Keep trying innit.

LIZ: I could find out about that IVF.

LIZ stops, turns to him.

LIZ: Give us more of a chance.

PAL: We don't need all that. Besides we're young, that stuff's for old people, the ones who've given up.

LIZ: No, it's not.

PAL: Things are alright as they are.

LIZ: I could find out. No harm in finding out.

PAL: Supposed to be expensive.

LIZ: Be worth it if it works.

PAL: Now she's here, there'll be a wedding to sort.

LIZ: Cookie might lend us…

PAL: *(Interrupts/Firm.)* No! No way.

LIZ: I could ask my mum and dad.

PAL: They don't want no brown babies going round their house! Come on, we're trying aren't we?

LIZ: If I knew we definitely could... even if it's ages away, then I'd be alright, but it's not knowing when or if...

PAL: Stop worrying!

LIZ: I just wanna be somebody's mum.

PAL: What are you going on about? You're making it worse!

LIZ: I want a baby Pal.

PAL: Me too. I wanna be the same as other blokes. Pushing swings down the park, buying one of them off road three-wheelers, moaning about being knackered and getting old. It's New Year's Eve, come on, let's go and get hammered.

LIZ: Okay, I'm sorry!

He feels bad, pulls her towards him.

PAL: It's gonna happen. I know it.

He kisses her hard and passionately. LIZ withdraws, finishes clearing up. Covers her disappointment. MAJOR enters, he's holding his iPhone and grinning.

MAJOR: *(Reads.)* Happy New Year to the best dad in the world. Saved you a chocolate sprinkles Krispy Kreme. *(Looks up.)* That's my favourite! *(Reads.)* Love you Sim and Jas. *(COOKIE Enters.)* Remember don't pick us up before noon tomorrow and don't call us, we'll call you. DO NOT CALL, exclamation mark. Exclamation mark. Exclamation mark.

LIZ: You've got good girls Major.

MAJOR: Oh yeah. They make all the rubbish life throws at you seem worth it.

JEETO and REEMA enter. LIZ composes herself.

LIZ: *(To REEMA.)* Do you wanna come to the party?

COOKIE: She's not gonna wanna sing 'Auld Lang Syne' after 9 hours on Air India.

REEMA: I'm okay. It would be nice to go out.

PAL: We haven't got time for her to change.

LIZ: Well you look lovely as you are.

REEMA gathers her things.

JEETO: Reema isn't going.

LIZ: Oh.

REEMA's face falls. COOKIE enters.

JEETO: You look tired.

REEMA: But I'd like to…

JEETO: *(Interrupts.)* Sit down.

REEMA stares at JEETO, then sits.

COOKIE: Right then, let's move.

JEETO sits down.

JEETO: I'm staying with Reema. Here.

PAL: What?

COOKIE: What you on about? Everyone'll be waiting for you to do your boliah *[songs]*. They'll wanna to hear that rude one, y'know about the testicles.

JEETO: *(To REEMA.)* You can see Big Ben on the television.

LIZ: Mum, I pressed your suit and everything!

JEETO: And Reema will help me write the cards for Daddy's patth. *(To REEMA.)* At the end of March we always do a khand patth *[religious service]* for their daddy in the house.

REEMA: Our custom is to do only one patth, the year after a loved one dies. Papaji held one at the Gurdwara.

JEETO: We make the langar *[meal]* here ourselves. You will see what customs money can buy.

COOKIE: But Inderjit's hired a chocolate fountain for the front room.

JEETO: I am tired of going to places on my own.

PAL: We're with you.

JEETO: *(Loud.)* Does anyone under this roof remember my husband?

COOKIE: You think you're the only one who misses him?

PAL: Mum, just come willya…

LIZ: All your friends'll be there.

JEETO: Oh yes, pointing their fingers and staring with their pitying eyes. Look at poor Jeeto, buchareeh *[poor thing]*. No husband, no grandson, Jeeto, alone with her bad kismet.

PAL: If Daddy didn't care what they say, why do you?

JEETO starts taking off her shoes.

JEETO: Reema will keep me company.

MAJOR starts to head out.

MAJOR: Happy New Year then.

COOKIE and LIZ follow.

LIZ: See you in 2014.

PAL turns to join them.

PAL: Happy New Year. *(Exits.)*

JEETO opens her bag, finds her husband's photo, puts it on the table next to her.

JEETO: You know when I danced with my husband I was the envy of all the ladies round here. Whenever we went to a party, the other ladies would be walking yards behind their men. But Daddy would hold my hand. Everyone would be looking, whispering – 'see what Gill Sahib is doing'? He'd laugh and say what was the point of marrying this beauty if I can't show her off. That man made my heart beat, he turned me into a somebody.

REEMA: *(Eyeing the photo.)* He was very handsome when he was young.

JEETO: Even more handsome when he died.

REEMA: Papaji cried for days after we got the news.

JEETO: We all cried.

REEMA: Poor Papaji, he has lost his brother and his son. And now I am here.

JEETO: Jiti didn't go to Bollywood did he?

REEMA shakes her head.

JEETO: Was he still taking nusheh *[drugs]*?

REEMA: *(Nods.)* Every drug he could lay his hands on. And drinking, all day and all night.

JEETO: Where is he?

REEMA: We don't know. Jiti took my wedding gold with him when he left. And his mother's. He has broken Papaji's heart.

REEMA starts crying to herself.

JEETO: Acha. *[I see.]* *(A beat.)* Now you and I are women without men.

REEMA continues to cry silently. JEETO eyes her gravely.

JEETO: Stop your crying kurreeh. No time for tears in UK.

REEMA gets up slowly to get herself a glass of water.

REEMA: Thank you Thyji. For bringing me here.

JEETO: Don't ever thank anyone in the family Reema.

REEMA: I promise I won't be a burden.

JEETO: Burden?

REEMA: *(Nervous.)* I have qualifications. Not just in teaching. I studied economics in college. I know I will have to work. And I'll work hard. Doing whatever, I don't care. I'd like to study some more? Not straight away. But one day. When I've saved some money. If that's alright?

JEETO: First, learn to make the chah.

REEMA: Chah?

JEETO: There's a pattheela *[pan]* behind you. And lachees *[cardamoms]* and longh *[cloves]* and tea bags on the second shelf.

REEMA slowly gets the stuff for the tea.

JEETO: You know I was born twice. Once when I came out of my mother. And then when a 747 landed at Heathrow Airport in 1969.

REEMA makes the tea. JEETO eyes her gravely.

JEETO: It will be the same for you.

Dina Carroll's 'Perfect Year' plays and fuses into…

SCENE THREE (MARCH)

… Sikh religious music. The Christmas decorations are gone and the furniture is pushed back.

White sheets cover the floor and the characters sit on them, hands clasped, legs crossed, heads covered, shoes off, backs to the audience. Music fades.

The Ardaas [Sikh prayer] comes through loudly on a speaker. The congregation stand and join in with the chanting. As it ends, they all bend down and put their foreheads to the floor.

They sit back down. A woman, possibly REEMA, enters carrying a pan of parshad [religious sweet food] and hands it out to the characters who accept it gratefully with both hands and then eat it.

A man, possibly MAJOR, gives out kitchen towels to the congregation. After they have eaten and wiped their hands, they stand, clasp hands and gather round the door to watch the holy book [unseen] being carried out of the house.

Music plays again. The men start removing the white sheets. LIZ and COOKIE are in the kitchen area, making chapattis and stirring huge pots of dhal and sabji. JEETO and REEMA fill thalis with the food and REEMA and the men exit to dole out the thalis to the congregation who are spread throughout the house. Trays of tea follow the thalis out. The actions are repeated so there is a sense of the serving of the congregation as is normal following the khand patth [religious service].

Music fades. The women are in the kitchen area washing up. MAJOR enters.

MAJOR: Binder and them lot want more gulab jaman *[Indian sweets]*.

LIZ: But the kids haven't had any yet.

Someone calls MAJOR from outside, he disappears.

JEETO: Give them to Binder.

LIZ: There aren't enough.

MAJOR reappears.

JEETO: Give them.

LIZ puts gulab jaman into a few bowls onto a tray. REEMA enters, goes to help the women.

MAJOR: And I need five more chahs.

COOKIE doles out five cups of tea onto the same tray.

MAJOR: Binder wants to know if she can take some gulab jaman home.

JEETO: Tell her yes.

MAJOR: And she asked for some sabji. I think she's got visitors later.

MAJOR takes the tray out.

JEETO: *(To COOKIE.)* Sabji pah *[put the sabji]*.

COOKIE puts everything into foil containers. The women carry on clearing up the food.

LIZ: What about Mum's wedding ring? Maybe Binder could have it melted down and made into a bangle.

REEMA and COOKIE laugh.

JEETO: Choop kar! In our culture we take care of people.

COOKIE: She means we have to look like we're taking care of them.

LIZ: Even the ones who hate us like Binder?

REEMA: We take care of them the best.

JEETO: Binder is my good friend.

LIZ: She always ignores me. And if she does talk to me, she never calls me by my name. It's just 'Nee Goreeh' *[Oy, white girl!]*

JEETO: Choop kar. The important thing is everyone came for Daddy.

COOKIE: He was never one for khand patths though was he?

JEETO: Your Daddy believed in God.

COOKIE: Course he did. He just didn't believe in the Gurdwara.

LIZ: He would have enjoyed seeing everyone.

COOKIE: For about five minutes. By this time, him and Uncle Hothi would have sneaked off to the pub, lining up the whisky chasers…

JEETO: Is this the day to be talking about the pub?

MAJOR enters.

COOKIE: Well he would have.

MAJOR: Binder's asking if there's any dhal left.

JEETO: *(Angry.)* Does Binder want the chooni off my head?

LIZ: How come she's still here?

JEETO: *(To COOKIE.)* Dhal pah. *[Put the dhal.]*

MAJOR: Her and Inderjit are doing Zumba on the Wii. They're practising figures of eight. *(Demonstrates.)*

PAL enters with his head covered. He carries a couple of empty thalis over to the kitchen area.

PAL: I sorted the giani *[priest]*.

COOKIE: How much?

PAL: Twelve hundred.

LIZ: Pal!

REEMA: It's too much. In India nobody bothers with this ShowSha.

PAL: Only cos you're all skint! Gianiji did Daddy's first patth and last year. And today everyone's been saying how beautiful the kirtan was so I reckon he's due a rise. Anyway I can afford it.

COOKIE: *(Mimics.)* Anyway I can afford it. Stop showing off willya!

PAL: Just cos I fancy giving the man a tip…

JEETO: Gianiji is not a waiter at Pizza Hut. That money is going to the Gurdwara, to the men and women who do Guruji's work.

PAL: I've had a good few months haven't I Mum?

MAJOR: Oh yeah?

PAL: You see it pays to think strategically. Be open to new ideas.

LIZ: Reema's been doing the late shifts. She's been working really long hours haven't you Ree?

PAL: I've been training her.

REEMA: Training for what? I sit on the till, drink coca cola, moan about Wayne Rooney with the mentally ill goreh.

LIZ and COOKIE laugh.

PAL: Good honest work that is. Hard work.

REEMA: Teaching is far more challenging. Now that is hard work Birji.

LIZ: Bet you were a great teacher. Really caring.

REEMA: I was okay.

PAL: No money in teaching though is there?

Buoyant PAL hugs his mum.

PAL: Best start to the year we've ever had!

LIZ: Mum, you could at least say well done!

JEETO: *(Exasperated.)* Well done. Well done. Congratulations. You are the best. Okay. Happy now?

REEMA starts pouring out cups of tea onto trays. JEETO inspects the trays and addresses PAL and MAJOR.

JEETO: Offer the men first.

REEMA hands a tray to PAL, another to MAJOR. They exit. JEETO adjusts her chooni.

JEETO: I'll go and ask Gianiji if he needs anything more.

COOKIE: *(To REEMA.)* The last time she did that he went home with the microwave.

JEETO: Cookie, you come with me.

COOKIE: Why do I have to?

JEETO: To pay your respects.

COOKIE: Mum! He's... weird.

JEETO: Chull! *[get a move on!]*

COOKIE finds her chooni [scarf]. JEETO scans the kitchen area. Eyes LIZ.

JEETO: If I had left the sink like this, my mother-in-law would have cut my throat.

LIZ: I'm doing it!

JEETO and COOKIE exit. REEMA smiles at LIZ. As they talk, they clear up and put the furniture back into place.

REEMA: Have you spoken to Birji yet?

LIZ: Not yet. But he won't say no, not now he's in the money. I mean he can't, can he?

REEMA: Of course not.

LIZ stops, touches her tummy.

LIZ: Can you imagine feeling that little thing ticking inside you. You know I've already planned how I'll tell Pal, if... if it finally happens.

REEMA: You mean if you find out you're pregnant?

LIZ: I'll book a table for two at The Mandarin, and arrange it with the manager beforehand so when the waiter lifts the lid off the crispy duck, my pregnancy test will be sitting on top of the pancakes.

REEMA: But won't you have urinated on the test?

LIZ: Pal won't mind. He'll be over the moon when he sees them two lines.

REEMA: I see.

LIZ: Me and Pal, perfect in every way. Except... this one... The doctors call it unexplained. I reckon, this way... well, it might be the only way...

REEMA: You should talk to Pal Birji.

LIZ: Oh I will.

REEMA: Talk to him soon. You're a good person Liz. You shouldn't miss your moment.

LIZ: *(Pensive.)* No. *(A beat.)* Hey, you'll have to help me when it's born.

REEMA: Oh... I don't know anything about babies.

LIZ: I always wanted to be a young mum. And I'm not as young as I'd like but I'd hate to be one of them old ones. I see them every day picking the kids up from nursery. They're so worried about everything, tired and scared cos they know what life's really like. I don't wanna know about all that yet. D'you know what I mean?

REEMA: I don't want children.

LIZ: Course you do!

REEMA: I've never... I mean I don't feel... maternal...

LIZ: Only cos that Jiti put you off. Who'd wanna reproduce with him?

REEMA: He wasn't a bad man. But he was already married to the bottle.

LIZ: Like Daddy.

REEMA: Drink gave Jiti the freedom to dream. Always dreaming he was, anything to get away from the routine.

He hated all the chores Papaji made him do, hated the farm… he just wanted something different…

LIZ: Right.

REEMA: I understand him better now I'm here.

LIZ: How's that?

REEMA: See the power you people have running your shop!

LIZ: Us lot?

REEMA: Sometimes… I wonder if I could do something else… go to another place…

LIZ: Like where.

REEMA: America.

LIZ: You mean teach out there?

REEMA: I've had enough of working for others. One day… I'd like to set up my own business. Possibly… a bookshop.

LIZ: Oh, I can see you doing that.

REEMA: Honestly?

LIZ: For sure. You're a big hit with Pal's customers and you've always got your nose in a novel.

REEMA: But I would need more qualifications, capital. My own money.

LIZ: Money isn't everything.

REEMA: You think?

LIZ: You can still be poor and happy.

REEMA: Then why don't you try it? Poor people are just the rich people who never happened. The ones who didn't take their chances. They end up passing time dreaming dreams that never come true. Wasting days and weeks, years.

LIZ: Are you serious about going?

REEMA: *(Nods.)* If I could get a job here first, I could pay for a course.

LIZ: You're working in the shop.

REEMA: A proper job. With a salary. If I had my own money I could pay Thyji rent, contribute to the bills. Save up for my MBA.

LIZ: You should tell Mum. Her and Cookie have been looking on the internet at boys for you.

REEMA: *(Shocked.)* Boys?

LIZ: Men I should say. Most are divorced.

REEMA: So they won't mind second-hand goods.

LIZ: Haven't they mentioned it?

REEMA shakes her head. Landline rings. LIZ answers it.

LIZ: Hello… Oh Sat Siri Akal Chachaji. Yes it's Liz. Lij. Lij! Pal's wife. How are you?… Pal's wife!… Liz!… Hang on, I'll get her.

REEMA: Can I talk to him?

LIZ hands her the phone and calls out of the door.

LIZ: Mum, phone call from India!

REEMA: Sat siri akal Papaji… Hahji… I miss you. Hah… yes, I am happy… but it's different… Hahji, how are you…

She continues talking quietly in Punjabi. JEETO enters followed by PAL who carries a stack of thalis.

LIZ: Chacha.

JEETO takes the phone from REEMA.

JEETO: *(To LIZ.)* Bathroom needs cleaning.

LIZ: What?

PAL: Binder's been sick.

LIZ: *(Heading out.)* Can't leave the work surfaces like that Reema, Mum'll start to self-harm.

LIZ exits. PAL hands REEMA the thalis. He tidies away as she washes up.

JEETO: *(Shouts into phone.)* Hahnji. Sat siri akal... Hah... Everybody came...

PAL: Will you stop shouting?

JEETO: *(To PAL.)* He is in India stupid! *(Into phone.)* Hahji... Oh Reema is fine. Working hard for the family... Very good girl... No, you cannot have her back... Acha... Acha... I see... Okay... I understand... Don't worry... I will talk to him... we will send you by the end of next week... Don't worry. Hahji... Hah... Everybody came... Hah... Sat siri Akal...

She replaces the phone.

PAL: Send what by the end of next week?

JEETO ignores him, busies herself tidying up.

PAL: Send what?

JEETO: The kauthee *[house]* needs rewiring.

PAL: The whole house?

JEETO: Yes.

PAL: But that's gonna cost a fortune!

JEETO: You've just been telling the whole world how much money you're making.

PAL: I'm not working day and night to chuck my profits down the black hole Chacha's digging for himself.

JEETO: Your Chacha needs our help.

PAL: He must be earning something from the land.

JEETO: Whatever he earns goes to pay his debts.

PAL: Why is he holding on to the land then?

REEMA: Because it's all he has left. You don't know what it's like over there.

PAL: Who's asking you?

REEMA: I'm just saying you don't know.

PAL: I know I'm maintaining a house I'm never gonna live in.

JEETO: I'm going to live there. One day.

PAL: What for?

JEETO: To be close to my relatives.

PAL: Come on Mum, they're all dead. Or living in Mississauga. *(A beat.)* Now Chacha's on his own, he can't cope. That house and that land's draining away everything we've got.

JEETO: You think when you fall on hard times, you give up? When Daddy died and you took over the shop and lost us money did I give up on you? No you stupid bloody bastard, I saved you! That land, that jameen, is Daddy's blood. Your blood. It's all that matters. And you fight to save what matters.

PAL: Thing is I turned it around Mum, I'm making more money than Daddy ever was. Maybe you just don't know when to stop fighting.

Silence. JEETO starts making more tea.

PAL: Uncle Hothi was saying a lot of people round here are selling their shares of land back home.

JEETO: Your blood has farmed that land for centuries. Now you want to hand it over to some stranger.

PAL: Who said anything about handing it over? And it doesn't have to be to a stranger. Bet there's someone in the village who could use it. Someone who's gonna be there and help Chacha. Think about it, if you sell your share…

JEETO: Sell my hissa?

PAL: Do something more interesting with the money. You're a sleeping partner Mum, you're no use to Chacha.

JEETO: Did I teach my son to talk like this?

PAL: It'll still be our jameen *[land]*. Chacha's not going anywhere is he?

REEMA: If you sell, the money lenders will get their claws into Papaji's land, bleed him for every rupee.

PAL: You don't know that! Mum, you could still go and visit, stay for as long as you like.

JEETO: Your daddy always said we would go back home, me and him. We'd visit all the Gurdwaras in the Punjab. Make our lives in that house.

PAL: He never went back Mum. Not once!

JEETO: That jameen, that house, is the memory of the future I should have had with your daddy. It's all I have left of him.

PAL: Then do what you want. Land's in your name. You do what you want with it.

JEETO: How did you learn to think like this?

PAL: What do you mean?

JEETO: Like a gorah. Talking like your chacha and your daddy mean nothing.

PAL: I'm not.

The fury rises within JEETO.

JEETO: You want to sell your daddy's land? Sell my land? To some haramzada nobody? Who do you think you are talking to? The next thing you'll say is you want to sell the shop.

PAL turns to face her.

PAL: I've sold it.

JEETO freezes. REEMA stares at PAL. Silence.

PAL: Haven't exchanged contracts yet but that's a formality.

JEETO: You… sold the shop?

PAL: My shop Mum. It's my business. Daddy put it in my name, remember?

Shocked JEETO sits down. She blankly turns to REEMA.

JEETO: Go and see if our guests need anything more.

REEMA exits. Silence. JEETO composes herself.

JEETO: Does Cookie know?

343

PAL: Nothing to do with Cookie.

JEETO: Do you know what it took for your daddy to own that shop?

PAL: Yeah.

JEETO: Why?

PAL: Cos I hate it. I've always hated it. Wandering round that Cash and Carry makes me want to kill myself! Checking and filling that stinking stock room... And waiting at that till like somebody's servant, having to be grateful that they're spending a couple of quid... people looking at me, talking to me like I'm a moron, some pindoo *[villager]* without a brain cell.

JEETO: Is that what you think of us?

PAL: It's what they think of us.

JEETO: Me and Daddy used to work 80 hours a week. Every morning getting goreh newspapers ready. Every night being breathed on by drunks. In the end he was so stressed... and tired... And you show no thanks. That man gave his life for you.

PAL: For me?

JEETO: Hah *[yes]*.

PAL: Daddy died because he drank too much.

JEETO: When a man works that hard he needs something to ease his mind.

PAL: Every night he'd sip his Bacardi bottle till the room started to spin. Then he'd start crying and want a hug and start singing *(Sings.)* 'Peenee peenee peenee peenee eh sharab.' *['Drink, drink, drink booze.']* An hour later you'd be walking around with a bucket of Dettol, mopping up his sick and piss.

JEETO: We made sacrifices so that you could have your life.

PAL: I'd come home from school with a love bite or homework or bruises on my face and you'd be stuck in that stock room counting tins of beans. You never bothered to talk to me or Cookie.

JEETO: So you are selling the shop because nobody talked to you? Are you a man or a little girl?

PAL: I didn't ask for any of it Mum. You just thought I wanted what you wanted. But you never asked me. I could have taken exams, gone to college even...

JEETO: Oh yes, because your grades were so good!

PAL: If I hadn't spent every school night behind that till they might have been better. You never paid any attention to what I was capable of. I could be working in the City now. Making a fortune...

JEETO: So we didn't make enough money for you? You had – DVD players, computers, games... anything you asked for. We let you marry your goree.

PAL: Is that what you think of her?

JEETO: No, it's what I think of you!

PAL sits down, tired of the argument.

JEETO: He put the shop in your name because he trusted you. He gave you the power...

PAL: Daddy never gave me no power. I took it. He would have done the same.

JEETO: *(A beat.)* Pal. *(A beat.)* Don't sell his shop. Please.

LIZ enters cautiously. She's carrying trays.

PAL: I'm building a nursing home. With Harj. We've been talking about it for months. Been to the bank with the business plan and they've said yes. We're gonna renovate a pub. The King George. Daddy used to go there on a Friday night when we were kids. Remember? It's like a cemetery now. We're starting small but we know what we want. There's a load of money in care homes Mum. I can do this. I want to show you...

JEETO gets up. LIZ starts clearing the trays. JEETO walks out. PAL composes a text on his phone.

LIZ: Do you think she's alright?

PAL: She'll get used to it.

LIZ: At least she's still got us lot.

PAL: Yeah.

PAL is checking his phone. He gets a text.

LIZ: Pal…

PAL: I'll see you later.

LIZ: Hang on…

PAL: *(Heading out.)* I'm meeting Harj.

LIZ: Wait…

PAL: He's got an uncle in India who might want to invest.

LIZ: Please! There's no time to talk to you any more.

He stops.

LIZ: It's just… now you're doing so well, I thought…

PAL: What?

LIZ: I thought… maybe… we could have a think, about that IVF. I got some leaflets and…

PAL: *(Interrupts.)* You're not still on about that are you?

LIZ: We didn't have the money before.

PAL: I need every penny for the business, you know I do.

LIZ: But it's what I want. And now you've sold the shop, Mum's gonna need something, she deserves something…

PAL: What the hell's it got to do with Mum?

LIZ: It's everything to do with her!

PAL: She's putting ideas into your head!

LIZ: Mum wants us to be happy.

PAL: We are fucking happy! *(A beat.)* Let's see where we are after the home's up and running. Yeah?

No response.

PAL: You're stressing yourself out Liz.

LIZ: It's not about the money is it?

PAL: I told you it is.

LIZ: Liar.

PAL: I've never lied to you. Never once in my life.

LIZ: You don't want a baby.

PAL: *(Exasperated.)* Fucking hell.

LIZ: Not like I do. What's the point of us?

PAL: Eh?

LIZ: What's the point of me being here? If you don't want the thing I can't live without. *(A beat.)* All I ever wanted was to get married and have kids.

PAL: I've gotta go.

He exits. LIZ watches him leave.

SCENE FOUR (JUNE)

JEETO sits on the armchair with her feet in the basin. She is half listening to the radio. She takes out the photo of her husband, beholds it lovingly.

The song 'Main Shayar To Nahin' from the film Bobby *comes on.*

Suddenly JEETO begins doing part of the notorious dance performed by Helen in the film. She does the moves perfectly and performs the love song to the photo of her husband. The song ends.

She turns off the radio and sits back down, dries her feet. COOKIE enters, talking on the phone, she's dressed in designer jeans, immaculately made up and carries a large tote. As she's talking, she takes out a laptop and sets it up on the table.

COOKIE: She's twelve, so it's got to be the shape of a twelve… I dunno do I? Whatever shape a twelve is!… Pink… Yeah… All the shades of pink you've got… Happy Birthday Princess Simmy… Not Simply!… Simmy!… All capitals… and tasteful yeah, none of that spidery lettering… S.I.M.M.Y… Y not I. Y… Alright… yeah… next week. Bye.

JEETO: Simmy must be excited about her party.

COOKIE: She's not bothered. Dunno why I'm bothering. We made do with a Victoria Sandwich from the stock room. Remember?

JEETO: Chah bunah *[make the tea]*.

COOKIE goes to put the tea on.

COOKIE: If you scroll down there's a cardiac surgeon and a couple of accountants. They're not catwalk material but then she's hardly Miss India.

JEETO: *(On laptop.)* The surgeon is aged seventy-five.

COOKIE: Well Reema's no spring chicken.

JEETO: And this accountant lives in Bangladesh. He is a mussulman *[muslim]* you stupid!

COOKIE: Major said he'd come back with Pal. What time is he normally home?

JEETO: Who knows? He lives on that building site.

COOKIE: Well he wants to make a success of it. And he's helping us out. I mean this contract for the bathrooms has given Major's business a proper boost.

JEETO: He never needed help before.

COOKIE: It's hard for builders these days. You don't know what these Polish cowboys are like. Major can't compete with their prices. *(A beat.)* Any word from Liz?

JEETO: She is still at her parents.

COOKIE: But she is coming back?

JEETO: Ask your brother.

COOKIE: You look tired Mum.

JEETO: My daughter-in-law should be here.

COOKIE: Isn't that Reema supposed to be keeping you company?

JEETO: She is helping Pal build his bloody home.

COOKIE: You can't blame him for wanting to do his own thing.

JEETO: *(On laptop.)* Funeral Director. Divorced. Bald. Good teeth.

COOKIE: She'll say no to bald.

JEETO: That girl is too fussy.

COOKIE: That's what I should have been.

COOKIE brings over tea and biscuits.

COOKIE: Has he shown you the pictures of the nursing home?

JEETO: On his bloody iPad.

COOKIE: Hasn't skimped on the decor has he? Always thought I was the one with the taste. But cream and mauve do work. Rooms look so fresh…

JEETO: Once the old people come the place will start to smell.

COOKIE: You're so bloody ungrateful, he's doing all this for you!

JEETO: I don't want to live in his smelly rooms. He can keep his gorah business! Old people should be looked after at home by their children.

COOKIE: He's gonna make more money than Daddy ever dreamed of.

JEETO: How much money do we need?

COOKIE: I dunno, more than we've got.

JEETO: I won't be here to spend it. You can't build a house with broken bricks. And if you do, the cracks will show.

COOKIE: You wanna stop watching that Star TV.

JEETO: I've told Chacha, and I have booked my ticket for December. One way. After I leave you will never see me again.

COOKIE: *(Sighs.)* I doubt that.

JEETO: What am I staying here for?

REEMA enters. Puts her bag down.

JEETO: Daddy put the business in Pal's name. I put this house in Pal's name. And I still have no grandson to look after.

COOKIE: You've got two granddaughters.

JEETO: I'm going back to my land, to rest my eyes on green fields.

REEMA: There are green fields here.

JEETO: People here don't love the land like they do back home.

REEMA: Love sometimes turns to hate.

JEETO: *(Indicates the laptop.)* Funeral director. Good teeth.

REEMA: *(Glances at the screen.)* Acha *[I see].*

JEETO: Time is running out Kurreeh.

REEMA: Time?

JEETO: You need to choose somebody. Soon.

COOKIE: *(To REEMA.)* Have you finished that course?

REEMA: I passed the NVQ Level One.

COOKIE: Get you, brainbox! I failed all my GCSEs. Is he gonna make you clean the toilets?

REEMA: No, the cleaner will do that.

JEETO: Indian girls have changed. They used to be glad to just be doing something. Did you know I cleaned toilets when I first came to this country?

COOKIE: Oh, where the hell is Major?

JEETO gets up, observes her hands.

JEETO: These hands won't clean toilets again. No sir! *(Gets up.)* Pushaab ondhe *[my wee is coming].* Reema, roti bunah *[make the roti].*

She exits. REEMA takes out an iPad Mini, opens it and starts typing.

COOKIE: Where did you get that?

REEMA: Birji asked me to check his accounts.

COOKIE: Why?

REEMA: Probably because I am good at mathematics and he doesn't have to pay me.

COOKIE: Right little mover and shaker aren't you?

REEMA goes to the kitchen, starts making roti.

COOKIE: Here's the invite to Simmy's do. *(Shows her.)* I've got caterers so us lot can relax and enjoy ourselves.

REEMA: Thought it was a children's party.

COOKIE: Yeah, but I've still booked a DJ and there'll be cava.

REEMA: I wasn't planning to come.

COOKIE: What do you mean?

REEMA: Why give them more to gossip about. Anyway won't be much fun without Liz.

COOKIE: Can't have everyone thinking we lock you up in the kitchen. And wear something decent. Buy a new suit.

REEMA: I don't have any money.

COOKIE reaches for the biscuit jar.

COOKIE: Daddy always made sure Mum had her emergency fund. *(Rummages.)* Is a hundred enough?

REEMA nods. COOKIE passes her the notes.

COOKIE: If it's not, tell me and I'll sort you out.

REEMA holds the money. She stares at it.

REEMA: I want… my own money…

COOKIE: You have been staying here for free.

REEMA: Free?

An angry REEMA shows COOKIE her floured hands.

REEMA: Since Liz went, who irons the clothes, washes the floor, cooks each meal? Who boils the water for your constant, endless bloody chah… you people have more chah running through your veins than blood!

COOKIE: Mum's trying to help you move on. Why do you think she's on Shaadi dot com every night? Least you get to choose. I never.

REEMA: You have a nice family. Big house, expensive car. Good business. In India, a girl might kill for your life.

COOKIE: Mum was always gonna find you a husband. She's giving you a leg-up back into the community. If that wasn't what you wanted, you shouldn't have come…

REEMA: This is the UK, I thought you understood about freedom.

COOKIE: Freedom? You have to make do. Get on with it, like everyone else.

REEMA: You can turn all your dreams into reality. Anything you want you get because you can pay for it!

COOKIE: You think I'm that shallow?

COOKIE takes over, starts making roti.

REEMA: What could there be Bhanji, that you don't have?

COOKIE: You said it love, I'm the chick who's got it all.

REEMA: Some people become accustomed to dissatisfaction.

COOKIE: Like I said, best to get on with it.

REEMA: What I don't understand is, why they don't change the circumstance of such dissatisfaction?

COOKIE: *(Stops.)* Expect it's like planting a bomb. On your life.

REEMA: I wish there were bombs being planted all over the world!

COOKIE takes vegetables out. Begins chopping. REEMA watches her.

REEMA: I'd like my own place.

COOKIE: Good luck. Go if you want.

REEMA: With two pounds in my pocket?

COOKIE: You're here for Mum until she finds you the right man. That's what Chacha thinks.

REEMA: What's this got to do with Chacha?

COOKIE: You're still his daughter-in-law. You leave this house and that's his izzat gone. His honour's all he's got left.

REEMA: I know about his honour.

COOKIE: Suppose you're not likely to see him again, so it doesn't matter.

REEMA: Chacha matters.

COOKIE: You're not even properly related, not by blood.

REEMA: Chacha is my family. *(Fierce.)* But you know, I have a right to be paid and to choose my future. *(A beat.)* Bhanji, you could ask Pal Birji for me.

COOKIE: Me?

REEMA: Stop one more woman from entering a circumstance she hates.

COOKIE: Nobody hands you life on a plate love. Ask him yourself.

REEMA: What would you do?

COOKIE: My time's gone…

REEMA: If you had your chance again…

COOKIE: *(A beat.)* I'd fucking grab it.

MAJOR and PAL enter.

MAJOR: Gonna be too cramped.

PAL: Shut up willya. Oy Reema, stick the chah on…

REEMA goes to make more tea. MAJOR's holding architect's plans.

MAJOR: Let me speak to the architect, if you add an extra 240mill…

PAL: They don't need a wash every day.

MAJOR: Who?

PAL: Old people.

COOKIE: Why not?

PAL: Tires them out.

MAJOR unfolds the plans, shows PAL.

MAJOR: There'll be a carer in there as well, I'm telling you, the extra 240'll make all the difference.

PAL: It's not the Ritz. Me and Harj looked round loads of care homes, the bathrooms are designed like that.

MAJOR: I've seen bigger kennels.

PAL: Regulation spec, the architect said.

MAJOR: There should be a certain amount of space between the toilet and the sink…

PAL: *(Interrupts.)* We need to get six residents on both floors.

MAJOR: What you charging per week?

PAL: Depends on their individual needs.

REEMA: Starts at seven hundred.

MAJOR: Seven hundred pounds?

PAL: Specialised care for Asians isn't it? All the carers speak the languages. Food's Gujarati or Punjabi. I'll even set a few fireworks off at Diwali. Reckon we can charge up to twelve fifty.

MAJOR: You're looking at more than ten grand a week.

REEMA: Income not profit. There are overheads, staff and associated costs.

MAJOR: Right.

COOKIE: She's got an iPad.

PAL: *(To COOKIE.)* Will you tell him?

COOKIE: *(To MAJOR.)* Just do what he says.

MAJOR: What do you know about fitting bathrooms? These plans aren't right.

PAL: If you don't want the job there's plenty who do.

COOKIE: Course he wants the job.

REEMA serves the tea.

PAL: They'll have enough space to soak their dentures. Come on Major, I want them to be happy, why do you think I'm doing this? *(Drinks tea.)* You'll make a packet.

MAJOR: Okay… okay.

Resigned MAJOR puts the plans down.

COOKIE: Who's doing your website?

PAL: Harj has sorted it. Reema'll show you.

REEMA shows them on the iPad. COOKIE and MAJOR are impressed.

COOKIE: Told you he knew what he was doing.

PAL: We've already had enquiries.

MAJOR: My bank manager said they weren't lending.

PAL: Business plan was spot on wasn't it Reema? And I had the capital from the shop.

MAJOR: This is a different league to the shop.

COOKIE: What did Harj put in?

PAL: His house.

MAJOR: His house?

PAL: As security.

COOKIE: Harj's house and the shop aren't enough to finance this business.

PAL: The bank gave us the mortgage to buy the pub. And we got an additional investor to fund the refurb.

COOKIE: Who?

PAL: Harj's Uncle Manjit. From India.

MAJOR: He's got this kind of money?

PAL: Uncle Manjit's Mr Big in telecoms in Amritsar. He reckons the future's in nursing homes. He likes us and the idea, wants to stay in the background while we do the leg work. Says we'll all make a fortune. And we will.

COOKIE: *(Impressed.)* You've worked out all your costings haven't you.

PAL: Course. Bank wouldn't have agreed to lend us otherwise.

REEMA indicates a page on the iPad.

REEMA: Staff/resident ratios, figures for the food and the domestics.

PAL: Show them the rota of nurses, there's a medical professional on duty twenty-four seven.

COOKIE: That's good innit Major…

REEMA: It's the law.

COOKIE: Sad though, packing all these budeh *[old people]* away like Christmas presents no one wants. I mean if you stuck Mum in there, she'd start a fire.

PAL: Not all Asian elders have kids to look after them. Even if they do, everyone's working nowadays. We can look after them properly, stop them getting lonely.

MAJOR: Haven't seen much of Liz lately.

PAL: Yeah, well… her mum's got… blood pressure.

MAJOR's phone rings. He answers it, goes off to the side.

PAL: *(To COOKIE.)* Hey, you'll have to organise a big do for the opening.

COOKIE: Leave it to me.

PAL: I know what people are saying. They're all watching to see what I do after the shop, waiting for me to trip up. They'll be waiting a long time. *(Finds papers.)* I wanna show Mum the letterhead. *(Shows cookies.)* See, they put my name on it and everything. *(Heads out.)* Bring some more chah up Reema.

He exits. REEMA gets a tea tray ready. MAJOR comes off the phone. COOKIE observes her husband.

COOKIE: Who was that?

MAJOR: Simmy, she's nervous about the party. Too much pressure…

REEMA exits.

COOKIE: I'm the one doing everything.

MAJOR: She needed to talk.

COOKIE: She never talks to me.

MAJOR: You're busy.

COOKIE: If you do a good job on these bathrooms you might get another contract. I could get a manager in the salon. Full-time. Then I can be at home more.

MAJOR: You hate being at home.

COOKIE's phone rings, it's on the table near MAJOR, he picks it up.

COOKIE: Wait, I'll answer it!

He answers it.

MAJOR: Hello… hello…

The other person rings off. MAJOR looks down at the phone. REEMA comes back in.

MAJOR: Your mate Tracey… Funny how she never wants to speak to me.

They stare at each other. He chucks the phone to her.

MAJOR: I'll meet you in the car.

He exits. COOKIE and REEMA exchange a look. REEMA clears up the tea tray.

COOKIE: Think you're noble do you? Sacrificing your life for Chacha.

REEMA: You know all about sacrifice Bhanji.

COOKIE: I never sacrificed anything love. I just didn't have the bottle to do what I wanted. I've turned an old barber's into the tackiest beauty salon in town. I've fed and clothed two kids who hate my guts. And I'm walking around on the arm of a man who I've never loved. That's my lot. Thing is I've got too much personality to feel sorry for myself.

COOKIE gets her bag.

COOKIE: I say, if your life's over why not kill yourself?

PAL comes back in.

PAL: Any more chah going?

REEMA goes to get him more tea. He composes a text. COOKIE eyes REEMA.

COOKIE: There's always a chink of light. If there wasn't, you wouldn't be breathing in and out.

COOKIE exits. REEMA watches her go. PAL reads through papers. REEMA slowly makes PAL's tea, takes it to him. Suddenly the cup falls from her hands to the floor.

PAL: What's wrong with you?

He clears it up.

REEMA: I'm sorry.

PAL: Uncle Manjit wants to see the copy for the brochure. We need to flag up the prayer room, outline dementia provision, mention the activities coordinator, that sort of thing.

He indicates the papers. REEMA stares at him.

REEMA: What do you think will happen to me, when you make a success of the home?

PAL: Dunno.

REEMA: I'm helping you for nothing.

PAL: You're living here for nothing.

REEMA: I deserve something. I must do.

PAL: Like what?

REEMA: When the home opens and the money comes, I want you to give me a loan for my MBA.

PAL: You that desperate for letters after your name?

REEMA: I'll pay you back. I swear. But I need to know.

PAL: *(A beat.)* Reckon you've earned it.

REEMA: You promise?

PAL: I'm not bothered what you do, as long as you pay me back.

REEMA: Thank you Birji… thank you… Knowing there's something to aim for makes a difference. *(Takes the papers.)*

PAL: Right.

REEMA: And doing a course like that, will give me chance. Being my own boss, it's what I've always wanted.

PAL: Lucky you.

REEMA: *(Flicks through papers.)* Your name on the letterhead, isn't that what you always wanted?

PAL: Yeah.

REEMA goes to make more tea.

REEMA: There's no sugar left.

PAL: Eh?

REEMA: Liz usually does the shopping.

PAL: Forget it.

He goes to the kitchen, finds a bottle of whisky.

REEMA: You must miss her. We all do.

He pours a glass, downs it.

PAL: Liz isn't interested in the business.

REEMA: Of course she is. You strike gold with the nursing home and she'll be here again, where she belongs.

He pours himself another glass.

REEMA: Are you listening? This house is Liz's house. You must find a way to get her. What about Simmy's party? Yes, that's it. You call her and tell her and she'll come. She'll come for Simmy.

PAL: I dunno.

REEMA: What do you mean you don't know?

PAL downs his drink.

REEMA: You've got to fight!

PAL: Maybe... maybe I can't have both. I mean Liz and the business...

REEMA: *(Interrupts.)* Harj's uncle is a multi-millionaire, and he believes in you. In this concept. He's chosen to invest in you and Harj. If it's not you, it'll be someone else. Could you bear that? *(A beat.)* You'll make more money in two years than your father made in his lifetime.

She and PAL stare at each other.

REEMA: Call her now. Invite her to Simmy's party.

She finds his phone, thrusts it into his hand.

REEMA: This is your chance. Take it!

PAL contemplates the phone. Lights down.

INTERVAL

ACT TWO

SIMMY's party. Bhangra music plays. Flashing lights. All the characters are dressed up to the nines and they dance enthusiastically. Music fades and they form a huddle around a huge cake. They all start singing Happy Birthday to SIMMY. The party goes on. To fade. Lights go down...

SCENE TWO

Later the same night, PAL and LIZ enter the Gill living room. He's wearing his suit from the party. LIZ is wearing a glam shalwar kameez also from the party. They are a bit tentative with each other, almost as if it's a first date.

PAL: Do you want a drink?

LIZ: Water please.

He pours her a glass of water, makes himself a large whisky.

LIZ: D'you think Simmy enjoyed herself?

PAL: Yeah, why not?

LIZ: She was sick in the toilets.

PAL: So was I.

Gives her the drink.

PAL: Thanks for coming. Meant a lot to Mum and Cookie.

LIZ: What about you?

PAL: Course me. *(Beholds her.)* You're beautiful you know that?

LIZ: *(Indicates her Kameez.)* Oh, I love this suit. Daddy bought it from Southall for me, after we got engaged. Remember?

PAL: I'm not talking about the suit.

LIZ moves away shyly.

LIZ: Reema said you're working together.

PAL: She's helping me out, with the home, you know.

LIZ: Makes sense. Reema's bright as a button.

PAL: She's hoping you'll be here in the morning. We all are.

Coy LIZ looks around the room.

LIZ: Feels strange being back.

PAL: Feels right to me. Been like me arm's missing.

LIZ: Stupid.

PAL: Nothing works without you. Never has. Since that first time I asked you to dance. Still can't believe you said yes.

LIZ: They were playing all them old tunes.

PAL: Teacher's favourites. So what if I asked you again now?

LIZ: Depends on the song.

PAL: Same one as back then. Just like I'm the same.

LIZ: You sure about that?

PAL: You know I am.

LIZ: What you waiting for?

PAL: Elizabeth Bradley, I've watched you singing in assembly, writing in history and titrating in chemistry. I know I'm a bit pissed but will you give me a dance? Please beautiful, perfect Elizabeth Bradley, one dance and I'll never bother you again.

He holds out his hand, she takes it.

LIZ: So you really want me to stay?

PAL: Never wanted you to go. *(Holds her close/Kisses her.)*

He turns the iPad on. 'True' by Spandau Ballet starts to play. They dance, it's as if they're back at the school disco where they first danced. They dance and kiss, dance and kiss. His phone rings. He turns it off, chucks it on a table. They carry on dancing. Suddenly the music is interrupted by a ping on the iPad which indicates receipt of an email. PAL stops when he hears the sound, but the music resumes and he goes back to dancing. They dance. Suddenly PAL breaks away from LIZ. He picks up the iPad, music stops, he checks his email.

LIZ: Pal!

PAL: Sorry, I just need to check something.

LIZ: I don't believe this!

PAL: I'll only be a minute.

LIZ: Can't you ever put that thing down!

PAL: I will, hold on…

LIZ: I wanna go to bed.

PAL: So do I.

LIZ: Come on then!

PAL: *(Reading.)* Harj needs some figures for tomorrow.

LIZ: *(Pointing at iPad.)* That thing, your bloody nursing home, won't make you happy.

PAL: After it's set up, we can afford to do anything, go anywhere. To the Maldives, I'll buy you a Maserati, you'll never have to lift a finger as long as you live.

LIZ: I'm ovulating!

PAL: We'll do it in the morning.

LIZ: I have to be at work at eight.

PAL: Won't take long.

LIZ: I need to lie still afterwards for at least half an hour.

PAL: Half an hour?

LIZ: So there's a chance of fertilisation.

PAL: *(Stops.)* Is that what you came back for?

No response.

PAL: *(Fierce.)* I asked you a question!

LIZ: Everywhere I go, I see mums pushing buggies, handing snacks to toddlers on them scooters. And on the news, they go on about how much ribena they can have and how you should read them fairy tales after bathtime. I could do that. I know about all that. I just need a chance.

PAL goes to the kitchen, finds a bottle of whisky, pours himself a glass.

PAL: So… that's the only thing you want from me?

LIZ: *(Upset.)* It's all I can think about. Wish it wasn't. But it is.

PAL: Do you love me?

LIZ: Yes.

PAL: I mean like you used to?

LIZ: Course I do.

PAL: You're enough Liz, you always have been.

LIZ: *(A beat.)* I need more.

PAL: Than what?

> *Silence.*

PAL: Go on, say it.

> *He approaches her.*

PAL: I'm sorry. Let's go to bed.

LIZ: I should never have come back.

PAL: I love you. I've loved you from that first moment.

LIZ: *(A beat.)* This… this is rubbish, it's rubbish… I'd better go.

> *She exits.*

PAL: Liz! *(Shouts.)* Liz!

> *PAL fights back tears, composes himself. Dressing-gown clad REEMA enters.*

PAL: We were talking and then… she went.

> *PAL swigs from the bottle of whisky.*

PAL: Can't she see the bags under my eyes? I mean I'm trying so fucking hard to make this work.

> *PAL finds another bottle of whisky, goes to leave.*

REEMA: Birji…

PAL: What?

REEMA: That bottle won't change anything.

PAL: Thing is, it does. For a bit. *(A beat.)* Thanks.

> *He exits.*

SCENE THREE (JULY)

Weeks later. Late evening. REEMA is on the iPad. JEETO is in the kitchen area. JEETO is serving up PAL's dinner. The atmosphere between the two women is heavy, tense. JEETO puts PAL's food on the table.

REEMA: Birji is late.

JEETO: What is there to come home for?

REEMA: Roti.

JEETO: Here is not like back home, men don't finish work when the sun sets. He has paperwork to do, internet, emails, Facebook, Google…

REEMA: Thyji, I told you we have computers in India.

JEETO: Hah, hah, hah *[yes, yes, yes]*, you know everything.

REEMA: And plenty of sharab in every pind. We don't need pubs for our men to be lost.

JEETO: You have been here long enough Kurreeh. Time you were married.

REEMA: I have work to do.

JEETO: Oh yes, no man is good enough for Reema! Is this how you were with Jiti? Moaning, groaning? It's up to a woman to keep hold of her man.

REEMA: That's not easy. You and me, we know.

JEETO: Kee?

REEMA: Both our husbands were drunks.

Suddenly JEETO stops dishing up.

JEETO: You're learning bad habits Kurreeh. Back home if a kurreeh like you talked this way to a budeeh *[old woman]* like me, that budeeh might kill her. Not with a knife or a pistol, but with one look from her eyes.

REEMA: Where is this back home you talk about? This place with green fields and the Pappar man and Gurdas Maan on the radio, where every day there is a wedding and ladies doing Gidha. In my Punjab, the men are running away from their birthrights, abandoning their women, drinking sharab *[alcohol]* all day and taking nusheh *[drugs]*, hanging themselves with their pugs *[turbans]*, because there's nothing. Nothing!

JEETO: When your heart is dark, all you see is darkness.

REEMA: And where is your light Thyji? Where is the light in this house?

JEETO: My daughter-in-law took it with her, the day she left.

PAL enters, he's on the phone.

PAL: Just tell him Harj… We can't have known, the survey said the electrics looked alright… Tell Uncle Manjit the subcontractor assured me it's gonna be fine, just might delay the alarm system by a few weeks… He's sent the first instalment hasn't he?… Gonna cost an extra few thousand that's all… Ok, yeah… you Skype him… tell him… tell him it's getting sorted.

He ends the call, opens his iPad, sets it up on the counter, starts typing.

JEETO: Roti?

PAL: Me and Harj had chips.

JEETO: Chips is not food.

PAL: Willya stop going on?

JEETO: You need to bring your wife home.

JEETO slowly gathers her bag and stuff together.

JEETO: Kurreeh, don't wake me in the morning.

She wearily heads to the door and goes upstairs. REEMA continues to clear the kitchen.

PAL: Dunno why the Indian's getting his Kachee in a twist.

REEMA: This is how it is. He wants to be kept informed.

PAL: He should trust us.

REEMA: Trust doesn't count in India, people believe in hard cash.

PAL: He's gonna get plenty of that.

REEMA: Harj's uncle knows. He's just making you sweat.

PAL: Yeah.

REEMA: Do you want to eat?

PAL: Later.

He gets up and goes to pour a drink from a bottle of Johnnie Walker Black Label. REEMA watches him.

REEMA: Can I have some?

PAL: What?

REEMA: Can I have a drink? Whisky.

PAL: Help yourself.

REEMA finds a glass, pours herself a drink. She downs it. PAL sits, continues to work on the iPad. REEMA fills her glass with more whisky.

PAL: Didn't realise you drank.

REEMA: My husband taught me. Do you remember him?

PAL: A bit.

REEMA: Jiti used to talk about you all the time. He looked up to you, like an older brother.

PAL: Me?

REEMA: He told me about the fun you had when he visited you all. Bowling, cinema, you watched *Matrix* didn't you?

PAL: Right, yeah.

REEMA: There is a photo of you and him together on Chacha's mantelpiece. From your day trip to London.

PAL: Oh yeah, we went to Buckingham Palace.

REEMA: No, it was the Tower of London. Don't you remember?

PAL: Was ages ago.

REEMA: Jiti said you used to have long talks.

PAL: Dunno.

REEMA: When he and Chacha argued, he would always say nobody understands me, except Pal Birji.

PAL: Did he?

REEMA: Chacha also thinks a lot of you. And your mum. He said you would look after me. Have you heard from Liz?

PAL stops for a second, then carries on typing.

REEMA: When they go, it's like they take your future with them.

REEMA pours more drinks.

REEMA: You know when Jiti left, I could have gone back to my own village, to my parents.

PAL: Why didn't you?

REEMA: Chacha.

PAL: He could have got a servant to clean the house and make roti.

REEMA: My parents were never interested in me. My sister was more beautiful and my brother was... the son made of gold. But after I was married Chacha treated me like I was his blood. He was the father I should have had.

PAL: *(Amused.)* What are you on about?

REEMA: After the home opens, I'd like to move out. I'll still work for you, hopefully... I'll be starting my course. But... you see, I'm worried about Chacha.

PAL: Once Mum's out there, she'll be making his roti, and I'll send her a few quid every month, whatever she needs, so Chacha's gonna be fine.

REEMA: It's not that.

PAL: What then?

REEMA: *(A beat.)* Can I tell you something?... Something I haven't told anyone.

PAL nods. REEMA watches PAL uneasily, walks round the room with her drink. Stops.

REEMA: Once, before Jiti left, he had been playing cards with some men from the village. He lost the game and owed them money.

Late one night I was sleeping and these men came to the kauthee *[house]*. They wanted their money but Jiti had gone out drinking, he was taking nushih *[drugs]* by then. I heard Chacha's voice and shouting on the verandah. I got out of bed and went outside. The men were drunk and one of them grabbed me, the others laughed and this man started pulling at my clothes, Chacha shouted at them to stop but they wouldn't.

I was screaming. Chacha went inside. They carried on laughing and... my hair came loose. The next thing I knew, there was a noise like a bomb and the man, the one who was holding me, fell back. I looked up and there was Chacha with his rifle. He shouted at them to go, to stay away from his land. The others took the dead one and went. They never came back. Chacha started crying and cursing Jiti. He said, you are my daughter now kureeh *[girl]*. You are my izzat and I am yours. We will protect each other's honour.

PAL: Chacha killed a man?

REEMA: He did the right thing. And I swore I would do the right thing by him. But now... if I leave here, his izzat will be destroyed. *(A beat.)* He is owed better than that. *(Drinks.)* I don't know what to do.

PAL: I'm sorry.

REEMA: Why should you know? All you consider is your self-advancement.

REEMA pours more drinks. They are both getting steadily drunker.

PAL: Is that what you think of me? I bathed my dad the last year of his life. Carried him to the toilet and dressed him every day so he could die at home. Even passed him a Johnnie Walker miniature so he had a smile on his deathbed. He told me to take care of the shop. To look after Mum and Liz. *(Drinks.)* My Dad and Chacha and all that lot, they have these expectations, you have to leave them behind.

REEMA: How do you learn to bear their disappointment?

PAL: Just… get used to it.

REEMA: It's different for you. Because you are a male. *(Takes his hand.)* We are both flesh and blood, see. We should be the same.

PAL: We are.

REEMA: Both drunk.

They laugh.

REEMA: Worth the same I mean. I want to be worth the same, as you.

PAL: You can decide what you're worth.

REEMA: Can I?

PAL: It's not a decision you should let other people make.

REEMA: *(Drinks.)* Didn't you ever want something different?

PAL: Had everything I wanted here. Thought I did.

REEMA: And you never want to escape?

PAL: Yeah. Yeah sometimes I do now.

REEMA: I don't think there's anything wrong with wanting more.

PAL: More?

REEMA: More than there is.

She kisses him. He retreats.

PAL: Wait, this isn't right…

REEMA: Sorry… I just…

They behold one another. She kisses him again. This time he responds. Lights slowly go down.

SCENE FOUR (NOVEMBER)

JEETO sits on her DFS chair. Her tabard and bag are by her side, her feet are soaking in a basin of water. Beside her, is the photo of her husband. She starts singing 'Mohabbat khi Jhooti' ['the lie that is love' – a famous hindi song] to the photo. PAL enters, takes out his iPad.

He's about to start typing but pauses. Finds a bottle of Johnnie Walker, opens it, pours himself a large tumbler of whisky. JEETO observes her son, puts the photo back in her bag.

JEETO: You used to want chah when you came home.

PAL: Uncle Manjit, he's doing my head in.

He swigs as he talks. Speaks quickly, almost to himself.

PAL: Sub-contractor's ready to fit the alarm system, but the Indian won't approve the overspend. Wants to know why we're so over budget. We've told him, it's cos the electrics were fucked and okay it's taken a few months, but it's sorted now. He keeps asking for the paperwork but we sent it ages ago. He's holding everything up and it's costing money. *(Pours another drink.)* Are you listening?

JEETO: Oh yes.

PAL: I mean there's gonna be setbacks, when you're doing, planning something on this scale… I've told Major. He thought he'd be starting next week… but he has to wait. Cookie's been kicking off saying he's bought the stock but what can I do?

JEETO: Harj's uncle is your boss.

PAL: He's not my boss, he's our partner.

JEETO: He has the biggest share.

PAL: Only cos there's no money in this fucking country.
(Swigs.) And you, you're not exactly helping.

JEETO: Me?

PAL: You and Chacha sitting on that land, holding onto three hundred grand that's not doing anything…

JEETO: Don't talk about my land.

JEETO starts drying her legs, puts her shoes and socks back on. PAL glances over to the kitchen area.

PAL: I'll have me chah now. Where's Reema?

JEETO: Reema is not a Kenwood Teasmade. You make the chah.

PAL: I can't make it like you lot make it can I?

He reluctantly fills a saucepan with water. Puts it on the hob and throws cinnamon, cardamom and a tea bag into the water. MAJOR and COOKIE enter with shopping bags.

JEETO: Chah?

MAJOR: Yeah go on Mum.

JEETO: Cookie?

COOKIE: Alright.

PAL: How long's this water supposed to take?

JEETO comes over, takes over the tea.

COOKIE: *(Takes her coat off.)* You heard from the Indian?

PAL: I'm sorting it.

COOKIE: Major's bought half the stock already.

She starts unpacking the shopping. PAL opens his iPad.

MAJOR: Not half!

COOKIE: Nearly half, you've ordered it.

PAL: You can start in the next couple of weeks.

JEETO: *(To PAL.)* Your wife is upstairs.

PAL: What?

JEETO: Collecting the rest of her things.

PAL: Why didn't you say?

He goes to rush out.

JEETO: Leave her!

He carries on, she blocks his way.

JEETO: I said leave her. She is talking to Reema.

PAL takes this in. He retreats.

JEETO: She'll come when she's ready. She is packing the rest of her things.

MAJOR: Didn't see her car.

JEETO: Her father is outside waiting in his car.

MAJOR: We could have given her a lift.

COOKIE: Yeah, her mum and dad are only up the road. We see them in Asda all the time. They never say hello.

MAJOR: Did she take her car when she went?

COOKIE: Course she did. It's her car isn't it?

MAJOR: *(To PAL.)* Stock's in the warehouse. No need to worry about the stock.

JEETO gives out the tea. COOKIE eyes PAL.

COOKIE: If you don't get a move on your grand opening's gonna be delayed. I've booked that Channi from Alaap.

MAJOR: I used to like him.

They drink their tea. JEETO dishes out biscuits. They eat the biscuits. COOKIE opens the last carrier bag.

COOKIE: What do you think? For Chacha.

She holds up a couple of shirts.

MAJOR: Not bad.

COOKIE: You'll miss it Mum.

JEETO: Kee? *[What?]*

COOKIE: Pal's opening. Got your plane ticket haven't you? You'll be sitting on Chacha's verandah staring at your green fields.

JEETO: I'm not going.

COOKIE: But I've bought these now!

PAL: I knew it.

JEETO: What did you know?

PAL: You go on about leaving and then you change your mind. Same as all the other times.

JEETO: This is different from the other times.

PAL: Five hundred quid down the drain, how stupid can you get!

JEETO: Remember who you are talking to!

373

PAL: Five hundred Mum!

MAJOR: Why Mum?

JEETO: Reema.

COOKIE: What about her?

JEETO: Says she is ill.

MAJOR: Eh?

JEETO: You haven't noticed? Pal?

PAL: No.

JEETO: Because you don't speak to her any more.

PAL: I'm hardly here am I? I'm busy.

JEETO: Always bastard busy.

COOKIE: What's wrong with her?

JEETO: She thinks she has been poisoned.

MAJOR: Poisoned?

JEETO: Says she has eaten bad food. Every day she lies in bed moaning, groaning… I force her to come downstairs and eat toast.

She turns to stare at PAL.

JEETO: You know that kureeh brought so many shalwar kameez from back home. All twenty-one suits from her wedding day. None of them fit her any more. Too tight. *(Slaps her own stomach.)* Here.

PAL: *(Light/Nervous.)* She wants to go on a diet.

JEETO: I have been watching her. *(A beat.)* Her shape is changing.

PAL: What you telling us for?

JEETO: Maybe you know why?

JEETO stares at PAL. Suddenly slaps him round the face. He keels over.

PAL: It was a mistake. One mistake…

COOKIE: Bloody hell!

MAJOR: So are you and her like…

PAL: No! It was only once, wish I'd never laid eyes on her. Mum…

JEETO has her back to PAL.

JEETO: I don't want to look at your face.

PAL: Don't say anything to Liz.

COOKIE: *(To PAL.)* You stupid idiot.

PAL: I'm begging you, please…

COOKIE: Why can't you think before… ?

MAJOR: Leave him…

COOKIE: … before you spoil things…

JEETO gathers her things together.

MAJOR: I said leave him!

COOKIE: And she's keeping it?

JEETO: She has no choice.

Silence. JEETO exits.

MAJOR: *(Sits down.)* Lot to take in this, isn't it?

A shocked PAL slowly composes himself. He goes to pour another drink.

COOKIE: You are unbelievable!

MAJOR: *(To COOKIE.)* You never made a mistake?

COOKIE: Not one this fucking stupid.

PAL: Nothing works without Liz.

MAJOR: *(To PAL.)* If you let her go now, give it some time, you never know, maybe she'll come back.

COOKIE: Don't give him hope. He doesn't deserve hope.

The door opens. LIZ enters. She's made up and smartly dressed, wearing an autumn coat. She holds a small suitcase. They stare at her.

MAJOR: Alright Liz.

LIZ: Alright Major.

COOKIE: How's your mum and dad?

LIZ: The same.

COOKIE: Do you want chah?

LIZ: No. Thanks.

She contemplates the space, walks over to the kitchen.

LIZ: It's been weird without me kitchen. *(Opens a cupboard.)* Oh, Mum's out of atta.

COOKIE: I'll get some.

LIZ: My mum and dad haven't got a thuva *[special roti pan]. (A beat.)* I'll have to buy one.

COOKIE finds the thuva under the cooker.

COOKIE: Take it.

LIZ: No I can't.

COOKIE: Go on, you have to have your roti.

LIZ takes it, puts it on the side. She observes the kitchen.

LIZ: I'm glad we got these units. They were pricey but they're so spacious. Me and Mum picked them out, just before our wedding wasn't it Pal?

PAL: Yeah.

LIZ: *(Picturing the memory.)* We sat on them thrones for the sagan *[blessing]*. Like Posh and Becks. Remember?

PAL: Course.

LIZ: We got twenty grand that day.

MAJOR: Twenty?

LIZ: Yeah.

MAJOR: *(To COOKIE.)* How much did we get?

COOKIE: Six.

MAJOR: Did alright didn't you?

PAL: *(Gets up.)* Liz...

LIZ: *(Interrupts.)* My dad said they should have kept the Asian kids separate from us at school, on the other side of the classroom, you know like the men and women are at the Gurdwara. *(A beat.)* But no one could keep us apart.

PAL: Never.

LIZ: I turned my back on my family for you.

PAL: I know.

LIZ: I learned to goon the atta, make tharka, do gidha with Mum. Daddy always said I was more Indian than you. *(A beat.)* Can I please have a photo of him?

COOKIE finds one on the sideboard, hands it to her. LIZ looks at it.

LIZ: I still miss him so much.

PAL: I know.

LIZ: Take care of Mum.

PAL: I don't want this. Please...

Emotion rises in LIZ.

LIZ: All the years we've been trying, and it happened for you and her... just like that...

REEMA enters followed by JEETO who is holding a blanket. REEMA has put on weight but looks washed out. She and LIZ eye one another uneasily.

LIZ composes herself.

LIZ: At moments like this, you realise... There really isn't a God.

LIZ turns to JEETO and touches her feet. She picks up the thuva and exits. The front door slams. Moments pass. PAL runs out after her. JEETO helps REEMA onto the chair, she covers her with a blanket. JEETO gets a glass of water and tablets.

JEETO: Chah?

COOKIE: Not for me.

MAJOR: I'll have another cup Mum. *(To REEMA.)* So... er... how are you feeling?

REEMA: Not good.

JEETO hands REEMA a glass of water and some pills.

JEETO: Take these.

JEETO puts more chah on the hob. PAL returns, he goes to pour a whisky. REEMA takes the tablets.

COOKIE: What are they for?

JEETO: She feels sick. All the time.

COOKIE: It's called something, when you're sick the whole time…

MAJOR: What, until you have the baby?

COOKIE: Yeah.

PAL points at REEMA, he's getting drunk.

PAL: She should be the one going.

REEMA: I am ready to face my shame. Let it torture me. Liz was my friend.

COOKIE: Friend?

REEMA: This thing inside me, this sickness, it's like a poison, yes that's it… a poison inside… destroying my whole body.

PAL: *(To JEETO.)* Her staying here's wrong.

JEETO: *(Shouts.)* She's staying! This is because of your wrong, remember? *(A beat.)* Cookie chah bunah. *[make the tea.]*

COOKIE takes over the tea. She serves MAJOR and REEMA.

JEETO: *(To PAL.)* I'll tell you how things are going to be.

She goes over to the kitchen area, pours his drink into the sink.

PAL: What are you doing?

JEETO then pours the rest of the bottle down the sink.

PAL: Mum!

She opens a cupboard, finds another bottle of whisky. He tries to get it off her, they struggle. MAJOR and COOKIE rush over.

MAJOR: Bloody hell Pal!

COOKIE: Stop it!

PAL is about to take the bottle from her when MAJOR drags him away.

JEETO holds up the bottle.

JEETO: *(Breathless.)* You put this down.

She pours the rest of the bottle down the sink. JEETO hurriedly finds PAL's work bag, opens it, produces his iPad, hands it to him.

JEETO: You take this thing, you go to work, you make that bloody nursing home into something. And then you wait for your child.

REEMA: If I'd found out before I could have got the poison out of my body.

JEETO: Choop kurreeh! *(To PAL.)* Something in this house has died, you killed it. And now a new time is coming.

PAL: I don't want it.

JEETO indicates REEMA.

JEETO: You don't have to share a bedroom.

PAL: I can't do this.

JEETO: *(Fury rising.)* You think I'm going to fall down after standing tall all these years? After being spat at by goreh and now pitied by my own people. You think I'm going to let you turn me into nothing? *(A beat.)* Now go to work. Go to work. Jah. *[Go.]*

Dishevelled PAL slowly composes himself. He gathers his iPad and other stuff together, walks out. JEETO pours tea into two cups, puts a couple of slices of bread in a toaster. Hands one cup to REEMA.

JEETO: Toast is nearly ready.

REEMA: I feel too sick.

JEETO: *(To COOKIE.)* Make sure she eats it.

JEETO heads out. COOKIE goes to stand by the toaster.

REEMA: I should never have come to this house.

COOKIE: That's a no-brainer. *(Takes out butter and a knife/To MAJOR.)* This is more Liz's home than Pal's, but he's still here.

MAJOR: It was her choice to go.

Toast springs up, she starts buttering it.

COOKIE: He should suffer for this.

MAJOR: *(A beat.)* And what should happen to you?

COOKIE: Eh?

MAJOR: You're worse than your brother cos you pretend to be something you've never been. And I'm as bad.

COOKIE: Major…

MAJOR: I let you pretend, cos I wanted to believe in you.

COOKIE: Nothing's ever happened… I mean I've never done anything… I swear…

MAJOR: It's in your head all the time though, isn't it? *(Loud.)* Isn't it?

She nods.

MAJOR: You don't deserve the life you've got.

He exits. Shocked COOKIE watches him go. She looks at REEMA who has not touched her toast.

COOKIE: Maybe you'll be the mothering type. Wish I was, but I wasn't.

REEMA: I was drunk that night.

COOKIE: You must have been to have fucked Pal. *(Indicates toast.)* Mum said you have to eat that.

REEMA shakes her head.

COOKIE: Eat it!

Nothing. COOKIE takes the toast and angrily forces it into REEMA's mouth. She resists, chokes and gags. They struggle and REEMA finally succumbs to chewing it.

COOKIE: I'm sorry but you have to.

An upset REEMA slowly eats the toast.

SCENE FIVE

Months later. Spring. The living area is adorned with blue baby stuff. Cards and flowers are on all the tables and in the kitchen area. A bouncer and changing mat are on the floor. JEETO puts sheets in a moses basket. She glances towards the photo of her husband which is placed prominently on a decorative table.

JEETO: *(Excited/To photo.)* Soon you will see him properly.

She holds up a blue baby gro.

JEETO: Five pounds in Asda. Binder was there, buying her lottery ticket. That dungar *[cow]* said to me, Bhanji, what is this kismet God has given you? I looked her straight in her small eye and I said God has given me a pottha *[grandson]*. If I die today my kismet has been more golden than I could have dreamed.

She goes over to the kitchen area and stirs a huge pot on the hob.

JEETO: How can there be shame in a baby? So new and perfect and untouched. *(To photo.)* He looks like you.

PAL enters, sees all the baby stuff.

PAL: Why's all the stuff down here?

JEETO: He is coming soon.

PAL: It's supposed to be upstairs. What's that smell?

JEETO: Panjiri. Atta, badam, ghee cooked up with sugar and more nuts.

PAL: I'll have some with me chah.

JEETO: It's for that kurreeh *[girl]*. If she eats it three times a day her milk will be rich and thick.

PAL: Might just have the chah.

He puts a pan of water on.

JEETO: If only Daddy could hold him in his arms.

PAL: He'd probably get pissed and drop him.

JEETO: Choop kar *[Be quiet]*. That boy is your future.

PAL takes his iPad out.

PAL: Here's the latest photos.

JEETO: *(Looks at the iPad.)* Bathrooms. Acha. Why so small?

PAL: Regulation spec!

JEETO: For a nursing home or a nursery?

PAL: Our Major's done a good job. And Harj reckons we're on track to open in eight weeks.

JEETO makes the chah.

JEETO: I thought we could go to the Gurdwara tomorrow.

PAL: What for?

JEETO: My grandson must have a name! The Giani will open the book and choose the letter. I have been praying for a G.

PAL: G?

JEETO: Gurgaggandeep Singh!

PAL: Bit long innit.

JEETO: My grandson needs something with impact.

JEETO receives a text, checks it, beams.

JEETO: Cookie… they are on their way.

PAL picks up his iPad, heads out.

JEETO: Where are you going?

PAL: Got work to do. I'll have me chah later.

JEETO: Aren't you going to greet him?

PAL: You're the one who wanted this Mum.

He continues out.

JEETO: I phoned Chacha.

PAL stops.

JEETO: He sends you budhaiya *[congratulations]*.

PAL: What have you told him?

JEETO: That you and Liz have a son. Why break one more heart?

PAL: You're mad.

JEETO: The boy is your blood.

PAL: I told you, she can stay here, and you can do what you want, but this is nothing to do with me.

JEETO: Then why do you care what I tell people?

PAL: Because it's a pack of lies! Chacha's gonna find out soon enough. Someone in the pind'll spread the gossip.

JEETO: Chacha will pretend it's not true.

PAL: What if he asks you?

JEETO: He won't.

JEETO pours out chah.

JEETO: We were talking the day he was born. He said now you have a son, things have changed.

PAL: What things?

She hands him papers from her bag.

JEETO: We both agreed it is time I put my land in your name.

PAL: You joking?

JEETO: Remember all the times you begged me for that land. Now you have shown me you can work like a dog, and suffer and suffer. You have earned it.

PAL: My business is what I've worked for. That land, your land, means nothing to me.

JEETO: It might to your son.

PAL: No. You keep it.

JEETO: Chacha sent all the papers weeks ago. *(Shows him.)* He was hoping for a boy. Please.

PAL: Why?

JEETO: It's the only thing Daddy can give him.

PAL looks through the papers.

JEETO: Sign, before he comes home. I want your daddy's heir to feel the power of his birthright when he comes through that door.

PAL signs the papers. JEETO puts them on the dining table.

JEETO: Now you have everything you wanted, this house, your business, your land, yes sir!

PAL: I still miss her Mum...

JEETO: Maybe next year we will all go to visit Chacha, take little Gurgaggandeep to visit your land...

PAL: I mean Liz...

JEETO: He will be walking by then, running! And his ticket is free until he is two. So we should go. We must!

PAL: Will you listen?

JEETO: I'm not interested in your memories!

COOKIE enters. She carries shopping bags and a car seat in which a baby boy sleeps.

COOKIE: Here's our little man!

She puts the seat down so the back faces the audience. JEETO is immediately flustered.

JEETO: Thail! [oil!] Where is it?

She covers her head with her chooni [scarf], rushes into the kitchen and pours a small amount of oil from a bottle of mustard oil into a bowl.

JEETO: Pani Barr mundhi dhee mayi, Sookha sookeh dhee noo ahah dhin aya [Pour the water, boy's grandmother, the greatest comfort has arrived on this day]

JEETO pours the oil down the frame of the door.

JEETO: Sagan [blessing] for my boy!

REEMA enters. She slowly sits down on the leather chair. She appears blank and uncomfortable. JEETO and COOKIE beam at the baby.

JEETO: Daddy number 2!

COOKIE: Spitting image.

PAL: Where's Major?

COOKIE: Gone back to your bathrooms, but he's been singing to him all morning. *(To baby.)* Hasn't he? Been singing? *(Chants.)* United! United! United!… Oh look he's smiling…

PAL: He's not.

JEETO: He is, he is. Smiling!

COOKIE/JEETO: United! United! United!

COOKIE: Major's already got him a football kit. Oh and I got him these.

She starts opening the shopping bags, takes out assorted baby clothes. JEETO squeals with joy. COOKIE holds up shorts and sunglasses.

COOKIE: For when he goes on holiday!

She holds up a tiny suit and tie.

JEETO: For when he goes to his office!

PAL: How much stuff does he need?

COOKIE: Shut yer mouth you!

In the kitchen area, JEETO puts Panjiri into a bowl.

COOKIE: I never appreciated Simmy and Jasmin when they were born. They just got on my nerves! I'm gonna make sure I enjoy my nephew!

JEETO: Nee kurrih.

JEETO hands the panjiri to REEMA. REEMA takes the bowl, starts eating with a spoon.

JEETO: Cookie, chah bunah.

COOKIE goes to make tea, JEETO goes to take the baby out of the car seat.

PAL: What you taking him out for?

JEETO: Choop kar *[be quiet]*.

PAL beholds REEMA awkwardly.

PAL: *(To REEMA.)* Are you alright?

No response. JEETO sings a boli [traditional song] to the baby. She dances a gidha [dance] as she sings.

JEETO: We'll go to the Gurdwara with him tomorrow kurreeh, to name him. What do you think?

REEMA: He'll need a name.

PAL's phone rings. He answers it.

PAL: Harj. What?… Yeah… When?… How come?

PAL picks up his iPad, heads upstairs.

JEETO: Cookie, give her chah.

COOKIE hands REEMA a cup of tea.

JEETO: Okay Kurreeh?

REEMA nods.

JEETO: When did you feed him?

REEMA: Before we left the hospital. It hurt a lot. I'm sore, nearly bleeding. They said I could give him formula in the bottles.

JEETO: Hurt is normal. My grandson wants his mother's dhood *[milk].*

(To BABY.) Do you want to see your house? Come, I'll show you your room…

She exits.

COOKIE: Give him a bottle if you like. I got you some powdered.

COOKIE unpacks it and puts it in the kitchen.

COOKIE: A little baby, makes you feel so hopeful. Like a new chance to get things right. You did well, with the pushing, you forget how bad it is.

REEMA: I hated it.

COOKIE: *(Nostalgic.)* Like being hit on the back with a lawnmower, again and again…

REEMA: The whole thing was… disgusting.

COOKIE: Have your chah.

COOKIE watches her as she drinks.

COOKIE: You'll have to get down them baby groups. Singing nursery rhymes and comparing dirty nappies. That'll cheer you up. *(She starts making a bottle.)* Mum'll help, and I will. Pal's home'll be open soon. Get involved again and you'll be rich.

Suddenly MAJOR bursts in.

MAJOR: Where's Pal?

COOKIE: Major?

MAJOR: Where the fuck is he?

COOKIE: Upstairs.

MAJOR opens the door.

MAJOR: *(Shouts.)* Pal! Get down here!

COOKIE: What the hell's wrong?

MAJOR: Pal!

He paces around, he's a bag of nerves.

MAJOR: Fuck, fuck!

A shocked PAL enters.

PAL: I just heard…

MAJOR: You bastard.

PAL: I didn't know, I swear…

MAJOR grabs him.

MAJOR: All the blokes who work for me, their families… they trust me, I've let them down, because of you…

COOKIE: Major, get off him!

She comes between them.

PAL: It's gonna be alright.

MAJOR: Fuck off.

COOKIE: Will you calm down? What's happened?

MAJOR retreats.

MAJOR: The payment for the plumbing and the fittings. *(He can't say it.)* Your cheque's bounced...

COOKIE: Right, well... sometimes it happens...

MAJOR: Accountant just rang me.

PAL: I'm sorting it.

COOKIE: *(To PAL.)* I mean it's just cash flow isn't it?

PAL: *(Agitated.)* Uncle Manjit never paid the second instalment.

COOKIE: What?

PAL: Told Harj he's still missing the paperwork. *(To REEMA.)* But we sent it ages ago, didn't we?

REEMA: I don't know.

PAL: What do you mean? I told you to...

REEMA: I must have... forgotten.

PAL: *(Shouts.)* You were supposed to send it!

COOKIE: Get it to him now and then he'll release the money.

PAL: *(Shakes his head.)* He's pulled out.

COOKIE: What?

PAL: And... and the bank are calling in the loan.

COOKIE: No, no... they can't be...

MAJOR: *(To COOKIE.)* So he can't pay anyone.

PAL: I'll fix it. Once I've spoken to the bank.

MAJOR: I spent tens of thousands on stock. What about our mortgage? The girls' future?

PAL: I ain't gonna let anything happen to you am I? Not to my sister, my nieces...

MAJOR: My dad spent half his life breathing in asbestos so he could leave me that business, you ain't gonna destroy it...

COOKIE: Course he won't. He said he's gonna sort it. Aren't you Pal?

PAL: *(To MAJOR.)* Yeah, once the bank visit the premises and see how close we are, it'll be alright. I'll convince them. I will…

COOKIE: Well go on then. *(Urgent.)* Go on!

PAL takes out his phone. Presses a button. MAJOR and COOKIE watch him. REEMA picks up the papers PAL signed for JEETO. Lights fade.

SCENE SIX

Weeks later. The once immaculate living area is a mess. Dirty dishes are piled up by the sink. The room now appears dated and drab, as if it's in need of a lick of paint. An exhausted looking REEMA wears baggy cheap sportswear. She sits blankly. JEETO comes in from work. She glares at REEMA, hands her a dummy.

JEETO: I said I don't want you giving him a dummy.

REEMA contemplates the dummy. JEETO takes off her coat.

JEETO: You should have tried longer with your own milk. *(A beat.)* Did Pal do the phone call?

REEMA: Not yet.

JEETO: *(Sits down.)* Did he take you to the Town Hall?

REEMA: I forgot to tell him.

JEETO: What have you been doing all day?

REEMA: I don't know.

JEETO: My grandson needs his father's name on his birth certificate.

REEMA: Maybe his father should give him his milk.

JEETO: What's wrong with you Kurreeh?

REEMA: I don't feel like myself today.

JEETO: This is your kismet. Plenty of girls have it worse.

REEMA: Plenty.

JEETO: Once this money business is finished, we'll go to India, visit Chacha. I already told him you are good with the baby. I said you are better than Liz.

REEMA: You shouldn't have said that.

JEETO: I have to prepare him, for what is to come.

REEMA: What is to come?

JEETO: When the time is right, I will tell him Liz has gone and that you are to be the mother. And you both need to start thinking about a wedding.

REEMA: Wedding?

JEETO: Someone has to wipe up this mess. *(A beat.)* Sometimes Kurreeh you just have to endure. Find a way of tolerating. Look at me, I'm the one who told Pal to do that phone call. You think I want that to happen. Do you?

REEMA shakes her head.

JEETO: Make sure you both go to the Town Hall tomorrow.

A dishevelled PAL enters. He goes to the kitchen area, starts making tea. JEETO joins him, starts making a bottle of formula.

JEETO: Time for your boy's dhood.

PAL: Can't anyone round here fill a dishwasher?

REEMA: I haven't had time.

JEETO: He's going to be big and strong…

PAL: Doesn't take long.

He starts filling the dishwasher.

JEETO: … like his Dhadha.

PAL finds empty biscuit wrappers.

PAL: You've got time to eat custard creams.

JEETO: Did you help Harj move?

PAL: Yeah. He hasn't even got that much stuff left, he's sold nearly everything. Never thought he'd be living back with his mum and dad.

JEETO: You never left yours.

PAL: That was my mistake. *(Indicates REEMA.)* Her coming over was yours.

JEETO: Don't blame her.

PAL: She sits there all day, doing nothing.

JEETO: She's depressed.

PAL: Who isn't?

JEETO: Once you speak to this man, you can pay Major, pay all your debts?

PAL: Yeah.

JEETO: Thank God, we've still got this house.

PAL: It's all we've got.

JEETO: When is he calling?

PAL: In a few minutes.

JEETO: Tell me his name.

PAL: Jarnail Singh.

JEETO: Atwal?

PAL: Yeah.

JEETO: Mohinder's son. They used to rent land from Chacha. You must know him Reema.

REEMA: Yes.

JEETO: How can that cunjar afford my land?

PAL: He's made it big. Runs a dairy outside Ludhiana.

REEMA: He's a thief.

PAL starts to pace around.

PAL: If we'd had more time we could have found another investor. Harj even said so. Bank should have trusted us Mum. I hate this fucking country. You can't do anything here. We were trying to think big, take a risk... be brave...

JEETO: *(Flat.)* You didn't have the money.

PAL: My nursing home's standing there empty. Fucking repossessed! Half finished. Nearly finished. Some fucker's gonna come and take it over and all the blood and sweat we put in… was all for nothing. They're gonna take my business, my place…

JEETO: Stop this moaning, groaning.

PAL: It's not right.

JEETO: Is it right that I have to sacrifice my land to keep this roof over our head?

PAL: *(Angry.)* Don't you think I'm ashamed?

JEETO: *(Furious.)* Don't you say that. Don't you let anyone hear you say that! I bear the shame on my shoulders because you are my blood and that boy is your blood. You bear it. You live with your shame and you sell my land to Jarnail Singh Atwal. You do the right thing for this khandan *[family]*. Pay your debts and we'll live on roti *[bread]* and dayhee *[yoghurt]* in this house. And one day we'll do something. We'll find something else.

The landline rings. They stare at it for a moment. PAL picks up the phone.

JEETO turns to PAL.

JEETO: You are the Sardar *[chief]* here now. Do what you have to do.

JEETO exits with the bottle of formula.

PAL: *(Into the phone.)* Hello. Yes. Okay. Five minutes. Tell him I'll be ready.

He puts the phone down. REEMA gets up and faces PAL.

REEMA: I've packed my bags.

PAL: What?

REEMA: I'm leaving.

PAL: You were gonna go before.

REEMA: This time it's real.

PAL: Where?

REEMA: Doesn't matter. *(A beat.)* She still loves you.

PAL: How do you know?

REEMA: If I leave, she might come back.

PAL: She ain't coming back.

REEMA: I need money, if I'm going.

PAL: Not much of that round here.

REEMA: Mr Atwal will pay you for the land. You could give me some.

PAL: Why would I do that?

REEMA: So we end this hell we are living.

PAL: No. No way.

REEMA: Then I'll still go. But I'll take my baby with me.

PAL contemplates all the baby stuff.

PAL: He... he belongs here.

REEMA: I can go anywhere, mothers in this country have rights. They get help.

PAL: You can't just walk out and take him.

REEMA: It's up to you.

PAL: You'll be okay. You're clever, you know about books and all that.

REEMA: My books don't mean anything any more. So... if you want him to stay...

She finds a piece of paper in her pocket. Gives it to him.

REEMA: I've written it all down.

PAL inspects the paper.

PAL: You've never seen this sort of cash.

REEMA: Maybe I will now.

PAL: I need every penny I'm getting.

REEMA: I won't be back.

PAL: And you'll leave the boy, just like that?

REEMA: I said I would didn't I? Please. I have to go.

PAL: When?

REEMA: Today. Mr Atwal will transfer the money over to you and you can put my share into my account.

She indicates the piece of paper.

REEMA: See. I've written it all down.

PAL: I don't get you.

REEMA: I want to start again. Like I was never born. Please let me. I made a mistake. So did you. You owe me. You know you owe me something.

PAL: So the money's what matters?

REEMA: No, but freedom in your country, real freedom, it costs.

PAL: Don't you care about your son?

REEMA: Don't you dare ask me that. You'll look after him. And so will Mum. *(A beat.)* Put my money in. And I'll go, nice, clean and simple.

PAL: What if I don't?

REEMA: I'll find someone who'll take him.

PAL: Someone?

REEMA: Rich women here like brown babies.

PAL: That kid's mine!

REEMA: But there's no certificate. We keep forgetting to go to the Town Hall you see.

PAL takes this in.

REEMA: Please. It's best. For everyone.

Silence. The phone rings. PAL lets it ring. REEMA exits. He takes out papers and looks through them. PAL picks up the phone. He's nervous as he speaks, becomes more tense as the conversation proceeds.

PAL: Hello... Hahnji... Yes... it is... Sat Siri Akal... Good to speak to you... yes, I've spoken to your associate many times... Yes Mr Atwal... Sorry... Uncleji... yes... It's a very fair sum... thank you... I've signed most of the papers, I was planning to scan them… and… of course, I'll send the hard copies as soon as possible…

REEMA comes back in with the baby.

PAL: My mother says Sat Siri Akal… Hahnji Uncleji… yes I have… nearly three months old now… we named him after my father… Avtar Singh…

REEMA puts the baby in its bouncer. She puts her coat on.

PAL: Well, once I sell this land, I can cover our debts… No sir… I'm hoping to build my business back up… you heard right sir… bad luck, some very bad luck… I'm trying to build a future for my son… absolutely sir… I want to be a good father and try to lead by example like my own father… direct transfer… right… yes… Hahnji… yes sir… my mother's explained to Chachaji that he can remain in the house.

REEMA picks the baby up, cradles it and waits, listening to PAL.

He's sure he's not selling his share… But there's nothing I can do… I'll see… No, he won't listen to me… that quickly?… I see… There's one thing Uncleji…

He stops. REEMA stares at her baby.

PAL: I need a bit more… *(Breathes.)* I need a bit more time… to tell you… I'm sorry… but… but, I've changed my mind. I understand Sir… I'm very sorry…

PAL puts the phone down, regards REEMA. He's breathless.

PAL: I can't sell that land. Not to Atwal. Not to anyone. It's my father's land you see. And it's going to be my son's land and Mum's going to go… and stay with Chacha, and he's been doing all that building work on the house and she keeps talking about staring at those green fields. It's all she wants, in her heart, and I can't deny her that… I won't… She deserves it.

REEMA eyes him. He scrunches up the papers, then turns to the kitchen cupboard, finds the biscuit jar, puts it on the table.

PAL: There's usually a couple of hundred in here. Have it if you want.

REEMA: You... you make sure you look after him...

After a few moments, she composes herself and hands PAL the baby. She opens the jar and frantically stuffs the money in her pockets. She exits. PAL is left with the baby in his arms.

SCENE SEVEN

The stage is transformed into a grubby, grim council flat. A vast expanse of space, bare and soulless. Someone left the dirty mattress they died on in a corner. Bits of litter here and there. Chintz curtains hang at the back, they are closed and cover a massive window. The layout of the space is the same as JEETO's house but the decor is a thousand times cheaper. The kitchen area is old-fashioned, modest. A suitcase and a black bag are on one side of the room. PAL and COOKIE enter through a door, with more black bags, a broom and cleaning materials. They put them next to the suitcase and black bag. COOKIE contemplates the space as PAL unpacks.

COOKIE: Tried not to look at it before.

She's almost in tears.

PAL: Stop it.

COOKIE: *(Composing herself.)* Can't bear the thought of you here.

PAL: The area's coming up.

COOKIE: A council flat Pal!

PAL: Ex-council, and we only just managed to afford it. Least I'm still a homeowner.

COOKIE: This isn't your home.

PAL: Course it is. Go and see, it's not so bad.

COOKIE disappears through the door. Once she's gone, PAL stops unpacking and beholds the room, he almost crumbles but holds it together. PAL removes kitchen utensils from a box, starts putting them away. COOKIE returns.

COOKIE: Her shalwars won't fit into that bedroom never mind the kameezes.

She picks up litter, starts sweeping up.

COOKIE: You can use our garage for storage.

PAL: We're lucky to have a place at all.

COOKIE gets a text.

PAL: Tracey?

COOKIE: No, er… me and Tracey aren't in contact any more.

PAL: How come?

COOKIE: Thought we were close, but really, we hardly knew each other. Fact is, she was a boring old cow. *(Texts back.)* Major says Mum's on her way, but he's staying downstairs.

PAL: What for?

COOKIE: Doesn't wanna leave the car.

PAL: Why?

COOKIE: He's not risking his laptop!

PAL: Tell him to bring it.

COOKIE: There's a gang out there!

PAL: Two kids playing football on the green bit! Mum's coming up on her own isn't she?

COOKIE: Well he's watching her, from the car isn't he?

PAL: *(Unpacking.)* Did he get that conversion job?

COOKIE: Yeah, and he's doing up those flats in Broad Green an' all. We've been lucky.

PAL: Yeah.

COOKIE: You know, he admires you, for what you did. We both do.

PAL: Right.

COOKIE: Think you're stupid. But we admire you.

JEETO enters with the baby in its car seat. She puts the baby to the side of the room. COOKIE feigns enthusiasm.

COOKIE: Bedrooms are nice! Bigger than you'd think! And you know Major's gonna sort out that kitchen, and the bathroom…

JEETO: Sabkoosh hohjooga. *[Everything will get done.]*

COOKIE: And me and the girls can hold a paintbrush.

JEETO takes out the photo of her husband, balances it on a kitchen surface [facing away from the audience]. She regards it for a moment then starts cleaning up in the kitchen. COOKIE receives another text.

COOKIE: I'd better go.

PAL: Don't you want chah?

PAL continues to unpack and JEETO carries on cleaning as they talk.

COOKIE: Jasmine's in a swimming competition. We're all going to watch. We'll come round after. Bring some dinner.

PAL: Okay.

COOKIE: Do you want Nando's or Domino's?

PAL: I'm not bothered.

COOKIE: Mum, Nando's or Domino's?

JEETO: Kooshvee *[Whatever]*.

COOKIE: Mum, decide! Which one do you want more?

JEETO: I don't know.

COOKIE: Shall I get Nando's?

JEETO: Okay.

COOKIE: Or Domino's?

JEETO: Okay.

COOKIE: Mum!

PAL: Get what you lot want innit.

COOKIE turns to go. She stops, turns to JEETO.

COOKIE: Mum…

JEETO: Hah?

COOKIE: Come and stay with us.

JEETO: *(Cleaning.)* A woman does not live with her daughter.

COOKIE: Please…

JEETO: Choop kar *[Be quiet]*… This place is a palace compared to the kamara *[room]* me and Daddy used to have. God has given Pal another chance, today he is born again.

COOKIE: Nandos it is then.

She exits. PAL unpacks, eyes his mother.

PAL: Harj's dad offered me a job.

JEETO: Acha.

PAL: Managing one of his pound shops. Wants me to keep on top of the stock. Do the Cash and Carry runs and all that. Monday to Sunday. I've said yes.

JEETO: Good.

PAL: But me and Harj aren't letting go. We'll have our business, even if it's not the nursing home, we'll open a dry cleaner's or a take away or something. We'll have it.

JEETO: *(Cleaning/A beat.)* They were advertising cleaning shifts at the hospital.

PAL: *(Stops.)* You said never again.

JEETO: We say a lot of things.

PAL: I won't let you…

JEETO: I've already started. Last week. Before I do the tea trolley.

She eyes his dejected countenance.

JEETO: You change that face boy. Your son has a home and you have a job and I have two jobs. You try something, build your business and when you make your money, then… then I'll go back to my land.

They stare at each other for a moment. The baby is unsettled. PAL picks him up. JEETO carries on cleaning. PAL walks him around for a while, soothing him. Eventually the baby calms down and PAL holds him up, just as JEETO previously described Daddy holding PAL up when he was a baby.

PAL: *(Soft/To son.)* What you thinking Son? What you gonna be? Whatever the hell it is, you find your way. Find it... we'll be watching...

JEETO: Put his clothes in my kamara.

PAL: He'll be alright in with me. *(To baby.)* Come on, I'll show you round your house.

He heads out.

JEETO: Pal.

PAL: *(Stops.)* Yeah?

JEETO: God will reward you... for my land.

PAL: My land Mum.

He takes the baby, exits. JEETO finishes cleaning up and opens the curtains. The view is surprisingly pleasing and almost resembles the green fields she has been describing in the Punjab. She takes it in, laughs to herself, laughs and laughs until she wipes tears from her eyes. She then moves to the kitchen area, takes out a pan, puts it on the hob.

JEETO: *(Shouts.)* Pal, chah peeneeyeh? [Do you want a cup of tea?]

Lights down.

THE END